I0761517

EL MUNDO ZURDO 7

SELECTED WORKS FROM THE 2018 MEETING OF THE SOCIETY FOR THE STUDY OF GLORIA ANZALDÚA

EDITED BY
SARA A. RAMÍREZ,
LARISSA M. MERCADO-LÓPEZ,
AND SONIA SALDÍVAR-HULL

aunt lute books
San Francisco

Aunt Lute Books
P.O. Box 410687
San Francisco, CA 94141
www.auntlute.com

Paperback ISBN: 978-1-879960-99-2
ebook ISBN: 978-1-939904-35-5

Cover design: Amy Woloszyn, Amymade Graphic Design
Cover art: "Lotería Nepantla," Celeste De Luna ©2018
Text design: Amy Woloszyn, Amymade Graphic Design
Typesetting: A.S. Ikeda
Senior Editor: Joan Pinkvoss
Artistic Director: Shay Brawn
Managing Editor: A.S. Ikeda
Production: Maya Sisneros, María Mínguez Arias, Cindy Ho, and Emma Rosenbaum

Library of Congress Cataloging-in-Publication Data
Names: Mundo Zurdo (Conference) (7th : 2018 : San Antonio, Texas) | Ramírez, Sara A, editor. | Mercado-López, Larissa M., editor. | Saldívar-Hull, Sonia, 1951- editor.
Title: El Mundo Zurdo 7 : selected works from the 2018 Meeting of the Society for the study of Gloria Anzaldúa / edited by Sara A Ramírez, Larissa M Mercado-López, and Sonia Saldívar-Hull.
Description: San Francisco : Aunt Lute Books, [2019] | Includes bibliographical references. | Summary: "This book is the 7th volume of an informal series of selected essays by scholars and artists presented at the 2018 meeting of the Society for the Study of Gloria Anzaldúa, a (roughly) biannual academic conference on the legacy of Gloria Anzaldúa." -- Provided by publisher.
Identifiers: LCCN 2019040126 (print) | LCCN 2019040127 (ebook) | ISBN 9781879960992 (paperback) | ISBN 9781939904355 (ebook)
Subjects: LCSH: Anzaldúa, Gloria--Philosophy--Congresses. | Anzaldúa, Gloria--Influence--Congresses. | Anzaldúa, Gloria--Study and teaching--Congresses. | Women's studies--Congresses. | Identity (Psychology)--Congresses. | Creation (Literary, artistic, etc.)--Congresses. | Minorities--Education--Congresses. | Hispanic Americans--Education--Congresses. | Borderlands--Social aspects--Congresses. | Mexican-American Border Region--Social conditions--Congresses.
Classification: LCC PS3551.N95 Z78 2018 (print) | LCC PS3551.N95 (ebook) | DDC 818/.5409--dc23
LC record available at https://lccn.loc.gov/2019040126
LC ebook record available at https://lccn.loc.gov/2019040127

Printed in the U.S.A. on acid-free paper
10 9 8 7 6 5 4 3 2

CONTENTS

EL MUNDO ZURDO 7

SELECTED WORKS FROM THE 2018 MEETING OF THE SOCIETY FOR THE STUDY OF GLORIA ANZALDÚA

OPENINGS

INTRODUCTION

WE NEED MYTHS/WORDS + MAGIC

SARA A. RAMÍREZ

> I write the myths in me, the myths I am, the myths I want to become. The word, the image and the feeling have a palpable energy, a kind of power. (Anzaldúa 93)

The 2018 Mundo Zurdo meeting of the members of the Society for the Study of Gloria Anzaldúa celebrated "a palpable energy, a kind of power" facilitated by the words, images, and feelings created by storyteller, poet, and philosopher Gloria E. Anzaldúa. The meeting commemorated not only the 30th anniversary of the 1987 publication of Anzaldúa's *Borderlands/La Frontera: The New Mestiza* but also the author's 75th birthday.[1] Because—according to her numerology—Anzaldúa's base (inner and outer) numbers were both seven, this seventh international meeting was quite a serendipitous gathering of nepantlerxs and borderlands dwellers, thinkers, writers, and artists.[2] This meeting was a testament to what Anzaldúa foresaw in the epigraph included above, as her words and images continue to impact how we think about present-day gender and sexuality, feminist praxis, education, art and performance, and, of course, borders. Anzaldúa's mythmaking indeed has the kind of power that will likely surpass the thirty years since the publication of *Borderlands*. The autohistoria-teoría's legacy was evident at the 2018 meeting, as conference participants applied Anzaldúan theories to present-day sites of activism such as education, art, and performance both in the United States and at an international level.

I often find myself asking what this great thinker—as she would have liked to be remembered[3]—would write today in 2019. Which words, images, and feelings would she use "to act and not react"—to use a significant phrase in her theorization of mestiza consciousness—in these current sociopolitical times (Anzaldúa 101)? As this seventh volume of *El Mundo Zurdo* goes to press, the media reports the massacre of "Hispanics" in El Paso, Texas, on a Saturday morning and the mass murder of people in Dayton, Ohio less than 24 hours later. *Beloved* author Toni Morrison has passed away. In Kashmir, there is a total communication lockdown and a curfew in place as the Indian government takes over Kashmiri lands. ICE arrests 680 undocumented workers at poultry plants in Mississippi, leaving many children without their parents. The EPA has reauthorized the use of cyanide bombs to trap and kill predatory animals. And this news comes in a single week. Immigrants, including children separated from their families, have been in cages for months. Hawai'ians have had to actively defend and protect Mauna Kea from the building of a thirty-meter telescope atop the sacred mountain. To say that we, Anzaldúan thinkers, writers, and artists, are in both mourning and outrage is an understatement.

Were she alive in these times, Anzaldúa would perhaps encourage us to consider, as she acknowledged in her writing notas,

> Words + magic gain significance in times of crisis. When old forms of life are in dissolution. Normal motives and incentives lose their efficacy. The prosaic and the matter-of-fact no longer satisfy. We need magic, the sense of the fantastic to lure us. We need incantations, myths to release our energies. (@dr_wease [AnaLouise Keating])

Words (read: action) are not sufficient. Petitions, for example, have not ceased gun violence in the United States. Magic alone is not enough. No matter how many #prayers we offer, hatred of the other still runs rampant. We need "words + magic" in the forms of incantations and myths to lure us toward a better world.

In *Borderlands*, Anzaldúa reminds us,

> Los que están mirando (leyendo),
> los que cuentan (o refieren lo que leen).
> Los que vuelven ruidosamente las hojas de los códices.
> Los que tienen en su poder
> la tinta negra y roja (la sabiduría)
> y lo pintado,
> ellos nos llevan, nos guían,
> nos dicen el camino.[4] (Miguel Leon-Portilla 125 qtd. in Anzaldúa 93)

As a sabia de la tinta negra y roja y lo pintado in her own right, Anzaldúa's words and magic culminate in the myths and concept-metaphors she developed throughout her career. *Borderlands* makes evident the myths in her, the myths she was, and the ones she wanted to become. This important text exemplifies the mythmaking, the magic + action, Anzaldúa calls us, her readers, to perform. Through *Borderlands*, she helps us rethink various concept-metaphors including Coatlicue, goddess of the Serpent Skirt, as a psychic symbol of Chicanas' dual natures; Malintzín, the indigenous woman accused of selling out her people to the Spaniards, as the victim of her people's betrayal; La Llorona/Cihuacoatl, the weeping mother who seeks her lost children and her possible antecedent, as a figure representative of depression and sorrow; nahualismo, the ability to shape-shift, as a practice that encourages us to sculpt our own souls; the new mestiza as a Chicana who tolerates ambiguity and "operates in a pluralistic mode" (Anzaldúa 101); and, most notably, borderlands, a concept that helps us consider the sociopolitical construction of geographical (Mexico-U.S.), psychic, spiritual, and sexual borders. Her myths and the practice of mythmaking guide Anzaldúa's readers toward molding the individual self into a cosmic Self and thus teaches us that our particularities are nuclei in a web of interconnectedness.

Borderlands reminds us that we, too, are the symbol-smith magicians who have been reading, teaching, noisily turning the pages of books. You and I have in our power the wisdom of writing and painting and creating. We take all our relations and guide them along the path. The SSGA meetings allow us to release the energies we have invested in la tinta negra y roja, en lo pintado, en lo encarnado amongst amistades.

ORGANIZATION OF THE BOOK

These energies, including the energies of *Borderlands* and the borderlands, bring us together and are invoked by the opening blessings Sandra Pacheco offered to our group on May 18, 2019. The spirits of our collective labor are represented here.

In the first section, titled "Philosophizing in the Borderlands," of this volume of *El Mundo Zurdo*, Mariana Alessandri investigates Gloria Anzaldúa's relationship to Søren Kierkegaard and argues that Anzaldúan thought can help us understand the Danish philosopher's work. Alessandri ultimately argues that Anzaldúan bridgework is a manifestation of Anzaldúa's faith. In the second essay, Cordelia E. Barrera describes how she has woven her creative nonfiction using Anzaldua's theories, especially those with utopian proclivities and impulses toward "social dreaming." In the next essay, Ricardo L. Franco considers the theological implications of Anzaldúa's work and pinpoints *Borderlands* as "a new grammar of the soul."

The second section, "Queering Nations and Imaginations," includes a duoethnography by Lobat Asadi and Mario I. Suárez, who delve into the shadow work of autohistoria-teoría and queer gender norms in order to investigate post-gender space and bodies that instill territorial fear. The authors posit their critical friendship as a cisgender woman and a transgender man as a form of protest. L. Heidenreich's opening plenary speech is also included within this section. Heidenreich offers insight into Anzaldúa's conceptualization of nepantla as "motion-change" and applies this understanding to the present-day shift to global capitalism. Heidenreich discusses the subsequent violence of this shift that has been met with resistance by people and organizations of el mundo zurdo, such as the Transgender Law Center. In the next essay, Camille Back critiques queer thought and praxis in France, which she argues is grounded in white U.S. queer theories that reproduce epistemic blind spots, and challenges us to consider the implications of redefining the genealogy of queer theory by beginning with Anzaldúa's "La Prieta" and *Borderlands*.

The next section focuses on "Expressions of Resistance in the Borderlands" and begins with a short statement by the curators—Eliza Pérez, Jess Gonzales, and Rebel Mariposa—of the art exhibit titled "Shadow Beast: Creating Sin Vergüenza," which took place at Galería Ecos de Voces y Arte (E.V.A.) in San Antonio, Texas. Fabiola Ochoa Torralba and Yvonne Montoya, two members of Decolonial Epistemologies: Dance Lab, each discuss their work as part of the contemporary dance group in their respective essays. Ochoa Torralba offers insight into their position in nepantla as a professional Latinx choreographer through a reflection on two workshops at the conference. Montoya documents the performance she enacted during the conference before examining the radical act of centering Xicana bodies, stories, and experiences in the field of contemporary dance. In essay 10, scholar, toy designer, and member of the Puro Chingón Collective Claudia Zapata details the philosophical influences that undergird the art of her designer toy, *Mundo Zurdo*, a three-dimensional glyph form of an Anzaldúan drawing. In the last essay of this section, Ewa Antoszek centers fiber artist Consuelo Jiménez Underwood's redefinition of the border in her *Borderlines* series and addresses how the artist contributes to the ongoing debate of the status of the U.S.-Mexico border.

The final section is comprised of "Testimonios of Healing, Persistence, and Feminist Praxis." Lilliana P. Saldaña and Sonya Alemán use an Anzaldúan approach to reflect on the Chicana feminist editorial praxis in their work with *Chicana/Latina Studies: The Journal of Mujeres Activas en Letras y Cambio Social* (MALCS). In essay 13, Victorria Simpson-Gervin employs Anzaldúan autohistoria-teoría as a testimonial of healing for her 11-year-old inner self. The essay that follows is also guided by the imperative to heal, yet writer Samantha Ceballos makes this effort through three poems that emphasize her roots in metaphorical and geographic borderlands. Essay 15 interweaves the voices of the Calmécac Collective, a group of indigenous and allied scholars who testify to the injustices they have experienced within academia and their revolutionary approaches to scholarship.

We conclude this volume of *El Mundo Zurdo* with Paola Bacchetta's closing plenary talk in which she offers great insight into the complexities of lovingly translating some of Anzaldúa's work into "French(es)," an essay that evidences that the palpable energy of Anzaldúa's magic and incantations has been able to cross oceans. As we did at the international meeting, we look to Sandra Pacheco for her words + magic as a closing ceremonia in line with Anzaldúa's visions for el mundo zurdo.

NOTES

1. The Society for the Study of Gloria Anzaldúa meets every 18 months, so we were not able to meet in 2017.

2. In her biography in *this bridge we call home: radical visions for transformation*, Anzaldúa indicates that according to her numerology, her inner and outer self are represented by the number seven. While SSGA has met eight times, this is the seventh international Mundo Zurdo conference. The first symposium, in 2007, was titled "Güeras y Prietas: Celebrating 20 Years of *Borderlands/La Frontera*" and all of the contributions were from within the United States.

3. See Mariana Alessandri's essay in this volume.

4. Those who are looking (reading) / Those who tell (or explain what they read) / Those who noisily turn the pages of the codices. / Those who have in their power / the black and red ink (the wisdom) / and that which is painted, / they take us, guide us, / tell us the path [my translation].

WORKS CITED

Anzaldúa, Gloria. *Borderlands/La Frontera: The New Mestiza*. 1987. 4th ed., Aunt Lute, 2012.

@dr_wease [AnaLouise Keating]. "Scholars and academics rarely associate Anzaldúa with magic." *Instagram*, 5 Aug. 2019, https://www.instagram.com/p/B0x6jfHApwv/.

OPENING BLESSING

SANDRA PACHECO

(Please stand, if comfortable doing so)
Feel your feet connecting to the ground
Feel your head reaching to the sky
Your arms slightly out, feeling the energy of those around you
Inhale slowly, deeply, go inward
I offer my corazón and spirit in this blessing with
respect for the diverse spiritual traditions we come from
May we honor the Ancestors of the land we stand upon
The Coahuiltecans, Lipan Apache, Tonkawa, Comanche and
the many other native bands that history attempts to erase.
Their spirits, we honor and remember
May we honor our spirit guides,
Tonantzin, Madre Tierra, Creador, Santas, Santos, Universe,
that which reflects back our divine light
May we honor our ancestors, the shoulders we stand upon,
the centuries of intergenerational love and resistance that runs in our venas,
Their wisdom guides us—speak their names
We welcome them in
May we honor our academic, creative, spiritual activist ancestor
Gloria Evangelina Anzaldúa

May our time together be a beautiful offering to her for all she has given us
May we honor the people of Gaza, Syria, Yemen and so many lands in turmoil,
so many precious lives lost
May their ancestors receive them with amor y luz
May we hold close our colleagues and friends who could not be here with us,
due to emergencies, deaths, and health matters,
We carry you with us; you will be missed
May we honor and call in the four sacred directions to our corazones, our beings,
East: Fuego, our Spirit
West: Tierra, our Cuerpos
North: Aire, our Aliento
South: Agua, our Sangre
As we begin our conference, may we do so with gratitude, gratitude for our
time together, for each other, for new friends and old, and especially for all the
labor and love that went into bringing us together.

PHILOSOPHIZING IN THE BORDERLANDS

"LEAVE OUT KIERQUEGARD"

READING GLORIA ANZALDÚA READING KIERKEGAARD

MARIANA ALESSANDRI

Scholars have yet to realize how profoundly Gloria Anzaldúa, the self-proclaimed "feminist-visionary-spiritual-activist-poet-philosopher," was influenced by 19th century Danish philosopher Søren Kierkegaard. That Anzaldúa considered herself a philosopher has itself largely gone unnoticed, but reading her as such would give scholars a new vantage point from which to analyze her work. Long before she died, Anzaldúa wrote her own obituary:

> *Here lies G.E.A., a great thinker, philosopher, writer and humanitarian who worked for understanding and peace between diverse peoples and groups. Era buena gente.* ("Obituary")

Philosophy riddles Anzaldúa's archives housed at the Nettie Lee Benson Latin American Collection, located on the campus of the University of Texas at Austin. In 1972, Anzaldúa made a "Program for the Year," which consisted of four categories: "Finance," "Personal Objectives," "Educational Objectives," and "Creative Projects," each containing two to four goals. "Philosophy" appears as a goal under the label "Personal Objective," alongside "diet," "dentist," and "self-psychology," instead of under the heading "Educational Objectives," which includes reading one page of French per day and reading contemporary American fiction ("Program"). This suggests that Anzaldúa saw the pursuit of philosophy as personal, not just part of her education. In another note, she identified philosophy as her favorite subject, along with psychology ("Favorite Subjects"). In another note, Anzaldúa asked herself: "what makes a philosopher?" and answered, "scholarly self-study" ("Philosopher"). While her philosophical proclivities have gone largely unremarked, her depression has been widely commented on; however, they are connected.

Anzaldúa found comfort for her depression early on in Kierkegaard. In her "Notes for a Memoir," possibly going to be titled "How Prieta Came to Write" (published posthumously as such in *The Gloria Anzaldúa Reader*), Anzaldúa wrote about herself in the third person:

> In her early years it was too painful to inhabit her flesh, fully. She was afraid of her impulses; she locked herself in a world of ideas. Books were her great love. In them she sought the answers to the riddles of life, of death, of immortality. Books were her refuge from a world in which she didn't belong. There was an escape from the intimacy of flesh struggling against flesh in pain, an escape to the cool distant regions of abstract thought. She buried her head in Kierkegaard's *Fear and Trembling* and *Sickness unto Death* and found a despair equaling her own. She became acquainted with the void. (*Reader* 235)

From her notes, it is also clear that Anzaldúa had intended to include Kierkegaard in *Borderlands/La Frontera*. The evidence comes in the form of a note to herself on the title page of a late draft: "leave out Kierquegard" ("Draft").

Before discovering their connection at the Benson Library, I had no idea how to reconcile my love for the dead white guy with my love for the Brown Chicana Feminist. As a Latina living on the Texas-Mexico Border where Anzaldúa grew up, I struggled to teach students philosophy in a way that would resonate with them. As part of a course I taught on the philosophy of Kierkegaard, some students and I attempted to uncover how and why he captured Anzaldúa's heart the way he had captured mine long ago and some of theirs that semester. In doing this research, I found my response to her obituary: I, too, would spend my time cultivating understanding between disparate pairs, in this case Anzaldúa scholars and philosophers who have never heard of her. I share my findings here. To give this pairing a visual element, two students of mine, roommates, simultaneously painted two portraits: one of Kierkegaard and one of Anzaldúa:

Fig. 1 Søren Kierkegaard (left) painted by Ilse Sepulveda Tuexi and Gloria Anzaldúa (right) painted by Bertha Cristal Reyna. Photo provided by Bertha Cristal Reyna.

These paintings remind me that we can bridge the most seemingly disparate elements, and, as a metaphor, it can give us courage to paint together other uncommon and unlikely pairs.

My essay has three parts: 1) the influence of Kierkegaard on Anzaldúa; 2) an existential lesson that Kierkegaard could have learned from Anzaldúa; and 3) an Anzal-gaardian interpretation of faith. As the story usually goes, people in the margins need to read the center but the center need not read work produced in the margins. I hope to reverse this by suggesting that Anzaldúa makes Kierkegaard (and philosophy) relevant and accessible. I begin with the story of Kierkegaard's influence on Anzaldúa.

THE INFLUENCE

Anzaldúa's love for Kierkegaard in particular began early, though scholars don't know how she got her hands on Kierkegaard as a child ("Childhood Memories"). In an interview with Ann Reuman, Anzaldúa said, "the intellectual, artistic identity that I have is very old. From the time when I was in elementary school I was this little kid that was carrying around Nietzsche, Kierkegaard, so I had that kind of identity" (Reuman 31). In a 1964 journal entry, she wrote, "reading Kierkegaard is like reading someone very close to me" ("Journal"). The 22-year-old Chicana wrote the following about the most famous journal entry of the 22-year-old Dane: "Kierkegaard, early in life, discovered that one must 'find a truth which is true for me—the idea for which I can live and die.' I don't know if I've found 'a truth which is true for me' yet" (Anzaldua "Journal"; Kierkegaard *Journals* 5 5100). Both authors seem to have found their truth in and by writing.

That Anzaldúa was influenced by Kierkegaard in particular, and philosophy in general, is evident, but she did not feel that philosophy or philosophers were open to her. She especially felt excluded from academia. About *Borderlands*, she wrote: "I wanted to be able to philosophize," but noted that "if you are a professor of color, you are required to write like a white professor" ("On the Process" 189). It's rare to see *Borderlands/La Frontera* taught in a philosophy class, and students sometimes have a hard time calling her a philosopher. First, she was a woman; next, she was a queer Mexican-American; and last, she only recently died. Likewise, students would not naturally assume that she would take refuge in someone like Kierkegaard: a male, white, straight, long-dead Dane. It would probably come as a shock to anyone who only reads *Borderlands* that Kierkegaard was ever there. But he was.

Kierkegaard appeared in a 1986 draft of the book. In a chapter titled *Movimientos de rebeldia*, under the subtitle "Intimate Terrorism," she wrote:

> Being "othered" means being identified by the admissable [*sic*] parts of myself—all others being repressed, hidden behind false faces. I was spit [*sic*] and the inadmissable [*sic*] part of me became "the other." Kierkegaard who taught me much about fear and dread would call this state of being "othered" a state

> of being in sin. The human will does not and has never been able to prevail when it pushes its insurgent parts down. ("Draft II")

By pushing some parts of herself down, Anzaldúa was technically in what Kierkegaard called "despair." And, by not accepting herself, she was also in a state of sin (Kierkegaard, *Sickness* 14). Anzaldúa's subtitle for this section is apt: it is *intimate terrorism* to repress oneself, to hide behind false faces. In her unpublished notes, she explained:

> When "othered," my self-psyche got repressed and hidden behind layers of masks and false faces and habits of evasion and of deception. It was "othered." This state Kierkegaard, a philosopher who shaped much of my early sensibilities, calle [*sic*] the state of being in sin. It was to the "I" of the masks and false faces that I was referring my experience to. So I had to dig my way to the surface, a couple of traumatic events and a near death on an operation table, a visit from Teo-Nanacatl, visitation of the goddess, shown the light on this hidden face of another I. ("Notes")

The masks that hid parts of Anzaldúa did not hide her state of sin, although she hid her awareness of it from her readers in subsequent versions by taking him out. After cutting Kierkegaard but before the final version, the sentence read: "the state of being 'othered' is the state of betrayal." *Movimientos de rebeldia* became chapter two of the final draft, omitting both Kierkegaard and sin. In the published version, she also rejected the term "othering" and settled on "rejection" and "betrayal." Chapter 2 of *Borderlands/La Frontera* is explicitly about rejection and betrayal, but it is now clear that it came from an internal dialogue Anzaldúa had with Kierkegaard on sin and despair. Now, every time I read "Intimate Terrorism," I know she is talking about Kierkegaardian despair.

In Anzaldúa's reading of *Sickness Unto Death*, sin equals othering, and othering equals rejection and betrayal. Anzaldúa might have been referring to the sin committed against her by her community in South Texas. We know she was othered for being queer, for not getting married, for reading philosophy, for going away to college, for becoming an academic. In the larger community, she was othered for not being queer enough, Chicana enough, Mexican enough, feminist enough, academic enough. But I think she was also referring to the way in which she betrayed herself by wearing "false faces." Her sin consisted of rejecting her most objectionable parts, or, in Kierkegaardian language, of willing not to be herself (Kierkegaard, *Sickness* 49-67). In the third section of this essay I return to the theme of sin as it pertains to my life as a Latinx philosopher in the footsteps of Anzaldúa. For now, I present Anzaldúa as a bridge-builder in a society bordered by walls. Kierkegaard could have learned something about ethics and religion from the life she lived.

AN EXISTENTIAL LESSON THAT KIERKEGAARD COULD HAVE LEARNED FROM ANZALDÚA

Had they had been contemporaries, Kierkegaard could have learned from Anzaldúa that bridge-building is an ethical act. She aimed to bridge the river that divides disparate perspectives in the following example from *Borderlands*:

> But it is not enough to stand on the opposite river bank, shouting questions, challenging patriarchal, white conventions. A counterstance locks one into a duel of oppressor and oppressed; locked in mortal combat, like the cop and the criminal, both are reduced to a common denominator of violence [...] At some point, on our way to a new consciousness, we will have to leave the opposite bank, the split between the two mortal combatants somehow healed so that we are on both shores at once and, at once, see through serpent and eagle eyes. Or perhaps we will decide to disengage from the dominant culture, write it off altogether as a lost cause, and cross the border into a wholly new and separate territory. (100)

Although in this passage Anzaldúa suggests the strategy of writing off the Anglo, in her real life she painstakingly chose the former option, bridgework. She refused the either/or that race offers and insisted on planting one foot in each world. In "To Live in the Borderlands Means You," she celebrated the borderlands as the place you can "put *chile* in the borscht, eat whole wheat *tortillas*, and speak Tex-Mex with a Brooklyn accent" (*Borderlands* 216). Bridgework is an ethical act, but it is also a spiritual act, one that requires faith. This is to combine Kierkegaardian language with Anzaldúan language, and to create a new bridge between philosophy and Anzaldúa scholarship.

AN ANZAL-GAARDIAN READING OF FAITH

The reception of *Borderlands/La Frontera* may well have taken a more theological turn if Anzaldúa had kept Kierkegaard in. "Sin" became "betrayal" when she deleted Kierkegaard, perhaps because she wanted to steer clear of traditionally Western theological language.[1] Even though she changed the terms, we now know when we read "betrayal" or "rejection" in *Borderlands*, Anzaldúa had in mind "othering," which was how she interpreted Kierkegaardian "sin."

Anzaldúa learned from Kierkegaard that it is a sin to "other" (to reject, to betray) parts of ourselves that are not acceptable to the public, as well as to "other" others. And she even managed to live differently as a result of thinking differently, which is a thoroughly Kierkegaardian prescription. Even though she never articulated it as such, I think she would agree with Kierkegaard that the opposite of sin is faith. I would call Anzaldúa's bridgework not just an ethical act, but a manifestation of her faith.

I can't speak for Anzaldúa, but I can apply her interpretation of "sin" to my own existential position as a Latinx Kierkegaardian philosopher with the hopes of unmasking a lesson on faith to be gained from reading Anzaldúa reading Kierkegaard.

Using Anzaldúa's interpretation, it is a sin to say that Latinxs shouldn't read people who look like Kierkegaard. It is a sin to "other" people, to reject them wholesale, to assume they have nothing to teach us or that they can't hear us or that they are against us. But I know many women of color who would roll their eyes if I suggested that Kierkegaard is meaningful today. Some of my colleagues outside of philosophy already balk at the idea that philosophy might have something to teach Latinx students, and they might say that Anzaldúa doesn't need validation by a dead white guy. They, like many, think philosophy is bankrupt, and I can't blame them since it is among the worst of all fields when it comes to diversity. They might accuse me of naiveté, perhaps even of adopting the master's (European) tools. The very teaching of Kierkegaard to a 90% Hispanic population is a colonial act, they might argue, suggesting that it is only my internalized racism that keeps me loyal to him. Why spend class time reading Kierkegaard when I could be employing "culturally relevant pedagogies"?

Academics tend to self-segregate, and thanks to Anzaldúa's reading of Kierkegaard, I now believe that sin lives in those spaces. Othering is everywhere. Us/them. *Pero me canso de oír esto*. Despite my affection for Kierkegaard (I wrote my dissertation on him), I had not been to a Kierkegaard conference in ten years. This was, in part, because the last one I went to was populated almost exclusively by older white men. What could this dying community possibly have to teach me? Would they listen to me? Us/them, *otra vez*. I learned from Anzaldúa's reading of Kierkegaard that avoiding these scholars on the assumption that they won't listen to me is a sin, too. I learned that my ethical duty is to build bridges, even to "them." Most importantly, from reading Anzaldúa reading Kierkegaard, I learned that building bridges is also a religious act, one that takes faith.

CONCLUSION: DESPAIR, REBELLION, AND FAITH

Before I discovered Anzaldúa's love of Kierkegaard, I felt sheepish about my own. I didn't abandon him but neither did I broadcast him, out of fear of being called out as colonized. At last I have Anzaldúa's blessing to publicly agree with something she wrote in private: "Kierkegaard is a terribly good writer" ("Journal"). Kierkegaard taught Anzaldúa and she taught me that othering—even academic othering—is sin, including when we other, reject, or betray ourselves. But here is another lesson that she could have taught Kierkegaard: rebellion is the answer to sin, though dialectically so. In her notes, Anzaldúa wrote, "sin: rebellion, willful estrangement, for acts of self-assertion, pride" ("15 Enero 85"). Rebellion seems to have both kept her in despair and helped her respond rightly to her self-othering. Anzaldúa's rebellion took the form of flaunting instead of hiding the "inadmissible" parts of herself. Addressing a mostly white group of writers at the University of North Dakota, she explained:

> I have to push the identities that they repress forward. When I'm in California I don't have to stress the queer. I live in the dyke capital of the world: Santa

> Cruz. In Texas…you know… Chicana/Tejana is ok but the queer me is not ok so I push that at them, at my family and at my communities. The race thing is what I push usually with people like yourselves because of people of color being so invisible. ("La Literatura" 00:34:00 - 00:36:00)

As a graduate student, I rebelled against the notion that because I was a woman I should become a scholar of feminism, and that as a woman of color I should only specialize in women of color. But I hadn't realized that I was othering others, and Anzaldúa gave me a Kierkegaardian framework to help me to stop. All renditions of despair, for Kierkegaard, have certainty at their core: I already know the result, so I justify writing people off. The description of faith that runs through many of Kierkegaard's works, on the other hand, hinges on uncertainty and vulnerability. Anzaldúa's reading made me realize that rebelling against certainty means having faith that all things are possible, that I don't know what others are thinking or intending. *Y con eso, ya pude respirar.*

When Kierkegaard wrote that love staves off despair in *Works of Love*, he meant that when we presuppose that love is present, we leave room for possibility, for surprise, for miracle, for breath.[2] Kierkegaard taught me *that* I should presuppose that love is present; Anzaldúa taught me *how*. This essay is an act of rebellious faith in the uncertain possibility that Kierkegaard matters to the Anzaldúan community, that colonialism is not the end of the story, that we have a duty to listen to the other, even if the other is white, male, or dead.

Anzaldúa was never supposed to read Kierkegaard, given her subject position as the poor daughter of Mexican-American farmworkers. But she did, and she left a crumb of him in her work, and now Latinxs who know nothing about Kierkegaard can have fun exploring the connection. This proposition is risky, since it rhymes with colonialism. But the stubborn fact is that the melancholy Chicana's heart resonated with the melancholy Dane's. The possibility against all probability that I have faith in is that scholars who have learned anything from Anzaldúa can accept that a few white males have influenced her, and that they're not all bad. We can all learn from Anzaldúa how to avoid othering the other, even in our own departments and universities.

NOTES

1. Anzaldúa might have intuited that she would have been heavily criticized for suggesting that she was in sin, since that would mean (to critics) that she was a victim of the colonization that was Christianity over Mexican Indians.

2. In *Works of Love*, Kierkegaard writes that it is a work of love to presuppose that love is present, and in *Sickness Unto Death*, Anti-Climacus compares "with God all things are possible" to breathing. For an elaboration on this theme see Cain, pp. 248-9, along with Kierkegaard's *Works*, pp. 224-7 and *Sickness*, pp. 38-9.

WORKS CITED

Anzaldúa, Gloria. *Borderlands/La Frontera: The New Mestiza*. 4th ed., Aunt Lute, 2012.

---. Childhood Memories. Gloria Evangelina Anzaldúa Papers, Benson Latin American Collection, University of Texas Libraries, the University of Texas at Austin. Box 32, folder 7. Copyright © Gloria E. Anzaldúa. Reprinted by permission of The Gloria E. Anzaldúa Trust. All rights reserved.

---. Draft. 1986. Gloria Evangelina Anzaldúa Papers, Benson Latin American Collection, University of Texas Libraries, the University of Texas at Austin. Box 32, folder 13. Copyright © Gloria E. Anzaldúa. Reprinted by permission of The Gloria E. Anzaldúa Trust. All rights reserved.

---. Draft II. 1986. Gloria Evangelina Anzaldúa Papers, Benson Latin American Collection, University of Texas Libraries, the University of Texas at Austin. Box 35, folder 5. Copyright © Gloria E. Anzaldúa. Reprinted by permission of The Gloria E. Anzaldúa Trust. All rights reserved.

---. Favorite Subjects. Gloria Evangelina Anzaldúa Papers, Benson Latin American Collection, University of Texas Libraries, the University of Texas at Austin. Box 108, folder 6. Copyright © Gloria E. Anzaldúa. Reprinted by permission of The Gloria E. Anzaldúa Trust. All rights reserved.

---. Journal. Gloria Evangelina Anzaldúa Papers, Benson Latin American Collection, University of Texas Libraries, the University of Texas at Austin. Box 105. Copyright © Gloria E. Anzaldúa. Reprinted by permission of The Gloria E. Anzaldúa Trust. All rights reserved.

---. 15 Enero 85. Gloria Evangelina Anzaldúa Papers, Benson Latin American Collection, University of Texas Libraries, the University of Texas at Austin. Box 32. Copyright © Gloria E. Anzaldúa. Reprinted by permission of The Gloria E. Anzaldúa Trust. All rights reserved.

---. La Literatura: Contemporary Latino/Latina Writing. 24th Annual UND Writer's Conference, 24 March 1993, University of North Dakota, Grand Forks, ND. https://commons.und.edu/writers-conference/1993/day2/3/

---. Notes. Gloria Evangelina Anzaldúa Papers, Benson Latin American Collection, University of Texas Libraries, the University of Texas at Austin. Box 109, folder 8. Copyright © Gloria E. Anzaldúa. Reprinted by permission of The Gloria E. Anzaldúa Trust. All rights reserved.

---. Obituary. Gloria Evangelina Anzaldúa Papers, Benson Latin American Collection, University of Texas Libraries, the University of Texas at Austin. Box 105, folder 3. Copyright © Gloria E. Anzaldúa. Reprinted by permission of The Gloria E. Anzaldúa Trust. All rights reserved.

---. Philosopher. Gloria Evangelina Anzaldúa Papers, Benson Latin American Collection, University of Texas Libraries, the University of Texas at Austin. Box 102, folder 5. Copyright © Gloria E. Anzaldúa. Reprinted by permission of The Gloria E. Anzaldúa Trust. All rights reserved.

---. Program. Gloria Evangelina Anzaldúa Papers, Benson Latin American Collection, University of Texas Libraries, the University of Texas at Austin. Box 32, folder 4. Copyright © Gloria E. Anzaldúa. Reprinted by permission of The Gloria E. Anzaldúa Trust. All rights reserved.

---. On the Process of Writing *Borderlands/La Frontera. The Gloria Anzaldúa Reader*. Edited by AnaLouise Keating. Duke UP, 2009. 187-197.

Cain, David. "A Way of God's Theodicy: Honesty, Presence, Adventure." *The Journal of Pastoral Care*, vol 32, no. 4, December 1978, pp. 239-50.

Kierkegaard, Søren. *Journals and Papers*. Edited and translated by Howard V. Hong and Edna H. Hong, Indiana UP, 1967-1978.

---. *The Sickness Unto Death: A Christian Psychological Exposition for Upbuilding and Awakening*. Edited and translated by Howard V. Hong and Edna H. Hong, Princeton UP, 1983.

---. *Works of Love*. Edited and translated by Howard V. Hong and Edna H. Hong, Princeton UP, 1998.

Reuman. Ann E. "Coming into Play: An Interview with Gloria Anzaldúa." MELUS, vol. 25, no. 2, June 2000, pp. 3–45.

APOCALYPSE OF HOPE AND THE QUEST FOR UTOPIA ON THE BORDERLANDS

CORDELIA E. BARRERA

This essay presents a brief foray into Anzaldúan theories that are linked to a utopian impulse and a spiritual ecofeminist perspective that does not polarize divisions between the political and the spiritual and is radical, democratic, and embraces processes that underscore alternative relations to nature.[1] The ideas presented here complicate the desire for a better world, what Ruth Levitas discusses as social dreaming, or the utopian proclivity for humans to wish for or dream of a better world by way of personal, transformative social action. Anzaldúa's writing shares elements of feminist utopias that imagine new psychological patterns and states of consciousness as the basis for profound social change. In this essay, I argue that Anzaldúa's spirituality is both apocalyptic and utopic for the ways that she unites social dreaming with transcendent idealism. Following Anzaldúa, this essay blends personal memoir and fictive forms within a utopic lens to suggest ways scholars might more broadly conceptualize an Anzaldúan spirituality so as to engage younger audiences in "work that matters."

The ideas outlined here are personal and experiential, fed by images and impressions that have compelled me to read Anzaldúa in terms of an apocalyptic disclosing of truths discredited by destructive patterns of thinking rooted in a patriarchal culture that devalues nature, difference, and paths to knowledge that foster duality. It's not a stretch to think of Anzaldúa's works as embracing the apocalyptic, especially when we consider that the etymological root of the term comes from the Greek *apokalypsis*, which means to "uncover" or "unveil." The term denotes a disclosure of knowledge through the imagery of the lifting of a veil that results in a revelation or previously undisclosed fact. Engaging apocalypse calls to mind imagery such as that found in The Book of Revelation with its emphasis on divulgence through dreams, visions, and altered states of consciousness. In religion and theology, "revelation" refers to the disclosure of some truth or knowledge through communication with a deity or other supernatural entity or entities. Although Anzaldúa does not communicate directly with a deity, she acknowledges the power of paralogical experiences, namely an encounter with an Earth Serpent, to imbue "a less literal and more psychic sense of reality" (*Borderlands* 61). What I'd like to suggest is that what Anzaldúa *reveals* to us in so much of her work, and specifically in the section of *Borderlands* titled "Entering Into the Serpent," is apocalyptic because what she is disclosing is a new way of thinking, and what is being revealed to us is the means by which we might realize these new thought processes.

For Anzaldúa, seeing through snake eyes, feeling snake blood course through her body, "entering into the serpent," as she calls it, is a process of abandoning the self, with all its destructive baggage that—as bystanders of systems we've inherited—we can slough off like old skin. Such a course is painful and is likened to death:

Dead,
the doctor by the operating table said.
I passed between the two fangs,
the flickering tongue.
Having come through the mouth of the serpent,
swallowed,
I found myself suddenly in the dark,
sliding down a smooth wet surface
down down into an even darker darkness.
Having crossed the portal, the raised hinged mouth,
having entered the serpent's belly,
now there was no looking back, no going back.
(*Borderlands* 56, lines 1–12)

Elizabeth K. Rosen makes the case for the apocalyptic impulse in postmodern works, much as Frederic Jameson makes the case for a utopian impulse—which is any undertaking for a better world in the broadest sense. Jameson, following Ernst Bloch, distinguishes between utopian programs that exist as forms of the literary genre of utopia and include depictions of new spatial totalities or societies, and utopian impulses, which are more generalized forms of social and individual practices that foreground liberal or social democratic reforms, emanate from the body, and seek to transform social totalities via ideology.[2] Alternatively, apocalyptic impulses help us make sense of dislocating historical events, as they reflect a despair that stems from social or historical disruption (xii). Post-apocalyptic narratives embed a break in the acknowledged order, and this break creates a space where—in the case of multiethnic fictions such as those of science fiction writer Octavia E. Butler—survivor heroes must embrace radical change if they are to survive. The significant element here is a rupture in a world order that provides a space for a *new* order. In the postmodern apocalypse, it's not only or necessarily a new world order that is revealed to us but, instead, a new way of seeing. Anzaldúa's ideas and language are apocalyptic because she calls for a rupture in the inner workings of the self, a change in how we access knowledge, how we engage with the spirit world, the numinous, the unseen and invisible. Perhaps most significantly, the hope that she envisions is an impulse—a utopian motivation—for a better world. This idea is exemplified in an interview between Anzaldúa and her fictional character, LP (La Prieta), who embodies Anzaldúa's ideas regarding shifting views of reality that ground egalitarian principles and deep ecological thinking into the fabric of her body and bones: "...this reality is not all it appears to be. There are cracks in the picture. Maybe other worlds exist and they sometimes bleed into this one through the cracks" ("A Short Q & A" 275). These are more than playful moments of engagement with a fictional character; rather, they are utopic imaginings that narrate freedom for women and non-human nature.

Readers not familiar with the means by which Anzaldúa links the power of human imagination to the transformative potential of the mind, body, and spirit often feel a sense of estrangement—a term borrowed from science fiction studies—when encountering her work. A foremost contemporary thinker of science fiction studies is Darko Suvin. For Suvin, sci-fi is about encouraging new ways of thinking about human society; he has labeled this idea of subversive thinking "cognitive estrangement." Works that cognitively estrange present alternative realities that directly contradict the status quo.[3] In this regard, Suvin is aligned with Octavia E. Butler, whose works illustrate how science fiction and speculative forms are ideal "exploring ground" for continued thought experiments as regards society, human biology, and human forms (brown 197). Butler's works, like Anzaldúa's—especially those that feature LP—engage with strategies of Self in which there is no dividing line between Self and landscape, the terrain beneath one's feet. For example, in an early essay titled "Cyborg Feminism," Catherine S. Ramírez juxtaposes ideas found within *Borderlands/La Frontera* alongside Butler's speculative works and Donna Haraway's "Cyborg Manifesto" to theorize a woman-of-color feminism that prioritizes the fluidity of the subject in terms of how these authors "expose ideology" and "denaturalize and relativize fictions" that have been upheld as fact (393). Ramirez's essay serves as proving ground for Latin@ speculative models theorized at length in the anthology *Altermundos: Latin@ Speculative Literature, Film, and Popular Culture.* Significantly, editors of *Altermundos* affirm that much of Latin@ speculative fiction is inherently utopic, an idea further articulated by José Esteban Muñoz's *Cruising Utopia: The Then and There of Queer Futurity*, republished in 2019 as a 10th anniversary edition.

Although there is little scholarship that develops insight into Anzaldúa's utopian proclivities, utopia's kinship with speculative forms provides a flashpoint by which to broaden new critical vocabularies and approaches to Latin@ speculative forms, as is evidenced by the inclusion of my author reflection and book excerpt in *Altermundos*, titled "*Becoming Nawili*: Utopian Dreaming at the End of the World." As indicated above, the present essay is both personal and experiential, as it describes Anzaldúan theories I weaved into my unpublished novel, *Becoming Nawili.* I wrote *Nawili* at a time when everything in my world had become poisoned and sick. In *Nawili*—as in Anzaldúa's stories about LP—there is no dividing line between the Self and *la tierra*, the earth that sustains all life. When my father inexplicably died and my personal world collapsed beneath my feet, I hungered to enter into the serpent, where "something must change/or I'd die" (Anzaldúa, *Borderlands* 57). I invoked Anzaldúa's *cenote*, that topos wherein she unearths a language "shared with the spirits of the trees, sea, wind, and animals. The language that speaks of what is other" ("Nepantla"). From the depths of *el cenote*, Anzaldúa pieces together the fragments of collective memories to re-write spaces of power and knowledge for Chican@s. I dove headlong into Anzaldúa's *cenote* and took Pepa—my novel's protagonist—with me; I kept her underwater for a year. In an audacious move, I had Anzaldúa's serpent swallow Pepa whole. Then I seeded her with the strength of the ancients—powers marked in the red and black ink of lost metaphors and primal memories—and injected her veins with the blood of ten thousand warrior women. She emerged a shape-shifting *nepantlera* able to fuse with the environment and other forms of life. *This*, I reasoned, was the future Anzaldúa's theories promised: a hopeful future bound by humanist connections and transcendent idealism rooted in respect for people and the planet. In *Nawili*, I wanted Pepa and the soil, sand, and water to reflect the concept of *in lak'ech*, the Mayan concept that translates as "you are my other self."

In many ways, *Becoming Nawili* is an angry novel. Still, because it is geared to a New Adult audience, it is full of hope and builds upon a narrative that directly overturns all-too-crushing patterns of global capitalism in which human needs and desires are easily subsumed by systems of profit at all costs. *Becoming Nawili* is a speculative Chican@ fantasy that takes place in the mid 21st century Borderlands, on the cusp of a new world order. It grounds an indigenous, matriarchal past to imagine a social and environmentally just future. *Nawili* opens in a world devastated by modern day "fracking" practices run amok. In the novel, the toxic waters of the Rio Grande both shelter and transform the young protagonist, Pepa. The act of drowning, falling into the earth is meant to mirror Anzaldúa's *cenote* and establish a link to unexplored indigenous knowledge and ancestral dreampools encased in cyclical time and within *la tierra.* As Pepa descends into the body of the earth, she unchains a utopic terrain of apocalyptic hope.

I am a product of the South Texas *monte.* Growing up in Laredo in the '70s and '80s, my friends and I prowled the *senderos* and explored miles of untamed *monte* fed by natural creeks and reservoirs. But Laredo's wild spaces, like those of

South Texas, are vanishing. In *Adios to the Brushlands*, Arturo Longoria bemoans the systematic clearing of native *chaparral* in South Texas by large-scale ranching and dry farming practices that exploded in earnest in the 1970s and '80s. But this was only the beginning. Today, the devastation of the *chaparral* in the name of oil and gas exploration and unbridled corporate interests is choking the lifeblood of the *monte verde* that is our sacred heritage as *texanas/os*. With the impending possibility of an expanded border wall and a looming, intensifying military presence, it remains to be seen how this unique biosphere will fare.

A few years ago, I found myself driving from Lubbock to Laredo almost weekly. My father was dead, and my mother was alone in the home our family had occupied for over forty years. The drive was surreal. The I-35 corridor, old Highway 83, and forgotten country roads on the outskirts of unexceptional towns like Asheron, La Pryor, and Carrizo Springs were thick with semi-trailer trucks, oil tankers, groundwater treatment trucks, wastewater treatment trucks, hazmat trucks, trucks full of sand, steel pipe, drill rigs, casings...and all those methane plumes that marked the escape of dangerous gases into the atmosphere. Rampant, unchecked industrialization and fracking had found a home in South Texas. My life, like the *chaparral* that formed an integral part of my identity, had become a place full of holes.

It was at this time that I became haunted by Anzaldúa's *cenote*. The *cenote*, deep and brimming in uncanny signs, was the place I wanted to drown. Perhaps, I thought, I could dive in, enter the serpent's belly the way Anzaldúa does in the "*sueño con serpientes*" section of *Borderlands* and emerge triumphant and transfigured from my sadness. Maybe here, I could coalesce the lost pieces of myself, fragments of both flesh and spirit rent asunder by the cage of a profit economy in which my father was a number and my *monte* was for sale. Lost in my self-reflexive malaise, I kept Pepa under the water for a year, where she would never drown but be reborn. Under the earth, where all was not lost, Pepa would unite the world of nature and the world of spirit; here she would encircle the numinous. This idea is in keeping with what Jane Caputi discusses as Anzaldúa's honoring of "downward pathways and shapeshifting as transformational" (186). Such paths to knowledge encompass veiled realms that are mythic, spiritual, and very powerful.

One of the most basic forms of utopian impulse is social dreaming, which Levitas suggests is "not just wishful, but will-full thinking" (88). Anzaldúa's vision of entering into the serpent allows her to see, feel, experience the world differently—healed and "through serpent and eagle eyes" (*Borderlands* 100-101). Social dreaming on the Borderlands is enmeshed in the idea that if all humans allowed themselves to be swallowed by the earth's serpent, "a massive uprooting of dualistic thinking in the individual and collective consciousness" could be actualized (*Borderlands* 102). This act presupposes an apocalyptic overturning of destructive patterns that keep us at odds, at war even, with the world around us. This sentiment is mirrored throughout Miguel López-Lozano's book on the history of utopian representation in Mexican and Chicano narratives, in which he discusses the use of apocalyptic imagery and images to suggest alternative models of development amidst the forces of Western industrialization and globalization. Similarly, Maxine Lavon Montgomery theorizes how, in African-American literary tradition, apocalyptic imagery constitutes visions concerned with the end of oppressive sociopolitical systems and regimes in favor of new world orders where racial and social justice prevails.[4]

In "Reading LP," a posthumously published short story collected in the *Anzaldúa Reader*, Prieta, one of Anzaldúa's alter egos found throughout her work, accesses another world through a common science fiction trope—the portal. In the story, this portal is a book. And through this portal, readers move alongside Prieta within an interior landscape. In her introduction to the story, AnaLouise Keating describes LP's journey as one surrounding an "unconscious subreality… an inner world of thought, where fantasy and dream states and the inner world of the spirit all converge" (250). When LP moves through this portal, she becomes embedded in the landscape and homes in on messages that she can hear, feel, and smell:

> She studies the landscape as she would a painting but she can't maintain the distance necessary to be merely an observer. She is embedded in it. To look at it is to look at herself. She could solve the mystery of what's just happened to her only if she could read the landscape, as if the land could give her a message through its feel, sounds, and smells (251).

LP both conceptualizes and travels within the interstitial spaces between worlds. Similarly, the world that emerges from the cinders of ecological catastrophe in *Becoming Nawili* embeds a transformative environmentalism, an actual ever-shifting landscape caught in the middle. Within this terrain, humans and animals must re-learn to relate to *la tierra* in a way that responds to it out of psychic and biological energy rather than physical force—a way of being that I argue is at the core of Anzaldúa's utopianism. In *Nawili* the landscape becomes sentient and changes to necessitate transformative, integrative, and participatory patterns of living. When writing the novel, I wanted to empty the landscape and then fill it. In this way, Pepa and all organic forms, must re-learn to commune with the landscape in order to survive. In "Reading LP," the landscape frames essential aspects of Prieta's human consciousness, incorporating imagery and feminist insights that recall preindustrial worldviews of the earth as a living organism and nurturing mother. The utopic impulse in *Nawili* is a direct parallel to the utopic impulses I believe undergird the most compelling aspects of Anzaldúa's canon, ideas that serve as a "lure and bait for ideology" and an allegorical outline for a better world (Jameson 3).

Scholars have begun to unpack theories and tropes associated with Gloria Anzaldúa's science fictional and speculative works, but there is little to no scholarship that develops insight into her utopian leanings. However, when we align Anzaldúa alongside the work of scholars and feminists who write from a spiritual ecofeminist perspective, women like Sally Gearhart and Marge Piercy, we broaden the base of critical approaches in the emerging canon of Latin@ and Chican@ speculative cultural productions. These authors complicate the impulse to social dreaming by creating new psychological shapes that favor interiority, communality, and relationships with the natural world, especially as they envision ways that states of consciousness and the power of the mind can trigger fundamental changes in society. When Anzaldúa states that part of the work of the *mestiza* consciousness is to engender a space—first individual, and then communal—that culminates in a vast uprooting of dualistic thinking in the individual and the collective consciousness, she is envisioning a future utopian temporality signified by the mutability of the mind and human nature. Ultimately, Anzaldúa's utopianism is a form of social dreaming that is capable of not just healing but renewing our waning natural landscapes—but only if difference and diversity are the compass that redirects our humanism in such a way that our primal ties to *la tierra* take center stage.

NOTES

1. See Catriona Sandilands, *The Good-Natured Feminist: Ecofeminism and the Quest for Democracy.* U of Minnesota P, 1999; Gwyn Kirk, "Ecofeminism and Chicano Environmental Struggles: Bridges Across Gender and Race." *Chicano Culture, Ecology, Politics*, edited by Devon G. Peña, U of Arizona P, 1998, pp.177-200; and Monica Sjöö and Barbara Moor, *The Great Cosmic Mother: Rediscovering the Religion of the Earth*, Harper, 1991.

2. For more, see "Varieties of the Utopian" in Jameson's *Archaeologies of the Future: The Desire Called Utopia and Other Science Fictions.* Verso, 2007; and Bloch's *The Principle of Hope*, Vols. 1–3. MIT Press, 1995.

3. See Darko Suvin, *Metamorphoses of Science Fiction: On the Poetics and History of a Literary Genre.* Yale UP, 1979.

4. See Miguel López Lozano. *Utopian Dreams, Apocalyptic Nightmares: Globalization in Recent Mexico and Chicano Narrative.* Purdue UP, 2008; and Maxine Lavon Montgomery. *The Apocalypse in African-American Fiction.* UP of Florida, 1996.

WORKS CITED

Anzaldúa, Gloria. *Borderlands/La Frontera: The New Mestiza.* 2nd Ed. Aunt Lute, 1999.

---. "Nepantla: Theories of Composition." 1995. Manuscript drafts. Box 61, folders 20–21, Gloria Evangelina Anzaldúa Papers, Benson Latin American Collection, University of Texas, Austin.

---. "A Short Q & A between LP and Her Author (GEA)." *The Gloria Anzaldúa Reader*, edited by AnaLouise Keating, Duke UP, 2009, pp. 274-275.

brown, adrienne marie. "Outro." *Octavia's Brood: Science Fiction Stories from Social Justice Movements.* Eds. Walidah Imarisha, adrienne marie brown, and Sheree Renee Thomas. AK Press, 2015, pp. 197-198.

Caputi, Jane. "Shifting the Shapes of Things to Come: The Presence of the Future in the Philosophy of Gloria Anzaldúa." *Entre Mundos/Among Worlds: New Perspectives on Gloria Anzaldúa*, edited by AnaLouise Keating, Palgrave, 2005, pp. 185-194.

Jameson, Fredric. *Archaeologies of the Future: The Desire Called Utopia and Other Science Fictions.* Verso, 2007.

Levitas, Ruth. *The Concept of Utopia.* Syracuse UP, 1990.

Ramírez, Catherine S. "Cyborg Feminism: The Science Fiction of Octavia E. Butler and Gloria Anzaldúa." *Reload: Rethinking Women + Cyberculture*, edited by Mary Flanagan and Austin Booth, MIT Press, 2002, pp. 374-402.

Rosen, Elizabeth K. *Apocalyptic Transformation: Apocalypse and the Postmodern Imagination.* Lexington Books, 2008.

ANZALDÚA'S SPIRITUAL VISION OF THE BORDERLANDS & CHRISTIAN SPIRITUALITY

RICARDO L. FRANCO

The work of Gloria Evangelina Anzaldúa (1942–2004) is difficult to classify. She is mainly known as a Chicana author, and her writings encompass a variety of genres such as poetry, fiction, autobiography, essays, and letters. Her theory has had influence in many fields and is being explored by diverse disciplines such as feminist, ethnic, literary, cultural, queer, pedagogical, and political studies.[1] However, despite the growing scholarly production around her work, very little attention has been given to the importance of her religious/spiritual contribution to the fields of religious studies in general and Christian spirituality in particular. Religious scholars David Carrasco and Roberto Lint Sagarana assert that while many scholars and writers "have focused on ethnic, gendered, and political elements" of Anzaldúa's work, "the heart of her portrayal of the borderlands is articulated, and must be understood, as a religious vision." ("Religious Vision" 224)

As early as 1995, Anzaldúa identified this fragmented reading of the various elements present in her work:

> The "safe" elements in *Borderlands* are appropriated and used, and the "unsafe" elements are ignored. One of the things that doesn't get talked about is the connection between body, mind, and spirit. Nor is anything that has to do with the sacred, anything that has to do with the spirit. As long as it's theoretical and about history, about borders, that's fine; borders are a concern that everybody

> has. But when I start talking about nepantla—as a border between the spirit, the psyche, and the mind or as a process—they resist. (Keating, "Risking" 7)

Anzaldúa points out how in academic settings this type of spiritual knowing is often associated with a "devalued form of knowledge" inferior to science and rationality ("now let us" 542). This resistance to the spiritual components in her work hindered, at least in the initial stages of development in the field of Anzaldúan studies, the exploration of her religious contribution. AnaLouise Keating affirms that Anzaldúa's spiritual vision is central to her lifework and cannot be ignored ("Risking" 8). Since her departure in 2004, there has been a growing discussion around the spiritual elements of her theories.[2] Nevertheless, in the words of Anthony Lioi, Anzaldúa's religious thought continues to be "the most undertheorized" aspect of her work ("Best" 73).

In *The Unassimilated Theorist*, Latina feminist and philosopher Linda Martín Alcoff praises Anzaldúa for the "unapologetic disclosures of her spiritual faith" (255), although she does not expand on the nature of Anzaldúa's spiritual faith. There are very few scholarly articles which consider the theological implications of Anzaldúa's work, and not a single study of any of her theories from the perspective of Christian spirituality, neither Catholic nor Protestant.[3] In this paper I first explore Anzaldúa's complex relationship with the Catholic Church of her upbringing. Second, I show how in her spiritual vision of the Borderlands, she drew on, among many other religious traditions, classical Christian spiritual writings and biblical passages, always contesting and subverting Eurocentric, male-dominated, and misogynistic interpretations and practices of the institutional Church. Finally, I argue that the language of *Borderlands* as a category of spiritual experience is a new grammar of the soul appropriate to name spiritual dimensions and experiences relevant to Latinx religious communities trapped and silenced within the limits of traditional Christian liturgy and spirituality.

ANZALDÚA'S EARLY RELIGIOUS EXPERIENCES: "...FOR THE MUSIC AND FOR THE INCENSE."

In a 1983 interview with Linda Smuckler, Anzaldúa informs us that she was born and raised in a "spiritual but not religious" family ("Spirituality" 79). She and her siblings were brought up in a tradition that blended indigenous religion and Catholicism. There was a Catholic church in Hargill, but they did not attend regularly. Anzaldúa and her siblings were all "baptized as Catholics and made the first communion and confirmation" ("Within" 94) but not because of any personal inclination or desire. They were simply "forced" to participate in these rituals, mostly because of the influence of their grandmothers (94). Anzaldúa comments that even at that early age, for her "the church felt very alien" and she would go only "for the music and for the incense" ("Spirituality" 79).

There was, however, an event that became decisive in Anzaldúa's assessment of the religious traditions of her family, and that was the death of her father, Urbano. She wrote a piercing short piece describing her internal processing during the wake and burial.[4] Years later, reflecting on the impact of this loss, she told Karin Ikas that "beginning with the death of her father and her *desencanto*," she was disillusioned with traditional Catholicism, and she rebelled ("Interview" 278). In her *autohistoria La Prieta*, Anzaldúa explains the implications of this *desencanto* in her religious thinking: "His death occurred just as I entered puberty. It irrevocably shattered the myth that there exists a male figure to look after me … I lost my father, god, and my innocence in one bloody blow" (40). For four years after the passing of her father, Anzaldúa "waited for the promises of religion to kick in, but its rituals didn't bring him back" ("Within" 98).

Out of this *desencanto*, Anzaldúa developed an important distinction between what she calls religious faith and spiritual faith. She thinks that "spirituality has nothing to do with religion" because, even though religion recognizes the presence of spirit, it "puts a dogma around it," eliminating "all kinds of growth, development, and change" ("Within" 98). For Anzaldúa, spiritual faith goes beyond any "personal representation of God" and it is a "real faith in the spirit" (98). Formalized religious faith, on the other hand, gives spirit "the wrong body, the wrong words, and the wrong forms" (98). The Church, she adds, "has taken the very essence of what spirit is and subverted it" (100). For this reason, in *Borderlands/La Frontera* she says, "in my own life, the Catholic Church fails to give meaning to my daily acts, to my continuing encounters with the 'other world.' It and other institutionalized religions impoverish all life, beauty, pleasure" (59).

Throughout all of her writings, Anzaldúa maintained this clear distinction between spirituality as a genuine expression of the soul, the inner self, the creative consciousness, and organized Catholic or Protestant religion with their dogmas, structures, and the body-spirit split. Her dislike of established religion and yet her appreciation for spirituality becomes clear in the 1983 interview conducted by Linda Smuckler where Anzaldúa unapologetically declares, "I hate Protestantism, I hate Christianity, I hate Judaism. Not the spirituality of it, but the establishment, the bureaucracy, the dogma" ("Spirituality" 94).

ANZALDÚA'S USE OF CHRISTIAN SPIRITUALITY: "I WANT TO TALK ABOUT THE BIBLE VERSE…"

Anzaldúa's radical position toward organized religion did not prevent her from crossing methodological lines and using authors, categories, and motives of Christian spirituality in her theories.[5] Sometimes she alludes to biblical expressions without quoting Scriptures, and this makes sense in light of the fact that in college she took two courses in Christian studies: The Life of Christ and The Bible as Literature ("Spirituality" 80). In her writing, she also refers to the spiritual experiences of classical mystics such as Sor Juana Inés de la Cruz, Teresa de Ávila, Juan de la Cruz, and Thomas Merton, the Roman Catholic theologian, mystic, and social activist. Furthermore, Anzaldúa intentionally engages in alternative and disruptive biblical interpretations of texts foundational to Christian theology. In an interview with Christine Weiland, she says:

> I want to talk about the Bible verse, "In the beginning was the Word and the Word was God." This statement before it got corrupted by the church fathers meant that in the beginning was the sound, the vibration—a rock, a plant, an animal, a human, a particular area. That vibration is like the song of its being, its heartbeat, its rhythm ... Spirit exists in everything, therefore God, the divine, is in everything—in whites as well as in blacks, rapists as well as victims; in the tree, the swamp, the sea ... Everything is my relative. The church has taken the very essence of what spirit is and subverted it. ("Within"100)

This is Anzaldúa's reading of the first verse of the gospel of John through the lens of Native American cosmology and epistemology, in opposition to the traditional theological interpretation by the Church in Greek philosophical categories. It is worth noticing here how she dialogues not just with a Bible verse but with patristic theology and its appropriation by the institutional Church.

But perhaps her most elaborate revision of a Christian theme pertains to the traditions around the symbol of Our Lady of Guadalupe. In the early 1980s, she said that the Virgen de Guadalupe had never really appealed to her ("Spirituality" 94). However, in her analysis of Mesoamerican mythology and Mexican/Chicana folk Catholicism in *Borderlands/La Frontera*, Anzaldúa considers La Virgen de Guadalupe the "central deity" connecting people of Mesoamerican ancestry to their Indian roots as well as their "spiritual, political, and psychological symbol" (*Borderlands* 49, 52). According to Anthony Lioi, in *Borderlands/La Frontera*, Anzaldúa "transforms, but does not abandon some of the central tropes of Catholic theology" ("Best" 75). Instead of saying that Anzaldúa does not abandon Catholic theology, it is more accurate to affirm that, in her approach, she aims to problematize doctrines which she never embraced in the first place. In her strategic reading, Anzaldúa retrieves the Mesoamerican roots embedded in the Christian icon and exposes the historical, theological, and linguistic dimensions undergirding the oppressive function of the symbol in Catholic/Protestant religion.

Another example of her alternative exegesis of a biblical text (Genesis 3) appears in her chapter "*now let us shift...the path of conocimiento...inner work, public acts*." Her analysis exposes with a sophisticated methodology the biblical roots and practical implications of one of the most fundamental doctrines in Christian theology, namely the doctrine of *original sin*. At the same time, she offers an alternative narrative—drawn from Mesoamerican cosmology—through which she reverts the paralyzing and oppressive effects of the Christian *myth of the fall*. This technique, which she calls spiritual *mestizaje*, "weaves together beliefs and practices from many cultures including elements of Shamanism, Buddhism, Christianity, Santeria, and other traditions" ("Foreword" 230), in order to subvert traditional modes of interpretation.

According to Christianity and other spiritual traditions, she explains, "the evil that lies at the root of the human condition is the desire to know" ("now let us" 542-543), and those female origin figures seeking alternative forms of knowledge, like Xochiquetzal or Eve, have been demonized and expelled from the paradise for seeking knowledge from *el árbol sagrado*. Backing this narrative, there is a suppressive politics of knowledge, the epistemological monopoly of those who are in power (male priests) and who control official laws "decreed by church and culture" (543). Against this myth, Anzaldúa articulates the counter-narratives of Cihuacoatl and Coyolxauhqui. She issues a call to "rewrite collectively the story of the fall and the story of western progress" (562).

In Anzaldúa's rewriting of these stories, Cihuacoatl, the goddess of origins, represents "not the root of all evil" but rather alternative ways of instinctual knowing that "fuel transformation" (543). Coyolxauhqui, the Mesoamerican moon goddess who, according to Aztec mythology, was butchered into pieces by her brother Huitzilopochtli, god of war, is also central to her theories. For Anzaldúa, putting Coyolxauhqui together—re-membering—is another way to gain "conocimiento," a strategy to seek "experiences that'll give you purpose, give your life meaning, give you a sense of belonging" (562). The collective rewriting of these foundational narratives must lead our communities "out of passivity and into agency, out of devalued into valued lives," and we should use this information "with intelligence, imagination, and grace, to solve [our] problems and create intercultural communities." (563) Again, here we see how Anzaldúa engages texts and theological categories of biblical mythology to put them in conversation with Mesoamerican mythology in order to contest traditional, misogynistic, Christian religious assumptions.

ANZALDÚA'S CONTRIBUTION TO CHRISTIAN SPIRITUALITY: "... HOW COULD I RECONCILE THE PAGAN AND THE CHRISTIAN?"

Anzaldúa's theoretical construction of the spiritual reverberations of *Borderlands* is unique and practically uncharted by theoreticians and practitioners of Christian spirituality. Although she clearly distanced herself from institutionalized Christian religion, her writings reflect an interest in addressing the important question she raised in *Borderlands/La Frontera* when she asked, "growing up between such opposing spiritualties how could I reconcile the two, the pagan and the Christian?" (60). The strength of her spiritual vision lies in the confluence of various streams of experience, religious traditions, and social milieu organized around an imaginary landscape and journey of the soul in the same tradition as that of Teresa de Ávila's mansions of the self. In Anzaldúa's religious vision, I have found the language to name *las vivencias* observed in Latinx religious communities of Borderlands dwellers, as well as to articulate a spirituality of ethnic identity and cultural affirmation in Latinx ministry. The language of the Borderlands as envisioned by Anzaldúa is a grammar of the soul appropriate to naming spiritual categories and experiences for which traditional Christian liturgical and spiritual nomenclature is insufficient.

In her theory, the geopolitical spaces of the Borderlands function as a threshold into existential, spiritual, and embodied realities shaped by the specific historical, religious, racial, and economic conditions of those who live simultaneously in diverse cultures. Borderlands emerge every time that people, institutions, and practices embedded in different worldviews and cultural systems collide. Borderland conditions are not limited by the geographical location of individuals, since in this theory the construction of borders as an analytical tool includes categories of linguistic, psychological, religious, gender, sexual, and ethnic experience.

NEPANTLA, LA FACULTAD, AND MAKING FACE/MAKING SOUL AS SPIRITUAL CATEGORIES

The space or locus for creative theological-spiritual reflection unveiled by Anzaldúa opens new ontological, epistemological, and ethical horizons particular to the spiritual topography of the Borderlands. Her imaginative constructions of Nepantla, La Facultad and Making Face/Making Soul are alternative ways of voicing this spirituality.[6] Nepantla captures the existential and ontological dimensions, the flesh and soul makeup of Borderlands people. Through La Facultad, Borderlands dwellers deconstruct Western epistemological patterns and traverse the porous boundaries of body, mind, soul, and spirit. Making Face/Making Soul is an ethical-based spirituality for individual and social transformation and political mobilization.[7]

With the category of Nepantla, Anzaldúa captures the existential landscapes and internal dynamics of my own Borderlands experience and the experiences of Latinx immigrant communities in ways I have not found articulated in any other spirituality. The permeability of the concept corresponds to the fluidity of the experiences it portrays, and, in turn, it allows space to interpret geopolitical, ethnic, linguistic, and historical configurations of the self. Nepantla also provides an ontological terrain wherein the epistemological strategy of La Facultad and the ethical imperative of Making Face/Making Soul can be deployed.

The theorization and descriptions of La Facultad validate ways of religious knowing generally overlooked or considered suspicious in academic discourses of Christian spirituality. In a culture based on the myth of the exactness and objectivity of the scientific method, La Facultad puts a question mark over this methodology by reclaiming the importance of imagination, intuition, and unconscious processes in the human endeavor of apprehending truth. La Facultad brings to the forefront questions about the spiritual meaning and role of the body, sensorial feelings, and gut discernment in the spiritual formation of individuals and communities.

The Mesoamerican spiritual practice of Making Face/Making Soul addresses a crucial need at the core of Latinx religious communities. Anzaldúa's description of brown faces as surfaces wherein social inscriptions and identity scripts are engraved is the most accurate diagnosis I have read of the predicament in which I see Latinx immigrant religious communities enmeshed. At the same time, it prescribes how to assert one's ethnocultural identity by carving out new faces and healing hearts and souls via the poetic-aesthetic spiritual discernment which the Nahua peoples coded by the expression *flor y canto*.

Anzaldúa's contributions in these three nomenclatures of spiritual discourse are transferable into categories of Christian spirituality. Further explorations of

Nepantla as locus of theological reflection, La Facultad as a category of theological epistemology, and Making Face/Making Soul as a practice of spiritual formation are still needed.

Perhaps no other of Anzaldúa's writings better depicts her vision of the spiritual journey through the topography of the Borderlands than "*now let us shift...*" In the estimation of AnaLouise Keating, this essay represents the culmination of Anzaldúa's personal, intellectual, ontological, and political journey ("Re-envisioning" xxvi). In this masterpiece—written only two years before her death—Anzaldúa builds on all her previous theories and aims to transform her personal life into a "narrative with mythological or archetypal threads not in the confessional tone...without victimization or sentimentality" (xxvii).

In "*now let us shift...*" Anzaldúa draws a route map through seven stages or "rites of passage" from *desconocimiento* to spiritual activism.[8] The stages point more toward an internal process of spiritual insight and transformation than to levels or steps in a linear progression of spiritual development as in traditional Christian spirituality. Anzaldúa's transformational ontology, epistemology, and ethics are woven through these stages in a balanced, tapestry-like combination of threads of *autohistoria*, cultural analysis, and theoretical approximation. The tone of the essay as a whole is imaginative, rich in metaphors, and recognizably liturgical. Anzaldúa's meditation on these rites of passage challenges the classical medieval spiritual itinerary based on the Triple Way (Purgative-Contemplative-Unitive) by offering human texture and social context to the analysis of the religious experience of peoples whose cultural, ethnoracial, and cognitive frameworks do not coincide with Western patterns of thought and religious worldviews.

CONCLUSION

Lioi considers Anzaldúa a "Catholic essayist." He explains, "If we hesitate to call Anzaldúa herself a Catholic, we are still left with her writing, which contains Catholic symbols, narratives, concepts, figures, and images in its deepest structures" ("Best" 74). Contrary to Lioi, I believe that the issue of religious affiliation should be differentiated from the methodologies and strategies of an author. Gloria Anzaldúa grappled critically with Christian texts and doctrines because of the importance of those traditions in the religious context she was trying to call into question, but she never ascribed herself or her writing to any particular religious group. Randy P. Conner describes her relationship with the Catholic Church as "complex" and "beyond the border of Post-Catholic identification" ("Santa" 197). This fact, however, does not diminish the importance of her contribution to the academic study of Christian spirituality. Her spiritual vision of the Borderlands experience offers a new frame of reference to develop creative personal and collective spiritual practices of social action and individual transformation. As has always been the case with those who venture to cross the borders of religious orthodoxy, after marginalization and condemnation, new generations recognize that those whom the Church called heretics were in fact visionaries and prophetesses. Anzaldúa's theories will continue liberating spirituality from the clutches of institutionalized religion.

> We are ready for change.
> Let us link hands and hearts
> together find a path through the dark woods
> step through the doorways between worlds
> leaving huellas for others to follow,
> build bridges, cross them with grace, and claim these puentes our "home."
> ("now let us" 576)

NOTES

1. See Mohammad H. Tamdgidi, "Re-membering Anzaldúa." This special issue of the journal *Human Architecture: Journal of the Sociology of Self-Knowledge* contains more than thirty articles by scholars of many disciplines who engage Anzaldúa's theories in their fields of research, theory, and practice.

2. See Anthony Lioi, "The Best-Loved Bones"; Carla Wilson, "The Liminal"; and Anne-Marie Bowery, "Voices from Within."

3. See for instance the works by Latinx biblical scholars and theologians Manuel Villalobos, "Bodies Del Otro Lado"; Mayra Rivera, "God at the Crossroads"; and Nancy E. Bedford, "To speak of God."

4. Gloria Anzaldúa, "People Should Not Die in June in South Texas."

5. For instance, she alludes to Sor Juana Inés de la Cruz ("now let us" 547); Teresa de Ávila (*Borderlands*, 176); Thomas Merton ("now let us" 572); and John of the Cross ("Daughter of Coatlicue,"45). Sometimes she uses biblical expressions without quoting scriptures, e.g., the tree of life ("Flights" 25); the mark of the beast (*Borderlands* 64); holy ground ("now let us" 558); the promised land (*Borderlands* 33); and speaking in tongues ("Speaking in Tongues" 26). In several of her writings she challenges traditional interpretation of the "fall" narrative in Genesis 3 and other biblical passages as well, see for instance ("now let us" 542-543, 573; "Within," 100; "Toward a Mestiza" 266. Finally, she takes theologically laden words such as conversion, spiritual re-birth, and resurrection and gives them new interpretations in light of her theories, see "now let us" 545, 554; and *Borderlands* 24.

6. Although Anzaldúa did not capitalize these terms in her writing, given their centrality and specificity as spiritual practices for my argument, I use capital letters to convey their particular meaning as categories of analysis.

7. For an extensive analysis of these theories through the lenses of biblical imagery, Christian theology, and Mesoamerican spiritual substrata, see Ricardo L. Franco, *Borderlands Spirituality.*

8. Interestingly, in Roman Catholic theology there are seven sacraments, each one identified with a rite of passage.

WORKS CITED

Alcoff, Linda Martín. "The Unassimilated Theorist." *PMLA*, vol. 121, no. 1, 2006, pp. 255-259.

Anzaldúa, Gloria. *Borderlands/La Frontera: The New Mestiza.* 4th ed., Aunt Lute, 2012.

---. "Daughter of Coatlicue: An Interview with Gloria Anzaldúa." Irene Lara. *Entre Mundos/Among Worlds: New Perspectives on Gloria Anzaldúa* edited by AnaLouise Keating, Palgrave Macmillan, 2005, pp. 41-55.

---. "Flights of the Imagination: Rereading/Rewriting Realities." *Light in the Dark/Luz en lo Oscuro: Rewriting Identity, Spirituality, Reality*, edited by AnaLouise Keating, Duke University Press, 2015, pp. 23-46.

---. "Foreword to *Cassell's Encyclopedia of Queer Myth, Symbol and Spirit.*" *The Gloria Anzaldúa Reader*, edited by AnaLouise Keating, Duke University Press, 2009, pp. 229-231.

---. "Interview with Karin Ikas." *Borderlands/La Frontera: The New Mestiza*, 4th ed., Aunt Lute, 2012, pp. 267-284.

---. "La Prieta." *The Gloria Anzaldúa Reader*, edited by AnaLouise Keating, Duke University Press, 2009, pp. 38-50.

---. "now let us shift...the path of conocimiento...inner work, public acts." *this bridge we call home: radical visions for transformation*, edited by Gloria E. Anzaldúa and AnaLoiuse Keating, Routledge, 2002, pp. 540-578.

---. "People Should Not Die in June in South Texas." *My Story's On: Ordinary Women, Extraordinary Lives*, edited by Paula Ross, Common Differences Press, 1985, pp. 280-287.

---. "Speaking in Tongues: A Letter to Third World Women Writers." *The Gloria Anzaldúa Reader*, edited by AnaLouise Keating, Duke University Press, 2009, pp. 26-35.

---. "Spirituality, Sexuality, and the Body." *The Gloria Anzaldúa Reader*, edited by AnaLouise Keating, Duke University Press, 2009, pp. 74-94.

---. "Toward a Mestiza Rhetoric: Gloria Anzaldúa on Composition, Postcoloniality, and the Spiritual." An Interview with Andrea Lunsford. *Interviews/Entrevistas*, edited by AnaLouise Keating, Routledge, 2000, pp. 251-280.

---. "Within the Crossroads: Lesbian/Feminist/Spiritual Development. An Interview with Christine Weiland." *Interviews/Entrevistas*, edited by AnaLouise Keating, Routledge, 2000, pp. 71-127.

Bedford, Nancy E. "To speak of God from more than one place: Theological reflections from the experience of migration." *Latin American Liberation Theology: The Next Generation*, edited by Ivan Petrella, Orbis, 2005, pp. 95-118.

Bowery, Anne-Marie. "Voices from Within: Gloria Anzaldúa, bell hooks, and Roberta Bondi." *The Gift of Story: Narrating Hope in a Postmodern World*, edited by Emily Griesinger and Mark Eaton, Baylor University Press, 2006, pp. 51-68.

Carrasco, David, and Roberto Lint Sagarena. "The Religious Vision of Gloria Anzaldúa: Borderlands/La Frontera as a Shamanic Space." *Mexican American Religions: Spirituality, Activism, and Culture*, edited by Gastón Espinosa and Mario T. García, Duke University Press, 2008, pp. 223-241.

Conner, Randy P. "Santa Nepantla: A Borderlands Sutra." *El Mundo Zurdo*, edited by Norma E. Cantú, et al., Aunt Lute, 2016, pp. 177-202.

Franco, Ricardo L. *Borderlands Spirituality: Practical Theology and Ministry in Three Latino Protestant Congregations.* Doctoral Dissertation, Boston University School of Theology, 2017.

Keating, AnaLoiuse. "Risking the Personal: An Introduction." *Interviews/Entrevistas*, edited by AnaLouise Keating, Routledge, 2000, pp.1-15.

---. "Re-envisioning Coyolxauhqui, Decolonizing Reality: Anzaldúa's Twenty-First Century Imperative." *Light in the Dark/Luz en lo Oscuro: Rewriting Identity, Spirituality, Reality*, by Gloria E. Anzaldúa. Duke University Press, 2015, pp. ix-xxxvii.

Lioi, Anthony. "The Best-Loved Bones: Spirit and History in Anzaldúa's Entering into the Serpent." *Feminist Studies*, vol. 34, no. 1/2, 2008, pp.73-95.

Rivera, Mayra. "God at the Crossroads: A Postcolonial Reading of Sophia." *The Postcolonial Biblical Reader*, edited by R.S. Sugirtharajah, Blackwell, 2006, pp. 238-253.

Tamdgidi, Mohammad H. "Re-membering Anzaldúa: Human Rights, Borderlands, and the Poetics of Applied Social Theory: Engaging with Gloria Anzaldúa in Self and Global Transformations." *Human Architecture: Journal of the Sociology of Self-Knowledge*, vol. 4, 2006.

Villalobos, Manuel. "Bodies Del Otro Lado finding life and hope in the Borderlands: Gloria Anzaldúa, the Ethiopian eunuch of acts 8:26-40, y yo." *Bible Trouble: Queer Reading at the Boundaries of Biblical Scholarship*, edited by Teresa J. Hornsby and Ken Stone, Society of Biblical Literature, 2011, pp. 191-221.

Wilson, Carla "The Liminal, the Luminous, and the Dark: The Path of Conocimiento and the Dark Night of the Soul." *El Mundo Zurdo*, vol. 5, edited by Domino Renee Perez, et al. Aunt Lute, 2016, 113-125.

QUEERING NATIONS AND IMAGINATIONS

QUEERING TERRORISM

DISRUPTING THE TERRITORIALIZATION OF GENDER THROUGH CONVERSATIONS ABOUT THE BORDERLANDS OF BODY AND NATION

LOBAT ASADI & MARIO I. SUÁREZ

INTRODUCTION

El Mundo Zurdo, the left-handed Anzaldúan world, nudges those concepts that have been neglected and hidden in normative society to shine light on the issues that remain dark, much like that which lurks in the periphery of Anzaldúa's writing—indigenous wisdom about gender. We, the authors, Lobat, a cisgender female, and Mario, a transgender male, investigate post-gender space by disrupting modern paradigms about what it means to be in brown bodies that instill territorial fear over the borders of nationality and gender. These lingering and disturbing issues of colonialism continue the oppression of brown women and transgender people. We assert that genderism and transphobia exist in our everyday spaces and conversations. Heteronormativity and nationalism alone may have the potential to impact identity, but when these norms are questioned through self-reflective shadow work, we learn to illuminate those engendered perceptions. Through duoethnography, our voices queer gender norms and expose how that queering can impact one's identity both with and without societal identifications. Thus, we reflect on our friendship as a heightened awareness in the form of binary resistance with respect to the interconnectedness of respective gender roles and expectations.

Anzaldúa (23) offers insights about a new indigenous mestiza consciousness that emphasizes intersectionalities that emerge from the physical and astral spaces of the borderlands and evoke non-binary paradigm shifts. Similar to control over female bodies, in order to control neoliberal economic gains, geographic borderlands have been created to legitimize poverty on one side and encourage working class labor under the premise of a more glamorous life on the other side of the Rio Grande River (Noguera 314). We argue that patriarchal figures of cultural domination have created fictitious explanations of gender which have caused binary terrorism in the bodies of people. Women are either fetishized or mutilated in order to possess and propel biopolitics (Puar 522). Thus, we attempt to merge indigenous knowledge, while acknowledging it is not monolithic, with Western thought that may have appropriated and commodified practices. This response comes as a result of the fetishism of the female body that has induced personal traumas, thus these power structures that control femininity must be deconstructed in order to complicate the current issues in gender that we have faced. We ask: What are some ways in which two people with seemingly different upbringings and backgrounds find similarities on issues relevant to ways of thinking about engendered discrimination?

METHOD

In typical ethnographies, participants state their gender and background to presume a so-called realist account (Denzin 4). That normalizing practice is part of a larger "crisis of representation" (Denzin 9) in which anthropology and its sibling ethnography have used to represent cultural phenomena. After four centuries of land occupation and the impact on people of color in North America, we have opted to draw upon indigenous knowledges to focus on our intersections as participants in this self-study. As gatekeepers of gender non-conformity, our respective yet dual self-exploration organically flowed into the shadow work of autohistoria-teoría (Anzaldúa 169) because it was an intervention "into and transformations of traditional Western autobiographical forms" (Anzaldúa 9). Realizing the potential of this assemblage, we decided to blend cultural and personal biographies with memoir, myth, personal (her)histories and storytelling in the form of a duoethnography.

Duoethnography, conceptualized by Norris and Sawyer, is a methodology rooted in post-colonial inquiry that stems from Pinar's process of self-reflection in curriculum studies known as currere, in addition to storytelling (Norris 233): "Their stories weave back and forth in juxtaposition to one another, creating a third space between the two into which readers may insert their own stories," (Norris 234). Through our conversations and re-storying, we discovered how we have both been living in "undocumented" bodies.

POSITIONALITY

Lobat is a cisgender woman, a naturalized U.S. citizen, hailing from the national borders of Iran, and is ethnically half-indigenous to Central Asia—the Lor Bakhtiari tribe. Mario is a transgender Latinx man from the Texas-México border, born to a Mexican-American mother and a Mexican father. When responding to this self-illuminating urge towards mutual understanding, both sensed a need for a critical friendship to develop as they met walking on the same path—in the between spaces. When concepts fail to describe one's state of existence, due to their systemic restrictions, spaces of liminality can emerge (McLaren 92). That is, we both occupy spaces between two different worlds or cultures. This crossing of dimensions, in which our hybrid identities are validated because binary dominant normativity does not exist, challenges Anglo structures and territories. Thus, border identity is an "anticentering experience" of postimperial spaces, while housing cultural possibility.

Intersectional (Crenshaw 139) peoples identifying as hybrids of Latinx, immigrant, subaltern, and especially transnational women of color, disabled women of color, and LGBTIQ+-identifying women of color have been omitted from common discourse. When intersectional identities cannot be placed in clearly defined binary categories, they may accrue less social and cultural capital within a nation (Bourdieu 17). Thus, people who live in the periphery are deemed to be inferior or unworthy through unspoken expectations and resultant judgement, which results in implicit oppression. The authors, embodying intersectional identities, inhabit the crossroads of their identities as a transgender man from the borderlands and a non-gender-conforming cisgender woman from Iran—in the Anzaldúan (243) sense of a Nepantla consciousness. This shape-shifting awareness may be a socio-spatial understanding of each one's marginalization. In this way, the multiple forms of oppression—social, cultural, national—that each person faced, was palpable. While developing a critical friendship, Mario's and Lobat's known yet unspoken spaces of existence emerged as sources of strength.

THE PHOTOVOICE PULSE STUDY

Initially brought together in 2016 by a study about the Orlando Pulse nightclub shooting in which 49 LGBTIQ+ people were killed, Lobat and Mario became inspired by reflections of the participants of the study. After interviewing the participants, Lobat and Mario shared their feelings with one another about gender, sexuality, and "outness." In this way, a parallel track of inquiry emerged and resulted in a duoethnography around personal feelings of liminality, queerness, and associations with the physical and mental borders of territory. Thus, two forms of territorialization emerged in this duoethnography, both of which fall under nation building: a) binary enforcement through cultural and medical oppression of bodies and b) hybridized identities disrupting the standards of nation-building.

LOBAT ASKS WHY MARIO DEVELOPED THE PULSE STUDY:

> The Pulse nightclub shooting has produced a different reaction for me (Mario) than it might for another person, as I am a Latinx transman from the Texas-México border. I still remember the day I heard about the Pulse nightclub shooting in Orlando, Florida. My wife, a cisgender female, and I had traveled

> to El Paso, Texas, for my top surgery with one of the premier surgeons in Ciudad Juárez, Chihuahua. Upon hearing of the news of the massacre, I remember crying at night for several days, watching the news and my social media newsfeed, hearing the stories of the victims. That could have been me or any one of my friends. I have always sought refuge in the lesbian and gay community, so I was drawn to this study in order to further understand how my LGBTIQ+ siblings processed their grief after the event.

MARIO ASKS LOBAT WHY SHE WAS DRAWN TO LGBTIQ+ RESEARCH:

> The Pulse study was like witnessing love conquer violence. I (Lobat) had witnessed how gender norms and human sexuality have been fought way before my own realizations by courageous, non-heteronormative souls such as those I was interviewing for Pulse. Through this work, I realized I have always questioned my expected role(s) and desires as a woman. Thus, I began to question whether in fact they were mine or the result of environmental brainwashing. I was inspired by the brave participants in the study and wanted to face my gender after having a hysterectomy in 2016. If the womb has been removed, what is the female body comprised of? Clearly, it is a bag of hormones coupled with societal expectations. When modern medicine removes these reproductive parts, they are, arguably, also removing the physical constructs of the female gender. Yet, we are still expected to perform and present as women.

TOWARDS NEPANTLA

Nepantla is a space where the queer become entrenched and thrive, and the pathway for artists to become shamans (Anzaldúa 181). Anzaldúa describes nepantleras as people who are mediators that can assist the passage into other worlds. For Anzaldúa, that third space may be unsafe but can also serve as a bridge where humans may find they have more in common with each other than previously anticipated (*The Gloria Anzaldúa Reader* 243).

Mario asks: "Is Nepantla a transition toward something? Is it okay for a person to remain in transition forever? In a way, is society working towards something that might not exist in the neo-colonial world?"

Lobat responds:

> Yes. The neo-colonial is meant to be closed off with defined, albeit arbitrary borders. Yet, Nepantla seems like an organic place you cannot access forcefully, that is why Anzaldúa said borderland artists could enter it. So, I am intrigued by the point you make about remaining in it. Have we always been ambiguous? We both suffered until we became comfortable with gender ambiguity, however. It is just that we are okay with that ambiguity at this point in our respective lives. I see that we both thrive in this intersection, yet the outside world struggles and thus we remain in Nepantla. For me I think it is also a place of refuge.

MARIO INTERROGATES THE SOCIO-SPATIAL UNDERSTANDINGS OF NEPANTLA:

> Some people prefer staying in that in-between for different reasons, some societal, some physical—those in third gender and with gender nonconforming identities. As such they are able to genuinely and safely be themselves. In El Mundo Zurdo, it could well be that one is always in a state of transition working towards something that we might never get to, whether it be equality, gender, anti-racism, or something else. How do you feel, Lobat, about being ambiguous in the neo-colonial world? Would you prefer to stay in Nepantla?

LOBAT ADDRESSES RESIDING IN A SPACE PERCEIVED AS BEING OF CONSTANT TRANSITION:

> While I am content with my decision to not procreate, not being able to fit into that maternal category causes judgment or I am simply omitted. I conceive of myself as post-female now and as such I seek refuge in Nepantla. Furthermore, I find that in la frontera where the transborderists reside, I can sit comfortably within that ambiguous space. Ironically, it is within this indeterminate vortex that I feel I am at home. I become lost in my memories of the deserts of the Middle East and recollect my father's stories about our tribe who lived off the land. The borders and barriers I live with today as a North American and as a woman confine me.

SKINWALKERS

Over one year of such conversations, Mario and Lobat shared creation stories and discovered that they both dwelled within Anzaldúan Mundo Zurdo, not as touristic trespassers, but as permanent residents constructed by a spell that was both physical and spiritual. They inhabited this space for different reasons, yet these very differences have become a source of comfort, too, so they stayed within the membranes of this Nepantla cell, exploring and comforting one another and have yet to leave. Mario, born of the borderlands, physically and spiritually, grew up within liminality as he always wanted to physically look more like his brother and not be confined to activities set for little girls. On the other hand, Lobat never felt like she fit into America nor that Iran was her home. She lived between and betwixt notions of home, identity, and, as she would later discover, heteronormativity. In fact, both had been living under highly policed, regulated, and monitored borders of so-called normativity within neoliberal borders of nationalism. Yet, in order to survive in the neocolonial world, they both respectively learned how to become skinwalkers.

An elder in the Lipan Apache tribe, Julia Nava, defined the skinwalker phenomenon as a person who is walking as a human on Earth, but is unconscious about what is happening to the planet because they are not fully awake. According to Nava, this is because they have "fallen in love with themselves as skinwalkers and perceive themselves as their assigned human skin on this planet" (interview). Thus, their ancestral stories have been lost because they desire their material stories and power stances more than the genetic, ancestral memories buried within the fibers of their skin. In a sense, Mario and Lobat may have been skinwalkers at one time. Yet, within the physical and astral spaces of Nepantla, they both faced gender rebirth(s) and unraveled their struggles to emerge as the artists of their own bodies and their creators of their own mythologies.

MARIO DISCUSSES FEMALE SOCIALIZATION FROM A LATINX TRANSMAN'S PERSPECTIVE:

> I have always been more comfortable working and speaking to cisgender women about my experience. Perhaps it is because I was brought up by mostly Mexican females, as a female, on traditional Mexican gender roles. As a result, I think I have always had difficulty being open about my experiences with cisgender men. I do not get the perception that you, Lobat, "claim to understand" me. I think you provide me with a space and an ear that permits me to be myself and to understand that while we have different experiences, there is a shared similarity. This, in my mind, is a way to move forward with a "queer connection," as we both have had ovaries. In my case, I have no need for the female reproductive organs in my body, as I do not plan on bearing children. So, because I cannot conceive in a "male" way nor impregnate a woman, I am not medically perceived as a male. Similarly for you, losing your ability to reproduce, in some way, seems to have affected your role of "womanhood" in the eyes of society.
>
> Undergoing a gender transformation for me (Mario), specifically, entailed that I undergo hormone replacement therapy (HRT). However, that is not always the case for every transgender person, as, depending on the access to resources, funding, education, etc., the person may choose to not medically transition. My ability to reproduce as a man was never an option, nor one that I intend to pursue in a biological female body. Again, that is not the case for every trans person, and I completely support my trans siblings that opt to give birth.
>
> Throughout my journey, I (Mario) have witnessed the extreme discomfort that comes from being ostracized as an "other," growing up in the Texas-Mexico frontera, not just on my part, but on those who were afraid to approach me in the earlier stages of my transition, as they could not determine whether I was a male or female. I always felt like I was a part of the land of los atravesados without a place to call home or feel safe. After HRT, as I began to be perceived more as a cisgender man, I found that it was better for my safety to not have to correct people about my gender all the time. The fact was that people's perception of me as a man did not incorporate the thought of what was lying under my clothing or the hormones medically injected into my body. That realization made me understand that you and I have much more in common than we initially thought.

LOBAT ENTERS A SPACE COMMONLY OCCUPIED BY THE LGBTIQ+ COMMUNITY:

> It is important for me to not colonize your space and your experience as a transgender man undergoing medical and physically manifest revisions to the exterior and interior of your body. To explain myself, I was never really consumed with child-bearing, while my family and society have been. Thus, after many years of being told I needed a hysterectomy and could not bear

children, I conceded. Soon afterwards, I began to wonder—could this death of a birthing opportunity be a rebirth of the Self? My composition of clothes, hair and make-up is a theatrical performance that I sometimes enjoy, but I recognize that it is simply a choice. I am but an entity inhabiting a human body in a form of post-gender stasis, when in fact society would have me weeping as Llorona.[1] However, you, Mario, are a source of strength for me because you proudly embrace your transgender body.

MARIO POINTS OUT POTENTIAL TRANSMAN AND POST-FEMALE DIFFERENCES:

While I do agree with you that gender is socially constructed in a way, I do not think that transgender people have an option of just presenting because we are the gender we know we are, even if others do not see us in that light. Within your line of thought, are you saying that transgender men or transgender women would also be post-male or post-female?

LOBAT CLAIMS DESCRIPTIVE TERMINOLOGY FOR HER CURRENT VIEWS ON GENDER ARE LACKING:

This awareness is what I call post-female, simply because it feels empowering to put a name on it rather than mourn procreation. Yet I cannot put other people into that space. Given our hormonal differences, as clearly demonstrated in biological women's abilities to conceive and associated medical interventions of fertilization, there are likely as many genders as there are people. In this sense, I feel some kind of kinship to transgender people. I also wonder if the fact that I feel post-female places me in an ambiguous, queer, Nepantla space. I have developed an awareness that I inhabit this body, meaning that this body is just a vessel for me. As such, I am performing for the world in the socially constructed ways dictated for this body. I now realize that the extent to which I present myself to the world is based upon gender norms imposed on me since birth. I am aware that I could wear a sexy dress and get one reaction or wear a man's suit and get another, but this gender fluidity does not bother me as it might a transgender person. Ironically, the fact that I still feel "right" in my body after surgical changes to my gender helps me understand how a transgender person could feel wrong in their body, pre-medical intervention. Maybe I am not alone in this feeling of kinship and gender exploration, but the fact that nobody is engaging cisgender women in these conversations keeps it out of public discourse.

In my post-female identity, I sense a type of gender stasis, where any impending gender roles or actions, are suspended. As such, you (Mario) and I met in a similar space, where we can peek behind the curtain at the clockwork of our social and cosmological origins that assigned our gender(s) by the Anglo-Saxon binary epistemologies that we both reside in, in North America. My concept of post-female existence acknowledges a difference between the mental and biological constructs of femininity. This aesthetic distance highlights the alienation that women like me feel within societal constructs.

ANZALDÚA ALSO EXPRESSED HER VULNERABILITIES AFTER HAVING HAD A HYSTERECTOMY:

The doctor played with his knife. La Chingada ripped open, raped with the white man's wand. My soul in one corner of the hospital ceiling, getting thinner

> and thinner, telling me to clean up my shit, to release the fears and garbage from the past that are hanging me up. (*The Gloria Anzaldúa Reader* 43-44)

Later, Anzaldúa re-storied the myth of Llorona to fit an image of her own life. Anzaldúa reimages the mythology in a poem, "The Postmodern Llorona," so that instead of being destined to roam the Earth and cry for her the children that she drowned, after being left by a man:

> La Llorona attends UCSC, goes on picnics,
> and to the movies.
> La Llorona writes poems.
> The dismembered missing children are not
> the issue of her womb—she has no children.
>
> (*The Gloria Anzaldúa Reader* 281)

The power to re-story oneself in an image that is positive and appealing rather than meeting the expectations of society can be a powerful tool.

CRITICAL FRIENDSHIPS AS SOCIAL ACTIVISM

Similarly, while Lobat's and Mario's voices may be unique in the connections made about the morphing of their bodies into new images, they may be filling a gap of silenced people through this previously undocumented knowledge of the connectivity between a cisgender female who has undergone a hysterectomy and a transgender male. To illustrate, Banerjea, Dasgupta, Dasgupta, and Grant assert that friendship can be "a mode of disrupting heteronormative ordering of life," (1). Lobat and Mario's friendship may have remained undocumented, but in order to push forward, we choose to look at the connectivity between a cisgender woman and a transman as a form of protest against binary genders and gender roles. Binary, heteronormative friendships are not faced with the same pressures to be gender- or sex-normative. Thus, by exploring the possibilities of increasing awareness about shared experiences between transgender people and women who can relate to being non-gender-conforming, an unexpected kinship and support system may emerge. Raffo (145) explains that critical friendship means "that literally, at the most cellular level, I become a part of you and you of me."

Likewise, friendship as critical activism that resists patriarchy's over-lording of gender roles must be questioned. Lobat's and Mario's analogous experiences, shared as friends, have bridged the divides that allow for each to embrace their respective space(s) in a world that shuns non-binaries. Deeming the act of friendship between a cisgender woman and a transgender man as transformative work, rather than standard responses that are within existent systems, creates a space to accept new ways of knowing, continuing, sharing and experiencing friendship.

Lobat queries critical friendships and wants to capture the process: "What is the way to move forward with our intersections of space, body, and societal-role assignments to create positive, uplifting assemblages such as ours?"

MARIO BRINGS PERSPECTIVE ON CRITICAL ALLIES AS A SUPPORT SYSTEM:

> Rather than *the* way to move forward, I would more than anything suggest *a* way forward, anecdotally, based on our experience working together. In our case, you were open to learning more about the queer community via this project, and put yourself in a position to be a learner rather than a researcher with all the answers. Particularly with queer theoretical perspectives, it is important to understand, I think, that there are some of us who fit outside the "box," or what is seen as "normal," such as myself—a transgender man, assigned female at birth, from the Texas-Mexico border, born into low socio-economic circumstances. In your own way, you also fit "outside the box," but in a different way than myself or other queer people. I think that having a sensibility that lends itself to not only being empathetic towards difference, but embracing it, is a possible way towards the mestiza consciousness that Anzaldúa talks about in *Borderlands/La Frontera.*

CONCLUDING THOUGHTS

Anzaldúa's Borderlands *as a compass.* These binary gender "contracts" impact biopolitics and nation-building (Puar 436) and are perpetuated by the medical industry and patriarchy. Lobat and Mario looked for historic and personal lived experiences within minds and bodies as a means to heal as well as forge their friendship. Through these muddy waters, the authors learned that each was been formed our respective spirits reaching for survival by (re)claiming bodies as nepantlerx[2] shape-shifters. Living in this colonial realm, instead of being exiled to la nepantlerx spaces, between and betwixt, fetishized and hated, pitied and scorned, both Mario and Lobat individually claimed nepantlerx lives as legitimate existences. Anzaldúa, from the Texas-Mexico border, was fascinated by how borders present a duality, that is, an us-them dichotomy. Anzaldúa writes:

> The U.S.-Mexican border *es una herida abierta* where the Third World grates against the first and bleeds. And before a scab forms it hemorrhages again, the lifeblood of two worlds merging to form a third country—a border culture. Borders are set up to define the places that are safe and unsafe, to distinguish *us* from *them* [...] *Los atravesados* live here: the squint-eyed, the perverse, the queer, the troublesome, the mongrel, the mulato, the half-breed, the half-dead; in short, those who cross over, pass over, or go through the confines of the "normal." (*Borderlands/La Frontera* 25)

OCCUPYING QUEER SPACE

Ahmed describes the normative as something that appears to keep the body "in-line" and as such can be reproduced and retraced with the confines of those lines, thus if something appears out of line, it disorients that picture:

> Queer is, after all, a spatial term, which then gets translated into a sexual term, a term for a twisted sexuality that does not follow a "straight line," a sexuality that is bent and crooked (Cleto 2002: 13). The spatiality of this term is not

> incidental. Sexuality itself can be considered a spatial formation not only in the sense that bodies inhabit sexual spaces. (66)

The non-heteronormativity of existing outside of a national confine, within the borderlands, offers the queer space that Lobat and Mario need to be emancipated from gender and gender expression dichotomies. Likewise, Puar (632) explains that while living in a capitalist world but abstaining from the normative narratives, cyborg, or modified, identities avoid social categories determined to dominate the body, as does the non-binary status. However, entering queer space by avoiding social categories often disorients expectations and may entangle race. Ahmed (68) examines proximity and distance as measures of orientation or disorientation as borders placed upon brown bodies in order to place them within reach of racial categorizations by the colonial constructs of whiteness. Similarly, the authors have faced this through being tokenized, feared, restricted and/or isolated in social discourses that they appear too "queer" to enter.

Throughout *Borderlands/La Frontera*, Anzaldúa constantly weaves a complicated conversation centered around borders, whether it be through the Coatlicue state, the mita' y mita', the hieros gamos, or the notion of the new mestiza, all versions create a third voice (a third perspective, or anything other than a dichotomy) by embracing indigeneity. Anzaldúa does this, in part, through a mix of English and Spanish writing, along with Nahuatl, without any translation for the colonizer. Instead, she embraces it in a rebellious manner, without regards to whether the reader may or may not understand. However, as a new mestiza, she embraces and has a "tolerance for ambiguity" (*Borderlands/La Frontera* 101). As a self-proclaimed "homosexual," Anzaldúa contends that the role of queer people, particularly queer people of color, is to "link people with each other—the Blacks with Jews with Indians with Asians with whites with extraterrestrials" (*Borderlands/La Frontera* 106-7).

LOBAT ADDRESSES BIAS TOWARDS IMMIGRANTS FROM THE MIDDLE EAST:

> I cannot tell you how many times I have had to explain my nationality or explain my national alliances. I vote, reside in, pay taxes to, and contribute to the betterment of the U.S., but because of the color of my skin, my unusual name and the fact that I won't lie about my place of birth, people tend to question me. I feel as though my entire right to exist is being questioned, being that I hail from the "Orient" seems to confuse people further because they exoticize, oppress and perhaps fear me and others from my ethnic background. Furthermore, I have expectations to behave, worship, reproduce, and enact the stereotypes associated with Middle Eastern women, which, as a hybridized identity, I am self-confined to. Perhaps my ambiguity and resistance to fit into molds is the reason that I feel more at home in the Texas borderlands, a place of perpetual strife, change, and a milieu of cultures, than many other places.

SPIRIT IN THE FLESH:

In deconstructing how our hybrid identities were able to explore the borders of body and nation, we see how flesh was the bridge that we, the researchers, used to potentiate a new feminist movement involving women and transgender men of color. Cleary, sociopolitical status, gender roles, and binational identities disorient the notions of gender. The reconstruction of socio-political and spatial memories in tandem with gender is what Cherríe Moraga names as a "theory in the flesh" (24). By interrogating the narratives of our bodies and including the violence, the neglect, and the remaining wounds, a pedagogy of deconstruction, yet hope, is formed as a middle ground. A man-made border presenting a male or female dichotomy has created and perpetuated the societal us-versus-them mentality. In fact, people who do not reproduce are perceived as a deficit to society and concepts of citizenship are questioned. Aspirations of dominant global security include reproduction and high birth rates as hegemonic constructs of nation-building. Thus, fertility, medicine, and heteronormativity are interrelated constructs of labor reproduction, which reply on the reproduction of humankind, explains Puar (77).

Through our experiences as self-sojourners, we identified a third perspective, the Coatlicue state, the ambiguity, and dwelled in it long enough to realize that there is more that connects us as human beings than we are taught. It is not in categories, rather, it is in how we perceive those categories, that we are able to come to terms that a woman is a woman whether she is born with or without the ability to reproduce, or with a vagina or a penis, as is a man a man. The societal view that only two genders exist, and blind adherence to this construct, has led to bathroom bans, military restrictions, bullying, lack of medical care and other unethical treatment of transgender and gender-nonconforming peoples. Ironically, the same argument from conservatives, who say that transgender people should accept the body they are born into, even though they feel unwell, is nullified when cisgender women undergo hysterectomies for similar (medical) reasons. This brings us to a crucial conundrum: when gendering a person, what is it that we consider—the gender identity or the sexual organs? In fact, Anzaldúa's non-binary New Mestiza consciousness provides a fluidity to gender and even ethnic boundaries, which can be defined as bodies, minds, and actual borderlands. This is the place of consciousness where "the Third World grates against the first and bleeds" (25). Situating borders as arbitrary ways of meaning-making sheds light on the restrictions of current epistemologies. This new consciousness allows us to analyze the ways in which we traditionally determine gender and gender roles, so that we can deconstruct them and reimage them under applicable lived experiences.

MARIO QUESTIONS LOBAT ABOUT GENDER NON-CONFORMITY:

> I see the point you are making here, and I get it now. My question to you is, do you think perhaps we have to use gender identity, or our sexual and reproductive organs? How about not at all? In effect, wouldn't that be de-centering colonial thought, by thinking of this in a neither/all-type of gendering(s)?"

LOBAT RESPONDS:

> I think this is a very personal choice based upon the actual body and spirit. I would not presume to know how to determine that for other people. For me, I think it emerged out of shamanistic means, shadow work, and other reflective measures. My father, born in a tent in Central Asia, a mystic and conservationist who was profoundly connected to our tribal ancestral land and values, guided my belief of the alliance of mind, body, and land. This may have set the stage for the hysterectomy to have a profound impact on my understanding of gender as territorialization of the body. Furthermore, I always recognized that the sacredness of reproduction to my ancestors and the land conflicted with my personal lack of desire and ultimate inability to reproduce.

NAVIGATING THE FUTURE:

The authors believe that we organically reached for what Anzaldúa (1999) calls the Coatlicue state through our intersecting states of existence and found that we were meeting one another in the la nepantlerx space. It can be perceived as pedagogy, as Reza-López, Charles & Reyes (2014) postulate, but we examine how the Nepantla plane may be triggered by life circumstances of liminality as opposed to a prescribed pedagogy. Mahicantuck, otherwise dubbed by colonizers as the Hudson River, is the "great waters in constant motion" or loosely the "river that flows two ways." Yet, it must have a parting point in the middle. This point may be inaccessible by skinwalkers, just as la nepantla is a space that runs, but is invisible to those who do not live under the duress of liminality and conflict. This magical space may have sparked our indigenous ways of knowing and invited us into deeper conversations about trust, friendship, and intersectional waterways.

It is the fear of strangeness, of that which is unknown and difficult to label, that causes humans to simultaneously abuse and enforce gender. This gender-policing behavior fails to assess how the medical industry conflicts with, yet perpetuates, gender biases. This combination of surgery and socio-cultural labeling coupled with epistemological theories of gender roles, makes for very restrictive identity construction. This volatile blend of physical and spiritual law and order is debilitating and causes further suffering for millions of people who simply cannot satisfy their socio-culturally inflicted obligations. Thus, queer, post-female, transgender and even Muslims, Iranian-Americans, Mexican-Americans, and other such misunderstood people fall into "undocumented" categories to be feared and perceived as deformations to nationalism. We are alienated at best, and pitied at worst. The fact that the word "alien" is a common word to describe immigrants evidences this ostracization from humanity.

Why accept the victimization when immunity comes from within the soul? Modern medicine and sociocultural norms should not have the privilege of dictating one's body. Any alternatives, such as skin-walking, to meet societal expectations of reproduction and binary bodies are far from self-affirming for so-called, undocumented bodies. Through this shadow work, we articulated our development and instincts about heteronormativity and the patriarchal dominance over planetary and physical geographies. Instead of being defeated by abnormality, we each saved ourselves by inventing concepts that were more positive and applicable to our lives. Instinctively knowing that Nepantla was the queer space we were both inhabiting, we reached out to AnaLouise Keating, a former writing partner and editor of much of Gloria E. Anzaldúa's posthumously published work, to address our conceptualization about the addition of the gender inclusive *x* to Anzaldúa's nepantlera. She asserted, "I agree that had GEA lived longer, she would have gravitated toward the 'x' for 'nepantleras,' (interview). The authors, through reimaging or transgendering each of our respective bodies, escaped into a stream of consciousness duoethnography that unraveled each one's gender liberation. Much like the revisioning of nepantlera into nepanterlx, our bodies have become our own through the (re)construction and empowerment of owning queer space.

NOTES

1. La Llorona is a ghost who mourns over the loss of her children in Mexican folkloric stories, including Gloria E. Anzaldúa's *Prietita and the Ghost Woman/Prietita y la Llorona* (San Francisco, Children's Book Press, 1995).

2. From this point on, we opt to use nepantlerx as an extension of Anzaldúa's nepantlera that may be more inclusive to trans people, nonbinary, and gender nonconforming folks.

WORKS CITED

Ahmed, Sara. *Queer Phenomenology: Orientations, Objects, Others.* Durham, Duke University Press, 2006. Print.

Anzaldúa, Gloria. *The Gloria Anzaldúa Reader.* Edited by AnaLouise Keating, Durham and London, Duke University Press, 2009.

---. *Borderlands/La Frontera.* 2nd Edition. San Francisco, Aunt Lute Books, 1999.

Banerjea, Niharika, Debanuj DasGupta, Rohit K. Dasgupta, and Jaime M. Grant, eds. *Friendship as Social Justice Activism: Critical Solidarities in a Global Perspective.* Chicago, University of Chicago Press, 2018.

Bhattacharya, Kakali & Keating, AnaLouise. "Expanding beyond Public and Private Realities: Evoking Anzaldúan Autohistoria-Teoría in Two Voices." *Qualitative Inquiry*, 2017, vol.1, no.10, pp 1-10.

Bourdieu, P. (1982). *Handbook of Theory and Research for the Sociology of Education* (1986), Richardson, J., (ed). Westport, CT: Greenwood, pp. 241-58

Crenshaw, Kimberlé Williams. "Demarginalizing the Intersection of Race and Sex: A Black Feminist Critique of Antidiscrimination Doctrine, Feminist Theory and Antiracist Politics." *University of Chicago Legal Forum*, 1989, pp 139-167.

Denzin, Norman K. *Performance Autoethnography: Critical Pedagogy and the Politics of Culture.* London, Routledge, 2018.

Keating, AnaLouise. Personal interview. 5 June 2018.

McLaren, Peter. *Capitalists and Conquerors: A Critical Pedagogy Against Empire.* New York, Rowman & Littlefield Publishers, 2005.

---. *Critical Pedagogy and Predatory Culture: Oppositional Politics in a Postmodern Era.* Vol. Taylor & Francis e-Library ed, Routledge, 2002.

Moraga, Cherríe. "Theory in the Flesh." *This Bridge Called My Back: Writings by Radical Women of Color.* Edited by Cherríe Moraga & Gloria Anzaldúa. New York, SUNY Press, 1981, pp 23-24.

Noguera, Pedro. "Reflexiones Pedagógicas Latino Youth: Immigration, Education, and the Future." *Latino Studies*, vol. 4, 2006, pp 313-320.

Norris, Joe. "Duoethnography." *The Sage Encyclopedia of Qualitative Research Methods.* Edited by Given, Lisa M. Los Angeles, Sage Publications, 2008. Print.

Norris, Joe & Sawyer, Richard. "Finding a Researcher's and a Teacher's Voice in a Plethora of Responsibilities: A Duoethnography in Administrivia." *Brock Education*, 2014, vol. 24, no. 1, pp 39-46.

Nava, Julia. Personal interview. 15 April 2018.

Puar, Jasbir. *Terrorist Assemblages: Homonationalism in Queer Times.* Durham: Duke University Press, 2007. Kindle.

Reza-López, Elva, Luis Huerta Charles, and Loui V. Reyes. "Nepantlera Pedagogy: An Axiological Posture for Preparing Critically Conscious Teachers in the Borderlands." *Journal of Latinos and Education*, 2014, vol. 13, no. 2, pp 107-119.

"LA SOMBRA Y EL SUEÑO"

LOOKING FOR QUEER HOPE IN TIMES OF EPOCHAL SHIFT[1]

L. HEIDENREICH

At first glance, our time appears to be an unqueer time—a time of capitalist exploitation, where bodies are of value only in their productivity. Yet a closer look reveals a weaving—albeit, at present, an unbalanced weaving—of economic consolidation and exploitation met by peoples' networked resistance. Trade agreements such as the North American Free Trade Agreement (NAFTA) and the Dominican Republic-Central American Free Trade Agreement (CAFTA-DR) tear down barriers to the movement of goods, generating movement of goods across borders and peoples from their homelands into export-processing zones or to the countries whose capital gave rise to the movement tearing at their homelands.[2] This violence is met by resistance on the part of transgender immigrants and transgender activists, el Ejército Zapatista de Liberación Nacional (EZLN), and labor organizers—all people of el Mundo Zurdo—who insist on shaping our age. In the words of Claire Joysmith, these are "nepantlan times" (97).

In this essay, I bring the work of Gloria Anzaldúa into dialogue with other philosophers of change and motion-change: Karl Marx, James Maffie, and the poets of Anahuac. I seek to take us on a journey through Anzaldúa's engagement with the philosophy of nepantla and then apply the philosophy to our current shift to global capitalism, which is a time of accelerated motion-change.

MOTION CHANGE: GLORIA ANZALDÚA, JAMES MAFFIE, AND MEXICA POETRY IN CONVERSATION

I did not come to an understanding of nepantla as motion-change through the work of Gloria Anzaldúa alone. As a person raised in two cultures and two faiths and queer and in the socio-economic margins of the US, I felt a connection with Anzaldúa's theory of nepantla from my first encounter with her work. It grounded me within a world of movement—at times, chaos—a third space not to be romanticized. Yet it was not until I encountered the work of James Maffie, the same year I was able to spend time with the Anzaldúa files at the Benson library, that patterns finally emerged for me to understand some of the archival work with which I had been engaged. For, while those of us grounded in theories of materialism hold that economic shifts and cultural shifts are intertwined, it was looking at the work of Anzaldúa, as it intersected with that of James Maffie, Karl Marx, and the poets of Anahuac, that I came to understand nepantla—motion-change—as the dynamic moving today's socio-economic shift to totalizing global capitalism.

Maffie, like Anzaldúa, returned to some of the roots of this nepantlan philosophy, concluding that nepantla, in the pre-colonial world, referred to "motion-change," what he describes as "middling, intermixing, and mutually reciprocating motion-change" (14). Such motion-change was critical to self-generation and generation, the creation of society and the world itself. The roots of the philosophy are deep, dating back to a time when philosophers were poets and poets were philosophers, writing:

> We only fill an earthly ministry, O friend:
> We have to leave the lovely songs we give...
> The flowers open their crowns, grow, germinate and bloom:
> From in you, poet, flower songs bloom and descend
> As rain and scatter over those destined to doom. ("Brief Songs" 2-3, 7-9)

This was a time when poets wove songs about this world and the next, scattered them over the people of an empire and watched them rain down (Vásquez 79). While those who received them were "destined to doom," the ideas and the poems were immortalized, passed down from generation to generation through Mexica school systems and through public ceremony (Curl 6-11; Maffie 2-3). In that world, poetry was the language of truth—*in xochitl in cuicatl*—flower and song. The poet-philosophers, *tlamatinime*, sought truth. Like philosophers from other cultures, they were concerned with knowledge, the nature of knowledge and the meaning of life (Vásquez 74-79; León-Portilla 102). It is possible that the philosophy of nepantla flourished in Mesoamerica long before the rise of the empire (León Portilla xvi, 23; Carrasco *Religions*, 30-45).

The Mexica people lived in the fifth age, or Fifth Sun, where inamic pairs of energy, all flowing from Teotl, wove their world (Vásquez 76; Maffie 14-24). Together the weaving of the inamic partners—creative and destructive—were/are nepantla. Nepantla was/is a middle space, but also generative motion. It wove the world, the physical-spiritual world of the Mexica people—of Anahuac. Theirs, like ours, was a world in motion.

TOWARD A NEPANTLAN LIFE OF GLORIA EVANGELINA ANZALDÚA

Centuries after the Spanish invaded Anahuac, nepantla would become central to the work of Gloria Anzaldúa. Drawing on and building upon Mexica philosophy and poetry, Anzaldúa came to articulate nepantla as "a limited space where you are neither this nor that but where you are changing" and, equally important, as "a way of seeing the world" (Anzaldúa, interview Ikas 13-14). Twelve years after the publication of *Borderlands*, she noted, "I'm taking [nepantla] into these other realms about how the universe operates and how life evolved" (Anzaldúa, interview Hérnandez).

Gloria Evangelina Anzaldúa was a daughter of the borderlands and of nepantla. Born into a share-cropping/field-worker family in South Texas, for the first six years of her life, she lived on the ranch settlement of Jesus María in South Texas, a place with no running water but rich in stories and narrative (Anzaldúa, "La Prieta" 221; Anzaldúa, Ikas 2). The elders in her family, especially her grandparents, told her stories, family histories, and tales of survival; and so the young Gloria learned to hear stories and to tell stories (Anzaldúa, *Interviews* 22-23). Yet it was as a young adult at Pan American University, she would later recall, that she forged the Chicana feminist mestiza consciousness that infused her later writings. This identity continued to grow and shift and redefine itself. But it was this time, while she was still working in the fields and going to school, to which she attributed her emerging mestiza consciousness. In her own words:

> I was a senior at Pan American University and I was still working in the fields. That struggle led me to consciousness-raising with feminists. When Cesar Chavez and the farmworkers in Texas were having talks, I would go to their meetings. La Raza Unida was growing strong in the sixties, and I participated in some of their conferences. At one point, the feminist movement and the farmworker's struggle and the Raza Unida struggle all came together for me. (Anzaldúa, interview Hernández)

This Bridge Called My Back: Writings by Radical Women of Color marked yet another turning point in her work. In it, she introduced concepts about movement, change, and revolution. As noted by Sonia Saldívar-Hull, "in 1979 she had already begun conceptualizing the new political, feminist philosophy, writing of the struggles of 'a colonized people throughout the world, including Third World Women in the U.S.'" (9). Much of this foundational work on identity is located in her essay "La Prieta," first printed in *This Bridge Called My Back*, in which she discusses El Mundo Zurdo, writing of our ability, as outsiders, "Third World women, lesbians, feminists, and feminist-oriented men of all colors," to band together and change the world (Anzaldúa, "La Prieta" 232). She argues "by changing ourselves we change the world…traveling El Mundo Zurdo path is the path of a two-way movement—a going deep into the self and expanding out into the world, a simultaneous recreation of the self and a reconstruction of society" (233).

In that same volume, in her very brief essay "El Mundo Zurdo: The Vision," Anzaldúa draws attention to the left-handed world of "the colored, the queer, the poor, the female, the physically challenged" (Anzaldúa, "El Mundo Zurdo" 218). She insists upon connections between and among those of us who live and move in El Mundo Zurdo, calling us to self-love, coalition, and revolution. This change and recreation within ourselves, and change and re-creation of the world around us, is a window into nepantla and the power of nepantla. As much as nepantla is motion-change, at times violent motion-change, we contain within ourselves the power to shape the weave of our time and the fabric of tomorrow.

If we return, then, to her last published essay, we can see that her discussion of nepantlan spaces as transition spaces, movement spaces, and sites of conflict is deeply rooted in her earlier work, from "La Prieta" and "El Mundo Zurdo" through *Borderlands* and numerous interviews throughout the 1990s. Thus, when, in response to the attack on the US trade towers and the rise of twenty-first-century violence, Clara Lomas and Claire Joysmith solicited testimonios from scholars and activists, Anzaldúa's focus drew our attention to the connections between the violence of the attacks and the colonial and imperialist violence that continues to shape our world (Joysmith and Lomas 21-23). Amid her critique, she once again suggests remedies:

> Nepantla is the space in-between the locus and sign of transition. In nepantla we realize that realities clash, authority figures of the various groups demand contradictory commitment... We're caught in remolinos, each with different often contradictory forms of cognition, perspectives, worldviews, belief systems—all occupying the transitional nepantla space... (Anzaldúa, "Let us be the Healing" 99)

Our world weaves itself into existence through struggle and we live in the midst of that struggle. As in the time of the Fifth Sun, and in the shift to monopoly capitalism, we live in a world of motion-change.

VIOLENT MOTION-CHANGE AND TRANS MESTIZA SURVIVAL

In her later years, as Anzaldúa wrote of nepantla as place and motion, she turned to the home of Sor Juana Inés de la Cruz as a generative space of nepantla. And so it is here, to the home of Sor Juana Ines de la Cruz, that I now turn our gaze. In her notebooks, Anzaldúa wrote of nepantla as space and a site of origin for the Zapatista movement. Building on the work of Julie Reynolds, she wrote of the town as the birthplace of Sor Juana, and the site where the Mexican government massacred members of the Fuerzas de Liberación Nacional (FLN), the movement born in the cities of Mexico that would be born again in the rural communities of Chiapas and the Lacandón jungle (Anzaldúa, "Exploring Cultural Legacies"). On February 14, 1974, as part of Operation Nepantla, federal troops invaded the general headquarters of the FLN, killing five members and arresting two others.

They proceeded to El Chilar, the FLN ranch in the Lacandón jungle, executing and disappearing much of the leadership. In its efforts to modernize the nation state, the federal government was in the midst of what is now known as Mexico's Dirty War (Herrera Calderon and Cedillo 1-18).

The late twentieth century was a time of hope, repression, and revolution throughout the Americas; with the Cuban revolution of 1959 and the Sandinista revolution of 1979, a loud and clear message reverberated throughout the hemisphere: resistance is not futile (Colectiva; Cedillo 149). In Mexico, even as this message was heard among multiple and diverse and dispersed communities, the federal and many state governments implemented neoliberal policies that reduced social programs and privatized communal land-holdings. Rural and urban resistance groups emerged, as did government repression of these same movements. The war lasted from 1964 to 1982, during which an estimated 3000 citizens were disappeared, another 3000 executed, and 7000 tortured (Herrera Calderón and Cedillo 6-8; Treviso 12-13). It was a time of nepantlan violence, and the revolutionary communities of the late twentieth century, including the Ejército Zapatista de Liberación Nacional, would be born from it, for, while historians mark 1982 as the close of Mexico's dirty war, the neoliberal policies displacing people continued and continue to date, with NAFTA as one clear example of this.

The effects of neo-liberalism, including NAFTA in Mexico, and CAFTA-DR throughout the Americas, created an increased movement of people not only within their nation-states but also from their homelands to the nations of the North. In Mexico, the dynamic was clearly recognizable among small-scale corn farmers. While US corn had begun to infiltrate the market the decade before NAFTA, with its signing, US corn and grain flooded the Mexican market, bankrupting hundreds of thousands of small farmers and cooperatives. Under NAFTA, the Mexican government was required to phase out subsidies to its corn growers; the US government made no promise to do the same (Bacon, *Illegal People* 62-63). According to Mexico's Ministry of Labor, from 1994 to 2012, 1,780,000 people left the countryside. It would be the men and women of families such as these that traveled north to EPZs and to the US in search of a livelihood (Quintana; Healey 23).

In Mexico, by the second decade of the twenty-first century, the initial displacement of small farmers slowed. Yet with approximately two million small farmers displaced from their livelihoods, the socio-political vacuums left from wide-spread bankruptcies, gutted social programs and disrupted cash-flows opened the doors to drug cartels (Ruiz-Marrero). With the collapse of the rural economy, cartels bought up property from those who went bankrupt. They expanded their ranches and built and expanded an infrastructure for production. They took over financing and lending and "diversified…beyond drugs, stealing machinery and equipment, robbing the wages of day laborers on pay day, requiring extortion payments from farmers and sales people" (Quintana). They brought in a reign of terror from which refugees today continue to flee. In this movement, as in the movement of the last epochal shift in capital, transgender lives were increasingly visible and vulnerable: "Transgender women [fell] victim to cartel kidnappings, extortions, and human trafficking" (Transgender Law Center and Cornell University Law 19-20).

Violence against transgender women was exacerbated under Felipe Calderón's "War on Drugs." With the rise of cartels in Mexico, Calderón gave targeted funding to the military to act as law enforcement in civilian matters. Soon violence against civilians in general increased, but especially against transgender women, making them targets for "arbitrary arrests, beatings, extortions, and robberies." In Ciudad Juárez, in 2007, military police assaulted a community of approximately 40 transgender women, leaving many hospitalized (Transgender Law Center and Cornell University Law 18-19). In Chihuahua, Mercedes Fernández, president of the Chihuahua Lesbian Gay Movement noted that transgender women "can't even go and buy their groceries because they are immediately transferred to the authorities where they are accused of engaging in prostitution. They take them away even if they are holding their grocery bags" (Transgender Law Center and Cornell University Law 19).

By the second decade of the twenty-first century, some of the displacement from NAFTA had slowed, yet immigration did not return to pre-NAFTA rates (Passel et al.). In relation, as immigration from Mexico slowed, neo-liberal trade agreements and policies, including CAFTA-DR, were signed by the US and the governments of Central America, and so movement continued. The disruption created by the intensification of neo-liberal social policies and trade agreements further marginalized communities already fragile from years of civil strife. Immigration from Mexico's neighbors to the south, from El Salvador, Guatemala, and Honduras, increased (Passel, "Written Testimony" 4; Amnesty International). Like Mexico, these countries faced similar challenges in the shifting weaving epoch of the late twentieth to early twenty-first century. Such challenges were rooted in the history of violence named by Anzaldúa in her last published essay, in which she wrote of the US "using the military to advance economic and political interests around the world," and "a history of colonialism, imperialism, and support of right-wing dictatorships at the expense of freedom and democracy (Anzaldúa, "Let us be the healing" 95). Like so much movement in this epoch of global capital, much of the movement was fueled by, with, and for US economic interests (Rafael Hernández 131-136).

FABRIC TORN ASUNDER: TOXIC PATRIOTISM IN THE POLICING STATE

Even while an increasing number of people, including LGBTQI people, have fled their homelands, the scrutiny under which all residents of the US live has increased, making undocumented immigrants perhaps more vulnerable to deportation than any time since the anti-immigrant sweeps of the 1930s. The 1996 Illegal Immigration Reform and Immigration Responsibility Act (IIRIRA) and its companion bill, the Anti-Terrorism and Effective Death Penalty Act, created a climate of crisis for all undocumented immigrants but especially for transgender immigrants. They reduced opportunities to seek relief from deportation at the same time that they expanded the crimes for which a person could be deported (Anello 365). Today, using a stolen social security number can be prosecuted as an aggravated felony (Mejívar and Abrego 1390). People can be deported for crimes of "moral turpitude" as well as felonies, and, in some states, felonies include non-violent crimes such as forging a check. The wide net of deportable crimes includes a number of survival crimes, or crimes in which an unemployed and/or marginalized person might engage in order to feed themselves (Gehi 315-346; Benson and Moore 23-33).

Six years after the 1996 Acts, on October 26, 2001, George W. Bush signed the PATRIOT Act, increasing state surveillance of all US citizens and residents and restricting the ability of people to immigrate to the US. The destructive weaving of the late twentieth century accelerated when, as part of the formation of the Department of Homeland Security, the INS was abolished and a new department, Immigration and Customs Enforcement (ICE), was created. Soon ICE agents would be collaborating with local law enforcement "to help facilitate deportations by assisting ICE in identifying individuals who have committed crimes, regardless of gravity, as well as by providing records of individuals who have been stopped, fingerprinted, and found not to have committed any crime" (González Fernández 4). Together the absorption of the INS into Homeland Security and the bolstering of border security brought with them increased surveillance of all immigrants and an exponential growth in immigrant detention.

The weave and battle of destructive forces continues in our time. A staggering amount of tax dollars are utilized in an attempt to stop the movement fueled by the nation-state and corporate politics. In 2014, with a budget of 3.6 billion dollars, the US Border Patrol had 18,156 agents along the US/Mexico border, equipped with ground radar, motion detectors, thermal imaging sensors, helicopters, drones, and more (American Immigration Council 3). Equally disturbing, the US federal government began pouring money into Mexico to turn back immigrants and refugees from its borders. As of October 2014, according to the American Immigration Council, the US had sent approximately $1.3 billion to Mexico to secure its southern border.[3] In Mexico, police and the military raid trains, restaurants, and hotels, and the government continues to work with companies that run cargo trains to increase their speed so that immigrants and refugees cannot use them to travel north (American Immigration Council 5-6).

Yet nepantlan times are not woven by destructive forces alone, but by creative and life-affirming forces that push through such destruction. Thus, amid the destructive forces of ICE and the flourishing of private, for-profit carceral institutions, positive forces reacted and pushed back and pushed through, creating counter-movements and counter-discourses and weaving a more livable world. Among these counter-forces was the Transgender Law Center and the many vectors of resistance it helped to fuel.

WEAVING THE SIXTH SUN: THE TRANSGENDER LAW CENTER

In 2001—initially under the umbrella of the Center for Lesbian Rights—the Transgender Law Program, which would become the Transgender Law Center, was founded five years after the passage of the Illegal Immigration Reform and Immigration Responsibility Act (IIRIRA) and the Anti-Terrorism and Effective Death Penalty Act of 1996 and one year after the Patriot Act. As noted by Christopher Daley, one of its founders, the groundwork for their work began decades before the birth of the organization itself. As with most efforts toward structural change, years of struggle at multiple levels was necessary before any kind of infrastructure could be developed. So it was that decades after the founding of Vanguard and the Compton Riots (1966), TLC began as the Transgender Law Project under the umbrella of the Center for Lesbian Rights (CLR) (Stryker 63-75; Daley "Trans Rights").

As noted by Ilona M. Turner, Legal Director for the Transgender Law Center, San Francisco had been at the forefront of transgender rights for decades (5-6). At the same time that the destructive forces of totalizing capital were gathering, human rights struggles were also creating sites of disruption and change in this often generative site by the sea. As early as 1961, gender rights were visible in a renewed call for human rights. In that year, the burgeoning homophile rights movement in San Francisco received a dramatic boost when the politically astute drag performer José Sarria ran for public office (Imperial Court). Roughly five years later, the Compton's Cafeteria Riot rocked the city.

San Francisco continued to be at the forefront of transgender organizing in the years to come. Following the riot, Conversion Our Goal (COG), one of the first transgender peer-support groups was founded, also in San Francisco, with the support of Glide Memorial; additionally, a police liaison, officer Elliot Blackstone, was assigned to address the needs of the homophile communities in the Tenderloin (Stryker 75). Such forces of change, pushing and weaving through the backlash of the Nixon presidency and into the backlash of the 1980s, would keep San Francisco at the forefront of transgender organizing and transgender rights for decades.

As time pushed forward, into the era of global trade agreements and hemispheric displacement of LGBTQI people, the City also continued to weave forward. As Ilona M. Turner, Legal Director of the Transgender Law Center noted:

> In the 1980s, San Francisco was also the home base of the first national organization that focused solely on trans men, FTM International, and in 1992, of Transgender Nation. The city…pioneered municipal protections for trans people including…enacting an ordinance prohibiting discrimination based on gender identity in 1994, and in 2001, becoming the first municipality in the nation to provide health insurance coverage for transition-related care for city employees. (6)

Grounded in this larger history of transgender rights and liberation, TLC emerged as a force within multiple vectors of movement. Shannon Minter had been working on transgender rights cases with the Center for Lesbian Rights, so when Christopher Daley was awarded a Tom Steel fellowship, he was able to build on that work (Daley interview). For the first three years of its existence, TLP operated under the umbrella of the CLR (Connell 1). Daley and Minter worked collaboratively, producing "Trans Realities: A Legal Needs Assessment of San Francisco's Transgender Communities," a study addressing immigration rights among the many critical needs of transgender people (Minter and Daley). In 2004, with Noemi Calonje, the immigration clinic coordinator at CLR, they represented Adriana Turcios as she applied for asylum (Transgender Law Center, "Adriana Turcios" 2). They later developed "cultural competency" training for immigration service providers and immigration attorneys (Transgender Law Center, "Immigration").

Yet, as the country moved forward regarding many aspects of gender rights, the rights of transgender immigrants, especially women immigrants, remained markedly lacking. As noted in *Authentic Lives*, the government, "increasingly recognized and upheld certain rights of transgender people, while continuing to sanction the horrific abuse of transgender immigrants held in detention centers across the country" (Transgender Law Center, "Fresh and Evolving" 3). And so, in 2014, TLC stepped up its efforts, hiring Isa Noyola, an activist and organizer with extensive experience working locally for transgender rights, to manage its outreach and programming (Transgender Law Center, "TLC Welcomes"). Her hiring exemplified the complex strategy that had come to dominate the Center, advocating and providing "legal assistance and information to transgender individuals and their families [and engaging] in impact litigation and policy advocacy to advance transgender rights" (Transgender law Center and Cornell University Law 4). Such advocacy would grow to be as broad as facilitating networking among transgender activists in the US, supporting protests at detentions centers, and finding pro bono legal support for transgender refugees even while continuing to engage in impact litigation.

Fresh out of college, Noyola had not intended to do national work; instead she had focused her efforts on local communities and local needs. She worked with Marci Ochoa at Proyecto ContraSIDA Por Vida, creating Habla la Jotería, a queer-and-trans-friendly ESL program. When Proyecto ContraSIDA closed its doors, she continued to work with El/La Para TransLatinas, where she did everything from database work to fundraising to program planning (Isa Noyola, Personal inverview). Noyola worked tirelessly, organizing protests at detention centers, heading education programs, and supervising projects. Her labor, like the work of queer Chicanas of the twentieth century, was clearly rooted in a "politics of necessity" (Moraga, "Entering the Lives" 21). That necessity became even more urgent with the murder of Ruby Ordeñana. Ruby was just 27 years old when she was killed. As noted in her Community United Against Violence memorial, she had "left her native Nicaragua in search of a place she could call home":

> She wanted to be able to live a life free of violence and stigma where she could express herself without fear for her safety. At twenty-seven-years-old, she had created her own family from various communities in the Bay Area. ("Demanding True Justice" 1, 3)

With Ruby's passing, Noyola ardently embraced El/La:

> I just really made my home at El/La where…it is in many ways a home for many of us…this beautiful respite and holistic space that we have created, in which we honor our community members that have passed and also honor our folks that are living by providing services and space and providing—un cafecito con pan, you know, in the everyday ways we build community. (Noyola, Personal interview)

Noyola's work with El/La would continue long after she joined the Transgender Law Center.

Yet, working in advocacy, Noyola noted the absence of trans women of color in leadership. As she continued her work, the absence became increasingly apparent, even in places and organizations dedicated to making policies and implementing change on behalf of transgender women. Thus, when the opportunity to work at the Transgender Law Center presented itself, she knew she had to make the shift. And so her outreach became more national in scope, even while maintaining her ties with local organizations (Noyola, personal interview).

At the time she was hired as Program Manager for TLC, Noyola had also been working as the Program Manager of LYRIC's LGBTQA youth leadership/workforce department. As she shifted to TLC, she continued to serve as a national advocate for El/La Para TransLatinas and on the steering committee of Familia Trans Queer Liberation Movement ("TLC Welcomes"). It would be only one year later that she would be promoted to Director of Programs at TLC. As the organization grew into its role as a leading "multi-disciplinary organization committed to creating concrete change in the lives of those whose members of our communities are most marginalized," it was nepantleras such as Noyola who held the experience, insight, and vision to facilitate that growth ("Isa Noyola becomes TLC Director of Programs"). Throughout the 1990s and into the twenty-first century, the motion-change within which Noyola moved, like the motion-change of the last epochal shift in capital, was/is not one to be romanticized. Her appointment, in fact, came within a context of multiple violences: physical and emotional violence targeting trans women and, in relation, spatial violence—destructive motion-change.

Motion-change in the form of spatial violence—gentrification—rocked the Bay Area, San Francisco, and beyond. Notably, some of the workers and families displaced from the fields of Mexico due to the structural adjustment programs of the 1980s and 1990s had settled in the Bay Area—into cities of movement

(*Causa Justa* 20). For cities, like the fields of southern Mexico, are not static spaces. Instead, they are "shaken up repeatedly by the dynamic forces of capitalism and modernity" (Richard Walker qtd. in *Causa Justa* 3). Thus, like the displacement of Mexico's farmers by neo-liberal policies and trade agreements, the gentrification of the Bay Area was also driven by shifts in global capital. Neighborhoods that had survived the urban gentrification movements of the 1990s were once again vulnerable. In this next wave of gentrification, even the landmark queer Latinx gathering place of Esta Noche closed (*Causa Justa* 3; Mirabal 12). As Noyola herself would later note, that was a time when gentrification in urban areas north and south was closing down queer havens; safe spaces for queers of color, clubs and LGBTQI centers that were once "spaces to mobilize and to organize" were no longer available (Noyola, interview by Goodman).

Today TLC engages in advocacy as well as direct actions targeting ICE and detention centers (Transgender Law Center, "Honor Trans Immigrant Lives"). As in their early years, when they worked in collaboration with organizations such as Community United Against Violence, the San Francisco Human Rights Commission, and the Asylum Project, today, they work collaboratively with the same organizations, but also in collaboration with Familia QTLM and GetEQUAL. It was working with Not1More Deportation, in collaboration with Familia QTLM and GetEQUAL that they successfully fought alongside Christina López for her release from the Santa Ana Detention Center (Minter and Daley 46; Transgender Law Center, "Victory for #FreeChristina"). The next year, they appealed a deportation ruling of behalf of Marianna, a transgender woman from Mexico who had fled the country, fearing for her life. Their appeal was successful and Marianna's case was remanded (Transgender Law Center, "TLC Challenges Order to Deport," "TLC Wins BIA Appeal").

And so the weave continues. Marianna's case was remanded, but only after she was detained for eleven months in immigration detention. With the success of her appeal, she still faced the long and difficult process of applying for asylum. Struggles for justice and struggles for profit clash and weave and create the world around us. In the twenty-first century, the forces of a totalizing capital continue to grow strong as the nation-state functions to facilitate the globalizing of capital, moving, controlling, and incarcerating bodies in its service. In this movement, it is the lives of queer mestiz@s, that become visible, but also vulnerable.

And yet there is hope. For the forces of mobilizing capital are met with resistance by labor movements and by the activism of organizations such as the Transgender Law Center, Causa Justa, and EZLN. The weave continues and we continue to strive to shape the weave—to build upon the work of nepantleras and nepantler@s past and present in order to shape a better present and a livable future—one where those of us who live in between genders, races, cultures and spaces—people of el Mundo Zurdo—might flourish.

NOTES

1. This article is part of a larger work, *Nepantla2*, to be released by the University of Nebraska in fall of 2019. The author thanks Nebraska for their permission to offer up this pedacito of the forthcoming book.

2. As noted by scholars as diverse as Saskia Sassen, and Flynn and Kofman, NAFTA and CAFTA-DR spurred movement both within the nation-states of the Americas and between nation states. Unequal power relationships between the nation-states negotiating the trade agreements resulted in the elimination of government subsidies to agriculture in developing countries, where similar action was not required in the US. Such disparities gave rise to the displacement families and agricultural workers throughout the south. This, in conjunction with increased foreign investment in Mexico and Central America necessarily gave rise to increased immigration north (Sassen 7-43; Flynn and Kofman 67).

3. While the Immigration Council did not provide a start date for their figures, the funding was allocated through the Mérida Initiative, signed into law by Congress in 2008. In 2011, according to Congressional Research Service, a new focus was added which included "improving immigration enforcement in Mexico and security along Mexico's southern borders…" (1).

WORKS CITED

American Immigration Council. *A Guide to Children Arriving at the Border: Laws, Policies and Responses.* 2015, http://immigrationpolicy.org/sites/default/files/research/a_guide_to_children_arriving_at_the_border_and_the_laws_and_policies_governing_our_response.pdf.

Amnesty International. *Report: No Safe Place: Salvadorans, Guatemalans and Hondurans Seeking Asylum in Mexico Based on their Sexual Orientation and/or Gender Identity.* November 2017, https://www.amnestyusa.org/wp-content/uploads/2017/11/No-Safe-Place-Briefing-ENG-1.pdf.

Anello, Farrin R. "Due Process and Temporal Limits on Mandatory Immigration Detention," *Hastings Law Journal* 65 (February 2014), pp. 363-405.

Anzaldúa, Gloria. *Borderlands: The New Mestiza.* 2nd edition. California: Aunt Lute, 1999.

___. "El Mundo Zurdo." *This Bridge Called My Back: Writings by Radical Women of Color,* edited by Cherríe L. Moraga and Gloria Anzaldúa, 1981. Third Woman Press, 2001, p. 218.

___. "Exploring Cultural Legacies," Box 112.2. Benson Collection, University of Texas at Austin.

___. Interview with Karin Rosa Ikas. *Chicana Ways: Conversations with Ten Chicana Writers,* by Karin Rosa Ikas. Nevada UP, 2002.

___. *Interviews/Entrevistas.* Ed. AnaLouise Keating, Routledge, 2000.

___. "La Prieta." *This Bridge Called My Back: Writings by Radical Women of Color,* edited by Cherríe L. Moraga and Gloria Anzaldúa, 1981. Third Women Press, 2001, p. 218

___. "Let Us Be the Healing of the Wound: The Coyolxauhqui Imperative—La Sombra y el Sueño." *One Wound for Another: Una Herida Por Otra,* 99.

Bacon, David. "Union Ballot Exposes NAFTA's Broken Labour Promises." *The Green Left* 28 March 2001. https://www.greenleft.org.au/node/25419.

___. *Illegal People: How Globalization Creates Migration and Criminalizes Immigrants.* Beacon, 2008.

"Brief Songs from the Nahuatl." *El Grito,* 5 no. 1 (Fall 1971), pp. 13-18.

Carrasco, Davíd. *Religions of Mesoamerica: Cosmovision and Ceremonial Centers.* Waveland, 1990.

Causa Justa. *Development without Displacement: Resisting Gentrification in the Bay Area.* Oakland, 2014, http://cjjc.org/wp-content/uploads/2015/11/development-without-displacement.pdf.

Cedillo, Adela. "Armed Struggle Without Revolution: The Organizing Process of the National Liberation Forces (FLN) and the Genesis of Neo-Zapatism (1969-1983)." *Challenging Authoritarianism in Mexico: Revolutionary Struggles,* edited by Fernando Herrera Calderon and Adela Cedillo, Routledge, 2012), pp. 148-166.

Colectiva. "Nepantla, la insurreccion de la memoria 1," YouTube, 18 January 2012. Artemusicayvide, https://www.youtube.com/watch?v=gDU8IjkUyiU. Accessed 13 March 2018.

Congressional Research Service. "Mexico: Evolution of the Mérida Initiative, 2007-2019." *In Focus,* 23 July 2018, fas.org/sgp/crs/row/IF10578.pdf. Accessed 8 January 2019.

Connell, Mikayla. *Legal Translations.* Transgender Law Center, Fall 2005.

Curl, John, editor and translator. *Ancient American Poets.* Bilingual Press, 2005.

Daley, Christopher. "Trans Rights Come of Age." *Transgender Law Center,* http://www.transgenderlawcenter.org/do/trans-rights-2006.html. Accessed 24 April 2006.

___. Personal interview. 7 November, 2006.

"Demanding True Justice in the Face of Violence." *Community United Against Violence Newsletter.* Summer 2007. http://www.cuav.org/wp-content/uploads/2012/09/summer-07-web.pdf.

Gehi, Pooja. "Struggles from the Margins: Anti-Immigrant Legislation and the Impact on Low-Income Transgender People of Color," *Women's Rights Law Reporter* 30 (Winter 2009), pp. 315-346.

González Fernández, Luz C. "Immigration Detention in America: Civil Offense, Criminal Detention." *Harvard Journal of Hispanic Policy* 26 (2013/2014), pp. 3-12.

Healey, Josh. "NAFTA Corn Fuels Immigration." *The Progressive* 77 no. 4 (April 2013), pp. 22-24.

Hernández, Monica. Interview with Gloria E. Anzaldúa, "With Heart in Hand/Con Corazon en la Mano, *Colorlines* October 20, 1999. https://www.colorlines.com/articles/heart-handcon-corazon-en-la-mano.

Hernández, Rafael. "Alliances and Dis-alliances between the United States and Latin America and the Caribbean." *Latin American Perspectives* 38 No. 4 (July 2011), pp. 131-136.

Herrera Calderon, Fernando. and Adela Cedillo, editors. *Challenging Authoritarianism in Mexico: Revolutionary Struggles*. Routledge, 2012.

Imperial Court de San Diego. "Empress I Jose Sarria: The Widow Norton." *Twenty Five Year of Noble Deeds: A Silver Jubilee History of the Imperial Court de San Diego*.

Joysmith, Claire. "'Let Us Be the Healing of the Wound': Anzaldúa's Post-September 11, 2001, Testimonial Vision." *Guerras y Prietas: Celebrating 20 Years of Borderlands/La Frontera*, edited by Norma E. Cantú and Christina L. Gutiérrez, Adelante Project, 2009, pp. 93-100.

Lara, Irene. "Sensing the Serpent in the Mother, Dando Luz a Luz la Madres Serpiente: Chicana Spirituality, Sexuality, and Mamihood." *Fleshing the Spirit: Spirituality and Activism in Chicana, Latina, and Indigenous Women's Lives*, edited by Elisa Facio and Irene Lara, Arizona UP, 2014), pp. 113-134.

León-Portilla, Miguel. *Aztec Thought and Culture*, trans. Jack Emory Davis. Oklahoma UP, 1963.

Maffie, James. *Aztec Philosophy: Understanding a World in Motion*. Colorado UP, 2014.

Mejívar, Cecilia and Leisy Abrego. "Legal Violence: Immigration Law and the Lives of Central American Immigrants." *American Journal of Sociology* 117 No.5 (March, 2012), pp. 1380-1421.

Minter, Shannon and Christopher Daley. "Trans Realities: A Legal Needs Assessment of San Francisco's Transgender Communities." *National Center for Lesbian Rights and The Transgender Law Center*, 2003, http://www.nclrights.org/wp-content/uploads/2013/07/transrealities0803.pdf.

___. "Creating a Transgender Law Project: Serving the Unique Legal Needs of the Transgender Community." *San Francisco Attorney*, June/July 2002, http://www.olender.pro/sites/default/files/Media/SFAM%20Jun%20Jul%202002%20-%20The%20Mess%20at%20INS.pdf, pp. 46-47.

Mirabal, Nancy Raquel. "Geographies of Displacement: Latina/os, Oral History, and the Politics of Gentrification in San Francsico's Mission District." *The Public Historian* 31 no. 2 (Spring 2009), pp. 7-31.

Moraga, Cherríe. "Entering the Lives of Others: Theory in the Flesh." *This Bridge Called My Back: Writings by Radical Women of Color*, edited by Cherrie L. Moraga and Gloria Anzaldúa, 1981. Third Women Press, 2001, p. 21.

Moya, Moya. *Learning from Experience: Minority Identities, Multicultural Struggles*. Berkeley: UP, 2002.

Noyola, Isa. Personal interview. 17 May 2016.

___. Interview by Amy Goodman. *Democracy Now*, 14 June 2016, http://www.democracynow.org/2016/6/14/activist_latinx_lgbtq_community_its_stories. Accessed March 9, 2018.

Passel, Jeffrey S. "Written testimony submitted to the U.S. Senate Committee on Homeland Security and Governmental Affairs Hearing on: Securing the Border: Defining the Current Population Living in the Shadows and Addressing Future Flows." *Pew Research Center*. 26 March 2015, http://www.pewhispanic.org/files/2015/03/2015-03-26_passel-testimony.pdf.

Passel, Jeffrey S. D'Vera Cohn and Ana Gonzalez-Barrera, "Net Migration from Mexico Falls to Zero – and Perhaps Less." *Pew Research Center*, 23 April 2012, http://www.pewhispanic.org/2012/04/23/net-migration-from-mexico-falls-to-zero-and-perhaps-less/. Accessed 4 March 2018.

___. "Unauthorized immigrant Population Stable for Half a Decade." *FacTank: News in the Numbers, Pew Research Center*. 22 July 2015. http://www.pewresearch.org/fact-tank/2015/07/22/unauthorized-immigrant-population-stable-for-half-a-decade/. Accessed 4 March 2018.

Pérez, Emma. "Gloria Anzaldúa: La Gran Nueva Mestiza Theorist, Writer, Activist-Scholar." *NWSA Journal*, 17 no.2 (Summer 2005), pp. 1-10.

Quintana, Victor M. "How NAFTA Unleashed the Violence in Mexico." *Americas Program*, 7 February 2014. http://www.americas.org/archives/11427. Accessed 12 June 2017.

Ruiz-Marrero, Carmelo. "Contra and Drugs, Three Decades Later." *The Louisiana Weekly*. 10 November 2014. http://www.louisianaweekly.com/contras-and-drugs-three-decades-later/. Accessed 12 June 2017.

Saldívar-Hull, Sonia. "Before Borderlands and Beyond: 'Making the World Luminous and Active,'" *El Mundo Zurdo 2*, edited by Sonia Saldívar-Hull, Norma Alarcón and Rita E. Urquijo-Ruiz. Aunt Lute, 2012, pp. 7-11.

Sassen, Saski. *Globalization and Its Discontents: Essays on the New Mobility of People and Money*. New Press, 1998.

Screaming Queens: The Riot at Compton's Cafeteria. Writ. and prod. Silverman, Victor and Susan Stryker. Frameline, 2005.

Stryker, Susan. *Transgender History*. Seal, 2008.

Tony Platt and Cecilia O'Leary. "Patriot Acts," in *Social Justice* 30 no.1 (2003), pp. 5-21.

Transgender Law Center. "Adriana Turcios," *Legal Translations*, Fall 2004, p.2.

___. "A Fresh and Evolving Perspective," *Authentic Lives* (2015), 3.

___. "Isa Noyla becomes Transgender Law Center's Director of Programs!" Transgender Law Center, 22 October 2015. https://transgenderlawcenter.org/archives/12113. Accessed August 4, 2017.

___. "Hundreds of LGBT People of Color and Immigrants to Rally at Texas Capitol." Press Release, 1 August 2017. https://transgenderlawcenter.org/archives/13974. Accessed August 4, 2017.

___. "TLC Challenges Order to Depart Transgender Immigrant Seeking Asylum." Transgender Law Center, 10 August 2017, https://transgenderlawcenter.org/archives/13978. Accessed 9 March 2018.

___."TLC Wins BIA (Board of Immigration Appeal) Appeal for remand for trans immigrant to apply for asylum." Transgender Law Center. October 18, 2017. https://transgenderlawcenter.org/archives/14065. Accessed 9 March 2018.

___. "TLC Welcomes New Program Manager, Isa Noyola." Transgender Law Center, 20 October 2014. https://transgenderlawcenter.org/archives/11172. Accessed 8 March 2018.

___. "Transgender Law Center Launches Trans Immigrant Defense Effort (TIDE)." 18 January 2017. https://transgenderlawcenter.org/archives/13494. Accessed 9 March 2018.

___. "Victory for #FreeChristina – Transgender Detainee Granted Bond." Transgender Law Center, 19 February 2016. http://transgenderlawcenter.org/archives/12536. Accessed 9 March 2018.

Transgender Law Center and the Cornell University Law School LGBT Clinic. *Report on Human Rights Conditions of Transgender Women in Mexico*, 2016, pp. 19-20. https://transgenderlawcenter.org/wp-content/uploads/2016/05/CountryConditionsReport-FINAL.pdf.

Treviso, Dolores. *Rural Protest and the Making of Democracy in Mexico, 1986-2000*. Pennsylvania State UP, 2011.

Turner, Ilona M. "Pioneering Strategies to Win Trans Rights in California," *University of La Verne Law Review* 34 (November 2012), pp. 5-22.

Vásquez, Francisco H. "Aztec Epistemology," *El Grito*, 5 no. 4 (Summer 1972), pp. 74-79.

UNSETTLING DOMINANT NARRATIVES

BORDERLANDS/LA FRONTERA AS A PATHWAY TOWARD A "NEW" PERSPECTIVE ON QUEER THEORY

CAMILLE BACK

In his 2009 El Mundo Zurdo plenary speech, titled "Santa Nepantla: A Borderlands Sutra," Randy P. Conner, an intimate and lifelong friend and *comadre* of Gloria Anzaldúa, claimed that she was probably the first one to use the term "queer" in an academic context, opening a space for discussion around Anzaldúa's contributions to the development of queer theories. This is the space I would like to reopen today. In most of queer theory's self-narratives, the first introduction of the terms "queer" and "queer theory" into the academic sphere is attributed to Teresa de Lauretis who coined the expression in "Queer Theory: Lesbian and Gay Sexualities" after a conference held at the University of California, Santa Cruz in 1990. However, there are other genealogies.[1] Gloria Anzaldúa clearly defines herself as queer since 1981 and the publication of "La Prieta" in *This Bridge Called My Back*, and later on, in *Borderlands/La Frontera* (1987). However, when formulating her queer theory, de Lauretis only briefly mentions Anzaldúa's work without even emphasizing her use of the term "queer" or discussing her work, which nevertheless constitutes a precedent to her own formulation.

This chapter is a genealogical effort that aims to highlight the precursory and groundbreaking role of Anzaldúa whose contributions to the elaboration of queer theories (like those of many other queers of color) have been erased from current genealogies. I'm not the first one approaching this issue, and my work is indebted to Randy P. Conner's "Santa Nepantla," José Esteban Muñoz's introduction to

Disidentifications, Michael Hames-García's "Queer Theory Revisited," Evelynn Hammonds' "Black (W)holes," AnaLouise Keating's insights in *The Gloria Anzaldúa Reader*, and Norma Alarcón, Paola Bacchetta, and Jules Falquet's introduction to *Les Cahiers du CEDREF* where an entire chapter of *Borderlands/La Frontera* was translated into French. Following and furthering their analysis, I would like to show, as Hames-García rightfully puts it, that queer theory has never fully nor adequately questioned the fact that it was founded on the erasure of an important collection of poetic and critical texts written by queers of color even though these works were sometimes included in genealogies for strategic purposes (28). This chapter therefore focuses on a critical analysis of some of the texts usually considered to be foundational texts and on the erasure of Anzaldúa's contributions to the elaboration of white queer theories but also on her use of the term "queer" through its articulation with some of the concepts she develops in *Borderlands/La Frontera*. The challenge is also to disrupt, question, and redefine queer thoughts and practices that, in France, were mainly developed from white US queer theories (thus reproducing blind spots in the analysis), and to intensify their scope starting from *Borderlands/La Frontera*.

UNSETTLING DOMINANT NARRATIVES

In 1981, Gloria Anzaldúa and Cherríe Moraga publish *This Bridge Called my Back*, where Anzaldúa's queer theorizing first occurs in a publication. From 1982 to 1986, Anzaldúa teaches summer courses in creative writing at the Women's Voices Writing Workshop at Oakes College at the University of California, Santa Cruz (UCSC). Teresa de Lauretis joins UCSC's History of Consciousness Department in 1985. In 1987, Anzaldúa publishes *Borderlands/La Frontera: The New Mestiza*. Later this year, the *Library Journal* selects *Borderlands/La Frontera* as one of the best thirty-eight books of 1987. In 1988, after applying unsuccessfully for the doctoral program of the UCSC's History of Consciousness Department, Anzaldúa is finally admitted to the doctoral program in the Department of Literature.[2] From April to June 1988, she is appointed Distinguished Visiting Professor in Women's Studies at UCSC, where she teaches the course "Women of Color in the U.S.: Third World Feminism Theory and Literature" and an *historias* creative writing seminar.[3] The various essays composing the 1991 special issue of *differences*, introduced and edited by Teresa de Lauretis, are produced in the context of a working conference on lesbian and gay sexualities that takes place in February 1990 at UCSC.

When formulating her queer theory, however, de Lauretis only briefly mentions Anzaldúa's work without even emphasizing her use of the term "queer" or discussing her work. The only mention of Anzaldúa's work in "Queer Theory" appears alongside the name of other queer of color writers during an overview that, above all, enables de Lauretis to contextualize her own work. Revisiting the stated goals of both the working conference and the special issue she edited, she recounts:

> In this perspective, the work of the conference was intended to articulate the terms in which lesbian and gay sexualities may be understood and imaged as forms of resistance to cultural homogenization, counteracting dominant discourses with other constructions of the subject in culture.
>
> It was my hope that the conference would also problematize some of the discursive constructions and constructed silences in the emergent field of "gay and lesbian studies," and would further explore questions that have as yet been barely broached, such as the respective and/or common grounding of current discourses and practices of homo-sexualities in relation to gender and to race, with their attendant differences of class or ethnic culture, generational, geographical, and socio-political location. (de Lauretis iii-iv)

While stating she wants to counter dominant narratives by integrating the positionalities and epistemologies of queers of color but also to problematize some of the constructed silences in the then-emergent field of gay and lesbian studies, de Lauretis participates in the erasure of contributions by queers of color, of whom Anzaldúa is only one example, to the development of queer theory, and avoids questioning her own practice. My purpose, then, is to deconstruct some of the constructed silences of queer theory, focusing in particular on the way in which erasure operates in some of queer theory's foundational texts.

(OUR) CONSTRUCTED SILENCES

I choose to focus my analysis on two important genealogical elements of queer theory, Teresa de Lauretis's "Queer Theory: Lesbian and Gay Sexualities" (1991) and Eve Kosofsky Sedgwick's "Queer and Now" (1993), for the direct relationship they maintain with Gloria Anzaldúa's work. In "Queer Theory," de Lauretis references *Borderlands/La Frontera* and *This Bridge Called My Back* but without mentioning that Gloria Anzaldúa (or Cherríe Moraga in "La Güera") uses the term "queer" in each of these two books, nor discussing her work in greater depth. At the same time, de Lauretis laments the fact that queers of color have not produced much theory and offers some explanations:

> Surveying the writings of lesbians and gay men of color, one does not find a comparable amount of titles or authors. In part this is due to their restricted institutional access to publishing and higher education, which has only slightly improved in recent years with small presses and great effort.
>
> But, besides the severe problem of institutional access, the relatively greater scarcity of works of theory by lesbians and gay of color may also have been a matter of different choices, different work priorities, different constituencies and forms of address. Perhaps, to a gay writer and critic of color, defining himself gay is not the utmost importance; he may have other and more pressing priorities in his work and his life. Perhaps a gay Chicano writer cannot identify with the white, middle-class gay community of the Castro for several reasons that are both socially and sexually overdetermined. (de Lauretis viii-ix)

I follow Evelynn Hammonds on her analysis of "Queer Theory" when she argues that, while noting the problems due to their restricted access to publishing and higher education (but also to academic positions), de Lauretis ends up attributing the lack of knowledge of the experiences of queers of color to queers of color themselves, to their personal choices rather than to the institutional racism, heterosexism, and the structural inequalities that operate within US society and the university (303). My point is that, besides being "symptomatic of a disjuncture [...] between the stated goals of the special issue she edited and what it actually enacts" (Hammonds 304), de Lauretis's essay is representative of a denial of the processes of erasure and epistemic violence that deeply structure queer theory. As Michael Hames-García reminds us in "Queer Theory Revisited," despite their initial promise, most of the texts that are now considered foundational for queer theory introduce the issue of race-racism-racialization only to underscore the lack of critical work that has been produced by queers of color (24). Most of them portray queers of color as bringing additional considerations (and raw material) to the central issues of gender and sexuality, without themselves ever fully integrating an analysis of race and coloniality in their own frameworks (Hames-García 29). On the contrary, the issue of the articulations of race and coloniality to sexuality and gender comes later and appears as a concern that queer theory intends to address (Hames-García 25). Both de Lauretis and Sedgwick's accounts "erase [queers] of color from the center of the debate in order to reintroduce them later at the margins of [queer] theory" (Hames-García 25) as this excerpt of "Queer and Now" indicates:

> At the same time, a lot of the most exciting recent work around "queer" spins the term outward along dimensions that can't be subsumed under gender and sexuality at all: the ways that race, ethnicity, postcolonial nationality criss-cross with these *and other* identity-constituting, identity-fracturing discourses, for example. Intellectuals and artists of color whose sexual self-definition includes "queer"—I think of an Isaac Julien, a Gloria Anzaldúa, a Richard Fung—are using the leverage of "queer" to do a new kind of justice to the fractal intricacies of language, skin, migration, state. Thereby, the gravity (I mean the *gravitas*, the meaning, but also the *center* of gravity) of the term "queer" itself deepens and shifts. (8-9)

In "Queer and Now," through daring linguistic contortions, the works of "intellectuals and artists of color" are positioned as posterior and external to queer theory. Sedgwick is writing in 1993, and "La Prieta" (1981) or even *Borderlands/La Frontera* (1987) are far from being recent works. If Sedgwick recognizes that Anzaldúa clearly self-defines herself as queer and that her use shifts the center of gravity of the term and deepens it, she does so precisely through some temporal distortion. In both Sedgwick's and de Lauretis's accounts, queer theory seems to have been developed by white theorists without significant participation by queers of color with the consequence that genealogies can be written without any reference to their work (Hames-García 24-25).

As a result of those false chronologies and repeated erasures, queer-of-color writers—whose works have too often been ignored, underestimated, or marginalized in current genealogies—are systematically rendered silent and left unread.

Such rewritings should at least be viewed with some suspicion regarding their political motivations and consequences.

WE ARE THE QUEER GROUPS

What would a rewriting of queer theories starting from "La Prieta" and *Borderlands/La Frontera* look like? What political dimensions of "queer" have been erased at the same time as the references to works by queers of color and to Gloria Anzaldúa's in particular? What "new" perspectives on queer theory does that alternative genealogy help reopen? What is at stake, indeed, in their erasure and in my rewriting?

Unlike the essays published in the special issue edited by de Lauretis, which rarely use the "queer" terminology she proposes as a discursive solution, I think that Anzaldúa's use of the term categorically deserves our attention. "La Prieta" (1981), "El paisano is a bird of good omen" (1982), *Borderlands/La Frontera* (1987), "To(o) Queer the Writer" (1990), and the poems "The Occupant" (mid-70s) and "The Coming of the World Surdo" (1977) each highlight Anzaldúa's formative role in the development of queer theories, particularly through her blurring and deconstruction of conventional gender roles, her lesbian feminist critique of heteronormativity, and her reformulation of the notion of identity, as well as the issues of political alliance-building and knowledge production. Her first use of the term "queer," which appears in "La Prieta," refers to her hormonal imbalance and to her subsequent early menstruations:

> What my mother wanted in return for having birthed me and for nurturing me was that I submit to her without rebellion. Was this a survival skill she was trying to teach me? She objected not so much to my disobedience but to my questioning her right to demand obedience from me. Mixed with this power struggle was her guilt at having borne a child who was marked "con la seña," thinking she had made me a victim of her sin. In her eyes and in the eyes of others I saw myself reflected as "strange," "abnormal," "QUEER" (Anzaldúa, "La Prieta" 199).

Since the very beginning, her theorization of "queer" goes beyond sexual and gender identifications. For me, her understanding of it is actually inseparable from the way she seeks to reconfigure identity. She invites us to think in terms of processes of identification and disidentification, positionalities, and movement. "Queer" appears indeed as an identificatory category and as a positionality (both position and positioning) rather than as an identity or an anti-identity. In "La Prieta" as well as in *Borderlands/La Frontera*, the term "queer" is often mobilized alongside other identificatory categories, differently marginalized (people of color, poor and working-class people, women, differently abled people, mestizas…):

> This is not new.
> Colored, poor white, latent queer
> passing for white
> seething with hatred, anger

> unaware of its source
> crazed with not knowing
> who they are
> choose me to pick at the masks. (Anzaldúa, *Borderlands* 193)

Anzaldúa leads us to seek commonalities and suggests that those subjects are co-constructed and produced (even differently) as marginalized by the white heteropatriarchy, and, therefore, that their struggles and processes of resistance are inter-connected. It's an interpellation to become aware of the multiple and situated power relations that are exercised simultaneously (and distinctively) on the subjects. Indeed, it seems to me that Gloria Anzaldúa conceptualizes power as a "co-formation" or co-construction, a terminology developed by Paola Bacchetta ("Co-Formations" 5-6). In Anzaldúa's work, "queer" is always employed in a context that politicizes it explicitly by anchoring it in a decolonial, anti-imperialist, and anti-racist agenda.

Just as it is impossible to read *Borderlands/La Frontera* out of its feminist and decolonial context, it is difficult to grasp the construction of the queer-identified subject in Anzaldúa's work apart from that of the "new mestiza." Subjects who identify as queer are inclined to develop "la facultad" and function as "new mestizas" or "nepantleras," mediators who facilitate the passages between the different worlds to which they belong and develop perspectives that allow them to reconfigure and transform these different spaces. This leads me to one of Anzaldúa's most precious contributions regarding queer theories: considering the queer-identified subject as an "atravesados," people "who cross over, pass over, or go through" (*Borderlands* 25). She underscores being queer as a permanent crossing but also as bridging worlds. I find this spatial dimension particularly interesting: "queer" evokes above all a position and a positioning in space (a positionality), something "across," "oblique," "transversal," "non-straight" as suggested by its etymology,[4] even before starting to mean "crooked," "twisted," or "fag":

> We are the queer groups, the people that don't belong anywhere, not in the dominant world nor completely within our own respective cultures. Combined we cover so many oppressions. But the overwhelming oppression is the collective fact that we do not fit, and because we do not fit *we are a threat.* Not all of us have the same oppressions, but we empathize and identify with each other's oppressions. We do not have the same ideology, nor do we derive similar solutions. Some of us are leftists, some of us practitioners of magic. Some of us are both. But these different affinities are not opposed to each other. In El Mundo Zurdo I with my own affinities and my people with theirs can live together and transform the planet. (Anzaldúa, "La Prieta" 209)

The queer-identified subjects, if they choose to function as nepantleras, to let their back be bridges and reinvest the strategic space of the borderlands, constitute these points of articulation and connectivity. Understood as a "mode of identification as relational as it is oblique" (Muñoz 127), especially with oppressions that may not be ours but are interconnected with ours, or as a mode of perception (a possible reading of the fiction "El paisano is a bird of good omen"), more than an identity, the term "queer" and the subjects it encompasses mark a field of connections, emotional, erotic and political, but also of affirmation of the difference within. El Mundo Zurdo represents the multiple spaces (always on the making) of community building based on affinities and commonalities rather than on similarities, which aims collectively at a revolutionary change. I think that one of Anzaldúa's most important contributions lies in the possibility of re-signifying differences as the principle for constructing inclusive and multi-issued alliances. Queer theories, in my understanding of Anzaldúa's work, are "theories in the flesh," theories "where the physical realities of our lives—our skin color, the land or concrete we grew up on, our sexual longings—all fuse to create a politic born out of necessity" (Anzaldúa and Moraga 19), deeply engaged in or with grassroots activism.

My belief is that queer theory's current genealogies, by erasing the contributions of Gloria Anzaldúa (and that of many other queers of color), contribute, above all, to the erasure of the anti-racist and anti-imperialist agenda that emerged alongside queer theories, uprooting the term from its decolonial context, from lesbians of color politics, and from a radical understanding of power in terms of co-formation, breaking the possibilities to create multi-issue and expansive coalitions.

May my work be a bridge.

NOTES

1. A similar point is made by Paola Bacchetta, Jules Falquet, and Norma Alarcón in the introduction to *Les Cahiers du CEDREF* (Introduction 10).

2. Anzaldúa was awarded her PhD posthumously. For more information on her dissertation project, see Keating, "Editor's Introduction: Re-envisioning Coyolxauhqui, Decolonizing Reality."

3. All of the details highlighting Gloria Anzaldúa's life come from the meticulous and illuminating timeline that AnaLouise Keating provides at the end of *The Gloria Anzaldúa Reader*.

4. As Sedgwick notes: "the word 'queer' itself means *across*—it comes from the Indo-European root—*twerkw*, which also yields the German *quer* (transverse), Latin *torquere* (to twist), English *athwart*" (Sedgwick, *Tendencies* xii).

WORKS CITED

Anzaldúa, Gloria. *Borderlands/La Frontera: The New Mestiza*. 4th edition, Aunt Lute, 2012.

---. "El paisano is a bird of good omen." *The Gloria Anzaldúa Reader*, edited by AnaLouise Keating, Duke University Press, 2009, pp. 51-69.

---. "La Prieta." *This Bridge Called My Back. Writings by Radical Women of Color*, edited by Gloria Anzaldúa and Cherríe Moraga. 4th edition, SUNY Press, 2015, pp. 198-209.

---. "The coming of el mundo surdo." *The Gloria Anzaldúa Reader*, edited by AnaLouise Keating, Duke University Press, 2009, pp. 36-37.

---. "The occupant." *The Gloria Anzaldúa Reader*, edited by AnaLouise Keating, Duke University Press, 2009, p. 22.

---. "To(o) Queer the Writer—Loca, escritora y chicana." *The Gloria Anzaldúa Reader*, edited by AnaLouise Keating, Duke University Press, 2009, pp. 163-75.

Anzaldúa, Gloria, and Moraga, Cherríe, editors. *This Bridge Called My Back: Writings by Radical Women of Color*. 4th edition, SUNY Press, 2015.

Bacchetta, Paola. "Co-Formations : Sur les spatialités de résistance de lesbiennes "of color" en France." *Genre, Sexualité et Société*, vol. 1, no. 1, 2009, doi:10.4000/gss.810. Accessed 11 September 2018.

Bacchetta, Paola, Falquet, Jules et Alarcón, Norma, editors. Introduction. *Les Cahiers du CEDREF : Théories féministes et queers décoloniales : interventions Chicanas et Latinas* états-uniennes, no. 18, 2011, pp. 1-40.

Conner, Randy P. "Santa Nepantla: A Borderlands Sutra" (plenary speech). *El Mundo Zurdo: Selected Works from the Meetings of the Society for the Study of Gloria Anzaldúa 2007 and 2009*, edited by Norma E. Cantú, Christina L. Gutiérrez, Norma Alarcón, and Rita E. Urquijo-Ruiz, Aunt Lute, 2010, pp. 177-202.

Hames-García, Michael. "Queer Theory Revisited." *Gay Latino Studies: A Critical Reader*, edited by Michael Hames-García, and Ernesto Javier Martínez. Duke University Press, 2011, pp. 19-46.

Hammonds, Evelynn. "Black (W)holes and the Geometry of Black Female Sexuality." *The Black Studies Reader*, edited by Jacqueline Bobo, Cynthia Hudley, and Claudine Michel, 2004, pp. 301-314.

Keating, AnaLouise, "Editor's Introduction: Re-envisioning Coyolxauhqui, Decolonizing Reality. Anzaldúa's Twenty-First-Century Imperative." *Light in the Dark/Luz en lo oscuro. Rewriting Identity, Spirituality, Reality*, by Gloria Anzaldúa, edited by AnaLouise Keating. Duke University Press, 2015, pp. ix-xxxvii.

Keating, AnaLouise, editor. *The Gloria Anzaldúa Reader*. Duke University Press, 2009.

de Lauretis, Teresa. "Queer Theory: Lesbian and Gay Sexualities. An Introduction." *Queer Theory: Lesbian and Gay Sexualities*, special issue of *differences: A Journal of Feminist Cultural Studies*, vol. 2, no. 3, 1991, pp. iii-xviii.

Moraga, Cherríe. "La Güera." *This Bridge Called My Back: Writings by Radical Women of Color*, edited by Gloria Anzaldúa and Cherríe Moraga. 4th edition, SUNY Press, 2015, pp. 22-29.

Muñoz, José E. *Disidentifications: Queers of Color and the Performance of Politics*. University of Minnesota Press, 1999.

Sedgwick, Eve K. Foreword. *Tendencies*. 1993. Routledge, 1994, pp. xi-xvi.

---. "Queer and Now." *Tendencies*. 1993. Routledge, 1994, pp. 1-20.

EXPRESSIONS OF RESISTANCE IN THE BORDERLANDS

CURATING *SHADOW BEAST: CREATING SIN VERGÜENZA*

ELIZA M. PÉREZ, JESSICA GONZALES, AND REBEL MARIPOSA

The art exhibit was about creativity and collaboration; we felt these two practices would be a way to honor the legacy of Gloria Anzaldúa. The exhibit was inspired by the writings of Anzaldúa in *Borderlands/La Frontera: The New Mestiza*, in which the author speaks to resisting limitations, ranging from the self-imposed constraints to oppressive societal and political restraints. We created a call for art asking for entries from all over the world and in all mediums of art. We received submissions of paintings, sculptures, installations, photographs, embroidery, music, videos, and more! We selected almost every piece submitted that fit the theme and essence of Anzaldúa's writings. Artists in *Shadow Beast: Creating Sin Vergüenza* were from California, Mexico, and all over Texas, including El Valle del Rio Grande, where Anzaldúa grew up.

While the selection process was not easy, the layout and display presented even more of a challenge. We selected many different types of artwork and then had to create a cohesive show that honored each piece. Together we laid the art out and moved pieces around countless times, yet in the end it was the works of art that spoke to us and told us where they wanted to be, and we honored their wishes and the spirits that guide us. We thought of how people would enter the room and move around; we wanted the pieces to take the viewer on a emotional and powerful journey. Moreover, as a way to give homage to our abuelitas' casitas, we displayed fabric art on a clothesline and used pinzas like our grandmothers would.

The fabric art danced to the rhythm of the gallery's fan and the wind from open doors. This was our way of honoring our ancestors and visualizing their work as art.

Further, we curated a photo opportunity by displaying "Shadow Beast: Creating Sin Vergüenza" in large text on a wall accompanied by lavender and aloe vera plants. This display encouraged visitors to take selfies and create their own documentation of their experiences.

Ultimately, we were inspired by the Shadow-Beast. Anzaldúa writes, "There is a rebel in me—the Shadow-Beast. It is a part of me that refuses to take orders from outside authorities. It refuses to take orders from my conscious will, it threatens the sovereignty of my rulership" (38). The Shadow-Beast is the ganas to get up in the morning and write the novel you need to write, it is the poder to self-reflect and dissect ourselves to evolve into the light the world needs, it is the brush stroke that creates worlds that speak volumes of marginalized stories, it is the movement of the body that shapes and embodies sacred dances, it is questioning authority and yourself, it is rebellion, it is challenging, it is creating sin vergüenza. This was the spirit of the exhibit and the energy we hoped would come through as visitors walked through the exhibit—breathing in copal, and being cleansed and blessed by the work these artists allowed us to share with the world.

WORK CITED

Anzaldúa, Gloria. *Borderlands/La Frontera: The New Mestiza*. 3rd edition, Aunt Lute, 2007.

DANCE EN NEPANTLA

FABIOLA OCHOA TORRALBA

The Decolonial Epistemologies: Dance Lab (DE:DL, comprised of Fabian Barba, Mireya Guerra, Yvonne Montoya, and Fabiola Torralba), has met regularly since 2016. Through monthly video chats, the platform brings together dancemakers from across the world of Latin American origin or descent. The purpose of these gatherings is to provide mutual support for the creative inquiry, scholarship, collaboration, and advocacy of choreographers in the field of contemporary dance. The DE:DL has supported the development of member projects such as Dance Lab Showing #1: Time, Space and Roots, Dance in the Desert, and the Latinx Choreographers Gathering (LCG).

The purpose of the LCG at the El Mundo Zurdo conference was to share our research with scholars who center the body and provide a space for in-person engagement between Latinx dance artists. The LCG consisted of a panel titled "Nepantla Embodiment: A Convivio of Latinx Dance & Performers" and two workshops, "Testimonials from the Borderlands: An Intercambio of Cuentos from Latinx Dance Makers" and "Open Studio: Decolonial Epistemologies Dance Lab." What follow are reflections about the first of the two workshops that followed the panel. While not intended to be a theoretical paper or a comprehensive account of the LCG activities, it offers entry into the nebulous positioning of Latinx choreographers in the professional field. Gloria Anzaldúa's concept of *nepantla*, a "threshold in the extension of consciousness, caught in the remolinos (vortices) of systemic change across all fields of knowledge," is a helpful framework for understanding how Latinx dance practitioners embody and reflect "the overlapping space between different perceptions and belief systems" that "exist beyond the subject-object divide, a way of knowing and acting on ese saber you call *conocimiento*" ("now let us" 541).

About a dozen individuals gather outside in an outdoor courtyard. They walk from all directions, weaving in through hot parking lot asphalt, corridors of hollow air conditioning, and steep flights of red brick stairs. I am standing at a foothill, encircled by tall buildings in all four directions, in front of a building entry, as I face the east. There are scattered trees surrounded by concrete that provide shady relief from the humid steam. Individuals continue to emerge walking from the horizon. They trickle in like water, falling into the mass. I am reminded of a particular choreography of arrival. Armed with bags, baskets of supplies, and trays of food, the gathering resembles that of ceremonia where dance is shared in prayer.

From the teachings of my community, Danza Conchero is a dance that has been kept alive through resistance. The native people of Yanaguana, what is now known as San Antonio, Texas, were surveilled for these practices and thus danced under guise for protection. Realizing my position at the bottom of the architecture, I remember learning about the priests who observed and monitored these dances. They overlooked spiritual ceremonies, often from above, only after granting permission to practice under their scrutinous eyes. These danzas, however, could only take place inside of missions or churches, which were often built over sacred places that had been demolished and occupied. Here we find ourselves again, I think to myself, at the bottom of one of the ivory towers.

More than a dozen people assemble next to me on the patio to form a circle. The bodies are of varying ages, shapes, and sizes. Some are dressed in clothing prepared for a traditional dance class with bare feet. Others wear blue jeans, finely pressed button-up collared shirts, slacks, fitted skirts, heels, and rubber-soled leather shoes. I recognize some as attendees and presenters of the El Mundo Zurdo conference. Others had arrived specifically to join the Latinx Choreographers Gathering.

Gloria Anzaldúa describes *nepantla* as the space between dichotomies, borders, and sociopolitical demarcations. The experiences of Latinx dancers and choreographers in contemporary dance similarly enact "una herida abierta" in a field dominated by Eurocentrism and Western ontology (*Borderlands* 25). The DE:DL aims to support choreographers and performers attempting to articulate their existence and bodily knowings in a space that privileges Whiteness. Comprised of Latinxs of various trainings, languages, ages, nationalities, marital and familial statuses, regional specificities, abilities, migration stories, class, genders, and sexualities, the DE:DL seeks to generate support for the development of work that reflects this space of ambiguity, this home we call *nepantla*.

The mix of academics, enthusiasts, and practitioners makes me nervous. I realize that I had recently and primarily been working with self-identified and technically trained dancers. I take off my guaraches to the feel the earth underneath, something that I have always found grounding. A few other participants follow my lead as I signal to everyone to form a circle. Noticing that some individuals are sitting in chairs at a distance, I wave at them to join in. I am met with resistance until they eventually scuffle in, still in their chairs, and with heavy bottoms. Sensing the immediate distance and tension of the bodies around me, I revamp what was supposed to be a roundtable discussion and begin the session the way that I was taught to open up space in círculo: with a blessing.

Despite the elaborate rituals of Danza Conchero, there can be a sense of informality in ceremony. Learning takes place through observation, deep listening, and simulation. The ego here is challenged by minimal step-by-step instruction and the invitation to make mistakes that are immediately corrected by maestros. There is no intention to know or expectation to know right away. As a result, individuals must invest heavily in ceremony before being invited to take on a particular role. Like a structured dance improvisation, knowledge and skill is based on the ability to respond to the moment and assess the energetic needs of the group. Each individual, then, is expected to find their own pathway and create their own relationship to the practice.

I light a small bundle of sage with fire and speak a few sentences before breaking the formation to walk inside. The participants face the inside of the circle, awaiting their turn in silence to be smudged. Slowly, I draw the sage one by one over each receiving body as I remember being taught. A faint stream of smoke encircles each person's toes, hips, back, arms, and head. This pattern continues across each of the bodies curving the traveling pathway in towards itself like a serpent. This continues until the sage returns to its beginning position in the circle.

I ask the individual next to me to continue this pattern and to continue the coiling. Slowly the bodies begin to alter their movement from standing to crouching and then touching the ground. This forces each person to acknowledge all sides of the bodies in front of them and the multi-dimensionsional space around them. Some individuals make larger motions by extending their limbs, spiraling their torsos, and turning their facings. The bodies seem to grow larger as each blessing becomes a dance and the caracol spiral increases energy in the space. As each person reaches their beginning place, the person next to them follows, and the spiral continues.

This is how I was taught to enter into dialogue with ourselves, the bodies around us, the trees, and concrete. Working in community has taught me that there are different ways to enter into space. *Ceremonia* has taught me that how you enter is just as important as the danza itself. We entered this circle in silence with our presence and full awareness. This place of knowing and not knowing is where ceremony collapses time, creating a space of no place where past-present-future exist simultaneously. *Nepantla* offers the possibility for the full intellect of our bodies and selves to be in relation, porous, ever shifting, and connected to the moment. Like writing, this practice can be positioned as the "blood sacrifice" that Anzaldúa affirms is required for creation to be, at once, of the "Earth's body—stone, sky, liquid, soil" (*Borderlands* 97). This *círculo*, the beginning place of this spiral, is where we begin to converge our bodies' knowings.

WORKS CITED

Anzaldúa, Gloria. *Borderlands/La Frontera: The New Mestiza*. 2nd Edition. Aunt Lute Books, 1999.

---. "Now let us shift...the path of conocimiento...inner work public acts." *This bridge we call home: Radical visions for transformation*, edited by G. Anzaldúa & A. Keating, Routledge, 2002, pp. 540-577.

WHO TAKES CENTER STAGE?

XICANA EPISTEMOLOGIES IN CONTEMPORARY DANCE

YVONNE MONTOYA

INTRODUCTION

DESLENGUADAS

The reading of this paper began with a dance performance. The performance I shared is an excerpt of a 15-minute solo dance piece inspired by Anzaldúa's writing "Deslenguadas." The dance tells the story of language loss and acquisition due to the implementation of Americanization programs in elementary schools in the Pojoaque Valley of Northern New Mexico in the 1940s. These Americanization programs came to Northern New Mexico during the building of the Los Alamos Scientific Laboratory, now known as the Los Alamos National Laboratory, where the atomic bomb was developed during World War II. Based on oral histories I collected from family members for my master's thesis, entitled *'ASINA NOS CRIARON': Contesting the Narratives and Claiming Place in the Atomic Age: 1912-1955*, the dance piece embodies the oral traditions of Northern New Mexico (Montoya 62-74). The dance consists of three sections representing three generations of women—my grandmother's, my mother's, and mine. Exploring how ancestral knowledges and embodied memories are passed down generationally through movement, the piece opens with the younger generation and progresses back in time. I open the piece with a dancer, in this case myself, representing my generation moving to the excerpt of Anzaldúa's "How to Tame a Wild Tongue" (58). I chose this text not only because of my background as a student, researcher, and lecturer of Mexican American Studies, but also because this passage poetically captures the essence of what I felt in my attempts to learn the Spanish language in college.[1]

THE PERFORMANCE

Academics, artists, and students are seated in a classroom at Trinity University. Desks are arranged in a deep semicircle. The audience is facing the front of the room where a large, intimidating desk stands; behind it, a lowered screen projects a PowerPoint with the title "Who Takes Center Stage?: Xicana[2] Epistemologies in Contemporary Dance." Seated in the back of the room, I stand up and open Rubén Cobos's book, *A Dictionary of New Mexico & Southern Colorado Spanish*, to a random page. As I begin to walk, I repeatedly attempt to pronounce the word "Deslenguadas" in the broken and accented Spanish of someone who learned the language as an adult. I pay special attention to the places where my tongue shamefully betrays me as a non-Native Spanish speaker—the diphthong and the pronunciation of the Spanish "d." I sound out "gua...gua...gua.." and "d..da...d... das…" over and over as I walk barefoot, slowly, from the back of the room, into the negative space created by the desk's semicircle. I walk towards the large desk in the front. I stop about a foot away from the desk with my back to the audience, say "Deslenguadas" once more, then slam the book shut and quickly roll to the floor, beginning a phrase of movement inspired by classical modern dance aesthetics.

The dance continues with a focus on lines, abrupt movements, and my body repeatedly coming in and out of the floor. There is no music; the only accompanying sound is my voice, spoken word, as I recite an excerpt of "Deslenguadas" from Chapter Five of Gloria Anzaldúa's *Borderlands/La Frontera: The New Mestiza*, "How to Tame a Wild Tongue" (58). I move through space in linear floor patterns, which are juxtaposed by small circles I draw around my nose with my right hand or on the floor with my feet as I complete tight and restrictive half pirouettes or chaîné turns. Legs and arms, moving like knives, execute sharp stabbing movements; my feet alternate between rigidly pointed and tightly flexed. Feet leave the floor during various kicks and extensions from both standing and lying positions. There is one jump in the piece, a turning calypso with one flexed and one pointed foot, that lands on the floor with a roll.

The book from which I was "reading" becomes a prop.[3] I open and close the book, drop it on the ground, leaving and returning to it various times during the piece. The book takes on several forms, including that of a heavy rock, a pillow, a drug, a sacred item with healing properties, and a knife. During the climax of the piece, I lie down, open the book on the floor, and rip out a page. Leaving the book on the ground, I clench the ripped page of the book in my right hand, wad it into a ball in my fist, then run around the space in a circular shape for the first time, breaking out of the rigid linear patterns. After a series of large classical modern soutenu turns, I say the last line of the Anzaldúa's excerpt, "We speak an orphan tongue," and then stuff the ripped page in my mouth ending the performance.

Afterwards, I walk to the large desk behind me, gagging, I remove the ripped page from my mouth, pick up my paper, and return to the performance space. Barefoot and winded, I begin to read the paper in a quick and theatrical manner. After finishing a page, I dramatically put it face down on a nearby desk and take a deep breath. The reading is almost acted as I share the paper in an animated yet casual manner as if I am retelling these experiences and ideas in an intimate setting with friends.

The following is the paper that was read after my dance performance at El Mundo Zurdo 2018. The paper examines the radical act(s) of placing Xicana bodies, stories, and experiences at the center of contemporary dance practice and performance.

DESLENGUADAS AND CRP

On May 21, 2017, I was invited to present the first section of "Deslenguadas" at a Critical Response Process training event at Arizona State University in Tempe, AZ. Critical Response Process or CRP is a structure for giving and receiving feedback developed by Jewish American choreographer Liz Lerman in 1990. CRP, developed to elicit constructive criticism that would inspire and motivate an artist to continue their work, was created as an alternative to dance's traditional, often harsh and demoralizing feedback practices. CRP is used in various disciplines, including but not limited to dance, creative writing, education, and science. Lerman facilitated the feedback session in which I presented my work. Although I received artistic feedback, the goal of this CRP session was a hands-on learning experience to train participants in the process of CRP by practicing CRP. It is important to note that the group of "respondents" participating in that CRP workshop were demographically similar to contemporary and concert dance audiences nationwide in that they were predominately white, middle class, and of the baby boomer generation. I was the only Xicana in the room. There were approximately five millennials, two of them women of color. I believe the respondents' reactions to my work are telling of the unique challenges and barriers specific to Xicanx dancemakers' experience in regard to their work and career.

"Respondents," as audience members are referred to according to CRP's structure of roles (Lerman and Borstel 14, 31-32), provided me with the following artistic feedback: inquiry into my first language, comments regarding the dirtiness of my feet, and stating that they felt "implicated" by the "we" and "you" statements from Anzaldúa's passage (Anonymous 3; Anzaldúa 58). In another session during that day-long training, one white male participant in particular displayed a great disdain for my work, indirectly insinuating that the piece is reverse racism. Rather than directly addressing this with me, however, this respondent expressed his concerns to the white male facilitator in the room.

I argue that the majority of the reactions and feedback I received regarding the piece was grounded in racism and racist attitudes toward Xicanx, Mexican-American, Mexican immigrant, and other Spanish-speaking populations of the Southwest region in general.[4] For example, the respondent who questioned my first language did so with a tone of romanticization and exoticization that can be likened to the tradition of the West falsifying and romanticizing non-Western cultures as described by Edward Said in *Orientalism*.[5] Simply put, this respondent assumed that I was an essentialized, racialized ethnic other performing for the white gaze. This assumption not only rendered the content of my work invisible but continued to center whiteness in dance spaces. Furthermore, I believe that the questioning of my language was grounded in the assumption that all Spanish-speakers are immigrants. While there are large, predominately Mexican immigrant Spanish-speaking populations in the Southwest, there are also significant Xicanx non-immigrant populations, such as the Tucsonenses in Arizona and my vecino, mestizo, and genízaro ancestors in Northern New Mexico, who speak various degrees of Spanish.[6] In general, non-immigrant Xicanx communities in the Southwest are products of the Treaty of Guadalupe Hidalgo and the Treaty of La Mesilla and the "ceding of approximately one third of Mexico's northernmost territory" and its people to the imperial expansion of the United States (Montoya 32). Exoticization and otherization of Spanish-speakers continue to combine with the mainstream narratives of Latinx diasporas and immigration stories, which largely erase non-immigrant Xicanxs in the Southwest from both contemporary and historical narratives, thereby rendering non-immigrant Xicanxs' lives and experiences invisible in our homelands.[7] This continues to serve the myths of Manifest Destiny and the Wild West by reinforcing the idea of Xicanxs as perpetual foreigners and the West as an unpopulated, empty, barren wasteland.

Another example of respondents' feedback grounded in racism was the comment regarding my feet. In general, modern and contemporary dancers perform barefoot. Following this dance tradition, I perform "Deslenguadas" with bare feet. The day of the CRP training, I performed on a filthy floor that left my feet noticeably dirty. Audience members saw the bottom of my feet when I kicked, jumped, and extended my legs during the piece. One respondent believed that this was an artistic choice, that I intentionally dirtied my feet for the performance to signify "poverty" (Anonymous 2). I conclude that after hearing the excerpts of Spanish in Anzaldúa's passage, the respondent drew a connection between the Spanish language and stereotypes of Latinxs as "dirty, unclean and unsanitary" and projected these stereotypes on to my work (Bender 11).[8]

LA TROQUITA

Shaken and upset, I drove back to my home in Tucson reflecting on the experience. Lost in thought, I remembered another instance when white audience members showed similar reactions to my work. In 2015, I staged a work in progress entitled "La Troquita," which celebrated the cruising culture of 6th Avenue in the City of South Tucson, AZ, during its heyday in the 1990s and 2000s. The piece was staged as part of a larger show, "Dancing the Mural," which was the culmination of a two-year residency and participatory dance theater and mural project spearheaded by the dance company I founded and direct, *Safos* Dance Theatre.[9] The "Color the Mural/Dancing the Mural" project was grounded in Participatory Action Research (PAR) methodologies to ensure that both the community mural and dance pieces were co-developed and co-created with the communities of South Tucson.[10] City of South Tucson community members of all ages up to 88 years old voted on the theme and design of the mural, painted the mural, and performed onstage alongside professional artists during the unveiling. Community members selected the representation of a classic 1965 Chevy CT lowrider truck for the mural and requested the honoring of cruising culture in the performance. I partnered with community members Florencia,[11] who worked as a dramaturg on the piece providing consultation on costuming, dialogue, and movement, and Salvador Angulo, the owner of the truck.

The piece was received with polarizing audience reactions and reviews after its debut. Most Xicanx, Latinx, and people of color in the audience identified "La Troquita" as their favorite piece. However, a group of predominately white, baby-boomer, cisgender women, who represent mainstream dance and art gallery audiences in Tucson, strongly disliked the piece. Similar to my experience presenting work at CRP, the disgruntled audience members did not directly inform me of their opinions, and rather chose to share them with my one white dancer who did not perform in the piece. This company member, concerned about the opinions and experiences of the white audience members, shared this information with me using a tone of a reprimand for offending audience members she knew and invited. I hypothesize that the white mainstream dance audiences who expressed disdain for this piece had little to no experience with cholo cultures other than media representations that, in general, create and reinforce stereotypes of Xicanxs as thugs or gangbangers. I also believe that white audiences were uncomfortable with the aesthetics that were centered in this performance. For example, the beginning of the performance featured dancers speaking in Caló and Spanglish. The tattooed, curvy, and stocky bodies of the dancers were adorned in bold colored cholo-inspired costumes complete with Dickies, bandanas, heavy black eyeliner, dark lipstick, and hoop earrings. Furthermore, the performers had a range of skin colors (light skinned to dark brown) that is reflective of the City of South Tucson and surrounding communities. In general, bodies, aesthetics, and themes such as these are not seen, much less centered, in contemporary dance. As such, I believe experiencing a celebration of cruising and cholo cultures in concert dance offended white sensibilities unaccustomed to experiencing these aesthetics and cultural representations in dance concerts and beyond.

Video Clip of La Troquita

At this point, I play the excerpt of La Troquita. The clip opens with the image of a light blue 1965 Chevy CT truck driving up a dirt driveway and onto a concrete slab. The backs of audience members' heads are seen as the truck pulls into position. The four performers are seated in the back of the truck. The clip fades into a shot of movement. One dancer is on the concrete slab doing 1990s inspired hip hop. A second dancer is on the truck doing ballet and classical modern style movement and dancing with the truck as if they are partners in a pas de deux. A third dancer is walking along the edge of the truck bed and climbing through the window into the front seat. The musician sits in the back of the truck and plays along with Zapp and Rogers' "No Bounce to the Ounce" on a French horn. Then, two of the dancers join in unified movement on the truck bed as the truck's hydraulics inflate, moving in sync with the dancers. Dancers then roll and jump off the side of the vehicle onto the concrete slab as the bags deflate. The clip fades to black. The video clip of "La Troquita" was filmed in March 2015 when the piece was shown as a work in progress as part of the larger show, "Dancing the Mural," produced by *Safos* Dance Theatre.

Fig. 1 "La Troquita" by Dominic Bonuccelli. Image appears courtesy of *Safos* Dance Theatre

After pondering why "Deslenguadas" and "La Troquita" offended mainstream white dance audience sensibilities so, I concluded it was because these two pieces are blatantly grounded in Xicana epistemologies as they unapologetically place Xicana experiences, stories, and bodies in the center, both thematically and literally, as dancers take center stage.

XICANA EPISTEMOLOGIES IN CONTEMPORARY DANCE

DANCE GROUNDED IN LIFE EXPERIENCES OF XICANAS: XICANA NARRATIVES AND "HIGH" AESTHETICS

For the purpose of this analysis, I identify epistemologies in contemporary and concert dance as systems and methods that inform creative and choreographic processes and productions of knowledge(s). Delgado Bernal states that Chicana feminist epistemological frameworks are "grounded in the unique life experiences of Chicanas" and "give voice to Chicana experiences" (559, 558). Chicana feminist epistemological frameworks center Xicana experience(s), placing them in a "central position in the research" (Delgado Bernal 558). In concert dance, this means centering Xicana experiences and bodies in the embodied and practice-based research that occurs during the choreographic process. I will focus on two components of chicana feminist epistemology framework as introduced by Delgado Bernal in the article "Using a Chicana Feminist Epistemology in Education Research" to demonstrate how my pieces "Deslenguadas" and "La Troquita" are examples of Xicana epistemologies in concert dance. My analysis focuses on the following two components: 1) the grounding work in the life experiences of Xicanas, and 2) the questioning of the notion of objectivity and a universal foundation of knowledge, specifically regarding what the Western Eurocentric field of contemporary and concert dance defines as high aesthetics.

In general, concert dance across the U.S. is largely upper middle class and white (NEFA 27).[12] Additionally, concert dance leadership is largely comprised of cisgender white men who make up the majority of artistic and executive directors of large, touring dance companies, presenters, and renowned choreographers. On concert dance stages the world over, Western Eurocentric dance "high" aesthetics are characterized by young, tall, long, thin, white bodies with strong "technical" foundation, meaning years of training in classical ballet. The general assumption in dance is that long bodies with classical lines look best on stage. Additionally, what is considered high aesthetics in post modern and contemporary dance, at least in the Southwest region, is devoid of narrative and any expression of the face.[13] Indeed, dance pieces that use narrative or an expressive face are considered subpar and of lower aesthetic qualities. For the most part, in Tucson and Tempe, Arizona, where my work was shown, the communities of dancers, choreographers, and audience members are predominately white, middle class, and heterosexual cisgender females.[14]

"Deslenguadas" and "La Troquita" both embody and perform histories of lived Xicana experiences. As previously mentioned, "Deslenguadas" is based on both my family histories and my personal experiences. Likewise, "La Troquita" is largely shaped by the life experiences of dramaturg Florencia. Both these pieces exemplify Xicana epistemologies in that the pieces are "grounded in life experiences of Chicanas." These dances center Xicana bodies and reveal the complexities, diversities, and intersectionalities of Xicana experiences in embodied and artistic ways. Furthermore, both pieces use spoken word and narrative. I argue that the use of narrative in these dance pieces serves to further deepen and reinforce Xicana epistemologies in the work in so much as the spoken word literally gives voice to dancers while recorded narratives give voice to ancestors. Delgado Bernal states that a "unique characteristic of Chicana feminist epistemology is that it also validates and addresses experiences that are intertwined with issues of immigration, migration, generation status, bilingualism, limited English proficiency" (559). Indeed,

"La Troquita" showcases bilingualism as dancers speak in Caló and Spanglish, and "Deslenguadas" deliberately showcases a Xicana experience of bilingualism, limited English proficiency, and generation status. Furthermore, in addition to Anzaldúa's passage, section three of "Deslenguadas" features recordings of my great-grandmother, great-aunts, and grandmother sharing their experiences of the 1940s Americanization programs in their own words.[15]

Clip of Music

Approximately one minute of the score is shared with the audience during my presentation at El Mundo Zurdo. Excerpts included the testimony of my great-aunts María Adelia Roybal Baldock and María Diolanda Roybal García. A transcript of the clip played is listed below:

> *First grade was exciting because, I remember the teacher. It was exciting just to be able to go sit at a desk, see a blackboard, and learn. And I remember having to learn English.* —María Adelia Roybal Baldock.[16]

> *Not one word of English, and uh, this I'll never forget. We were told that if we spoke Spanish during class the teacher would write a little circle on the blackboard and we would have to stand there with our nose inside that circle, that was punishment (chuckling).* —María Diolanda Roybal García.[17]

The piece was composed by Samuel Peña using oral histories collected by me, the choreographer.

Featuring the voices of my ancestors as the musical score for my piece, I intentionally center the voices and stories of women whose experiences are largely unheard, unseen, and invisible in historical and contemporary narratives as well as in concert dance. Following a looser narrative, "La Troquita" is sprinkled with dancers talking amongst each other throughout the piece. This dialogue was largely scripted by Florencia who also coached dancers on both the intonation of the words and accompanying gestures. Thus, the dancers provided a platform for Florencia's unique voice. The use of spoken word and narrative in these pieces gives voice to Xicana experiences in the public sphere.

As previously mentioned, Western Eurocentric "high" dance aesthetics consider the use of narrative in dance as unsophisticated and of low aesthetic quality. On the one hand, continued use of narrative in my pieces counter concert dance's Western Eurocentric white aesthetic hierarchies and challenge universal dance knowledges. The downside of this practice, however, is that gatekeepers indoctrinated in Western Eurocentric forms would likely deem my work inferior and withhold funding and other resources needed to create more works.

DANCE QUESTIONING THE UNIVERSAL FOUNDATIONS OF KNOWLEDGE: XICANA BODIES AND "HIGH" AESTHETICS

Linda McDowell describes the body as the most immediate place and surface for social inscription (34, 51). This is doubly true for dancers who are judged not only for how their body looks, but also how it moves, the quality of training it received, and so on. As previously mentioned, there is a type of body that is considered ideal for dance, usually tall, long, young, and white. Of the dancers featured in the two pieces, "Deslenguadas" and "La Troquita," none were over five foot, four inches in height. Additionally, all dancers had "curvy," "stocky" bodies that are generally considered, at minimum, overweight for a dancer. In the article "Jennifer's Butt," Negrón-Muntaner states, "Like hegemonic white perceptions of Latinos, big butts are impractical and dangerous" (189). In general, there is no room for big butts or panzas in concert dance. Traditional dance paradigms regarding thin body aesthetics are reinforced through methods such as public verbal reprimands, as exemplified by a former dance teacher who repeatedly publicly shamed me in dance class, commenting that my stomach should not touch my leg when contracted over on the floor in second position.

Thin body aesthetics are also upheld by practices such as conditioning letters that dance schools, like the conservatory-based University of Arizona's School of Dance, send out to students they consider to be overweight. Even institutions that consider themselves to be progressive continue to center whiteness and uphold Western Eurocentric ideals and beliefs that only certain bodies, thin bodies, "can" dance. As a post-graduate fellow in dance at Arizona State University, I introduced myself to a professor on the first day of a 300-level dance class and was received with a disdainful, dirty look up and down my body followed by the statement that this was a "very advanced class." This microaggression not only reinforced Western Eurocentric aesthetic ideals that only young, thin, white bodies are welcome in concert dance spaces, but also served to marginalize and make invisible my curvy, short body while discrediting my experiences and expertise in the field.

Casting short, "curvy," "stocky" bodies is a practice in Xicana epistemologies because I am intentionally countering the "universal foundation of knowledge" in dance, according to which only long bodies look good on stage and thus deserve to be seen. In this case, "A big culo does not only upset hegemonic (white) notions of beauty and good taste" (Negrón-Muntaner 189), it serves as a practice in Xicana epistemologies centering the bodies that Western Eurocentric aesthetics marginalized and erase. Additionally, when I cast myself in pieces, I challenge Eurocentric forms even further because I am centering myself not only as short and curvy, but also as an older dancer in a field that values youth. Thus, centering Xicana bodies in concert dance stages and spaces challenges dominant Western Eurocentric dance standards, paradigms, and notions of "high" aesthetics while directly countering the erasure of Xicanx and Latinx bodies and experiences in the field.

Beyond the height and shape of my dancers' bodies, I further challenged the "universality" of dance aesthetics and hierarchies by casting dancers who, like me, began "technical" training, meaning indoctrination into Western Eurocentric ballet, at the age of eighteen. Regarding Xicanx dancers, at the very least, intersections of race/ethnicity, socioeconomic status, and lack of cultural competencies in dance mean that many U.S.-based Xicanx dancers begin "formal" classical ballet and modern dance training in their late teens. This is considered too late by most practitioners in the field. Indeed, popular dance literature states that ballet dancers are "often expected to be career ready by 16" (Dance Spirit, 2012). This practice disadvantages Xicanx dancers with limited or no access to studio dance classes until later in life. By purposefully casting dancers who began indoctrination into Eurocentric dance practices at a later age, I challenge Western Eurocentric aesthetic hierarchies by refusing to accept that concert dancers are only truly dancers if they acquire a specific level of training in exclusive Western Eurocentric forms.

Although the bodies I used in these pieces evoke strong reactions from white dance audiences for the abovementioned reasons, I acknowledge the cisgender privileges of the dancers in both "Deslenguadas" and "La Troquita." The fact that I know fewer than three Xicanx concert dancers in Arizona who are not light-skinned or cisgender is indicative of the continual idealization and reinforcement of rigid heteronormative Eurocentric aesthetic hierarchies in concert dance in the region. I also recognize that my light-skinned privileges allow for access to certain dance spaces that I might not access otherwise. However, my light-skinned privilege only extends so far, as certain features on my body, such as my dark eyes, thick, long hair, big butt, and curvy, short stature, mark me as a racialized ethnic other in dance spaces. Furthermore, my light-skinned privileges are complicated by my lived experiences as a Xicana living and creating art in the highly militarized U.S.-Mexico borderlands region in Tucson. Unfortunately, there is little room for multiplicities and plurality in concert dance today. There is much work to be done.

Both the Anzaldúa-inspired "Deslenguadas" and "La Troquita" place short, curvy, stocky dancers with no "classical" lines center stage in concert dance spaces to perform narrative-based work grounded in Xicana lived experiences. Doing so is a practice in Xicana epistemologies. Chicana and Native American scholar Inés Hernández-Avila states, "When I and other Native American women are central as subjects—as sovereign subjects—we often unsettle, disrupt, and sometimes threaten other people's, particularly many white people's, white scholars', white women feminists' sense of self as subjects" (qtd. in Delgado-Bernal 556). By practicing Xicana epistemologies in contemporary concert dance spaces, centering Xicanx bodies, I challenged the artistic/aesthetic sensibilities of predominately white dance audiences accustomed to witnessing whiteness, white bodies, and white experiences centered in and on dance stages. I argue that the strong reactions white audiences experience following the performance of these two pieces is because the work unsettled and disrupted their senses of self. Placing Xicana ("Deslenguadas") and Xicanx ("La Troquita") bodies center stage, using embodied knowledge and contemporary movement aesthetics of the Southwest region to share the stories of Xicanas, including my ancestors, and decentering whiteness on the concert dance stages upset dance hierarchies. Moreover, these pieces center Xicana narratives and voices that are largely absent and invisible in concert dance spaces, historical narratives, and collective imaginaries alike. This work not only centers Xicanas but challenges the invisibility and erasure of the non-immigrant Xicanx communities who have lived in the Southwest region for centuries.

CONCLUSION

Overall, this analysis begets the question "who is this for?" meaning who is the intended audience? When I create work, I do not think about, much less center, whiteness or white experiences. For example, when I chose Anzaldúa's passage to open "Deslenguadas" I envisioned the "we" and "you" statements from the passage as a conversation between Spanish-speaking and non-Spanish speaking Xicanx and immigrant communities in the Southwest. I believe my unconscious decentering of white audiences in my choreography is due mostly to my upbringing among predominantly non-immigrant Xicanx communities and in close proximity to many indigenous nations in Northern New Mexico. Additionally, my continuous residence in Xicanx and Mexican immigrant communities in Southern Arizona continues to influence my work. It is important to note that rural villages of Northern New Mexico and Southern Arizona, including Tucson, remained relatively isolated and were not overwhelmed by initial waves of Anglo settlement in the Southwest in the late 19th and early 20th centuries (Sheridan 2). I argue that the construction of mainstream U.S. whiteness as idealized and upheld in concert dance is a recent arrival to the Southwest, especially to places like Tucson and Northern New Mexico. I believe that, in general, mainstream U.S. whiteness and white aesthetics, especially those in regard to body, were introduced to the area during the Americanization programs of the 1940s (Montoya 66-69).[18] As such, I argue that this specific construction of whiteness has yet to take root in the collective imaginaries of Xicanx communities in the Southwest and believe that the reason I do not center whiteness or white experiences in my choreography is a direct result of my geographic location(s).

I recognize that using Xicana epistemologies in my choreography could be to my professional choreographic detriment. During my post-graduate fellowship, two famous black choreographers, both elders, separately questioned me regarding the audience of my pieces. One said that work this specific will not be programmed in dance stages in New York. I recognize that yes, it is true that dance audiences, presenters, and programmers nationwide continue to be predominantly middle class, white, baby boomer, etc.; dancemakers who cater to those audiences are more likely to tour and thus have more sustainable careers. Nonetheless, I create work that is meant for my communities because I think it is important for the younger generation of Xicanx dancers and choreographers to see themselves in the work and to have role models from the same cultural background. Speaking from personal experience, it is difficult to identify mentors and elders from the previous generations in concert dance because there are few Xicanx practitioners, and even fewer reviewers, scholars, and presenters who write about concert dance grounded in non-Western Xicanx contemporary movement aesthetics. For these reasons, I am bucking the norms of dance scholarship and, as a practitioner, writing about my work. In conclusion, support the work of Xicanx dancemakers. You are my intended audiences.

NOTES

1. For this analysis, I focus on the Spanish language. However, it is important to note that there exists a multiplicity of indigenous languages in Northern New Mexico and throughout the Southwest region.

2. For the title of this paper, I chose to use Ana Castillo's spelling of Xicana with an "X" instead of a "Ch." Castillo incorporates the use of the Nahuatl "X" in the spelling of Xicana to honor the indigenous roots of Chicana identities. Furthermore, the "X" challenges binaries and calls for solidarity while rejecting separatist nationalist ideologies. For more information, see Castillo, Ana. *Massacre of the Dreamers: Essays on Xicanisma*. University of New Mexico Press, 1994.

3. I used the book *A Dictionary of New Mexico & Southern Colorado Spanish* by Rubén Cobos both when I was learning to speak Spanish and when I was conducting research for my master's thesis. I chose the book as a prop for the piece to symbolize the institution of education and the problematics of the institution in my family history. On the one hand, the 1940s elementary education Americanization programs that accompanied the fourth wave of colonization in Northern New Mexico literally beat the Spanish language out of my ancestors. On the other hand, I learned Spanish as a first-generation college student, which enabled me to speak with my great-grandmother and learn my family history. The painful irony is that the institution of education was used to both destroy and re-claim the Spanish language. The book also contains a regionally specific Spanish that I argue is a dying dialect, which adds an additional layer of meaning to the use of this specific book as a prop.

4. I am loosely defining the Southwest region as New Mexico, Arizona, Colorado, and Nevada, with emphasis on New Mexico and Arizona.

5. Edward Said defines Orientalism as "a manner of regularized writing, vision, and study dominated by imperatives, perspectives, and ideological biases ostensibly suited to the orient." For more information on "Orientalism," See Said, Edward W. *Orientalism.* Pantheon Books, 1978.

6. Regarding Northern New Mexico, see Montoya, Yvonne Marie. "*'ASINA NOS CRIARON': Contesting the Narratives and Claiming Place in the Atomic Age: 1912-1955.*" Master's thesis. University of Arizona, 2005. Regarding Tucson, see Sheridan, Thomas E. *Los Tucsonenses: The Mexican Community in Tucson, 1854-1941.* University of Arizona Press, 1986.

7. Latinx is a gender-neutral term that refers to the pan-ethnic group referencing the multiplicities of cultural, racial, and national identities of peoples of Latin American origins living in the United States.

8. For an in-depth analysis of Latinx stereotypes, see *Greasers and Gringos: Latinos, Law, and the American Imagination* by Steven W. Bender.

9. For more information regarding Color the Mural/Dancing the Mural visit http://safosdance.wixsite.com/color.

10. For more information regarding Participatory Action Research, see McIntye, Alice *Participatory Action Research: Qualitative Research Methods Series 52.* Sage Publications, Inc, 2008.

11. Per Florencia's request, I will refer to her by first name only.

12. For a recent analysis of national demographics of dance audiences, see "Moving Dance Forward: New England Foundation for the Arts' National Dance Project At 20 & Critical Field Trends" pg. 27 under the subheading "Context: National Dance Attendance Shows Modest Increases & Lack of Diversity."

13. In general, the terms post-modern and contemporary are used interchangeably in dance communities across the Southwest. Likewise, modern and contemporary may also be used interchangeably.

14. Currently, there is no research regarding aesthetics trends or the demographics of dance audiences in Tucson, Tempe, the state of Arizona, or the Western region at large. This is an area of study in need of resources and expertise. The statements in this section are based on audience surveys, on my lived experiences, and shared experiences with Xicana colleagues working in Arizona dance communities. More research is needed.

15. Due to time restrictions, section three of the choreography "Deslenguadas" was not performed at El Mundo Zurdo 2018.

16. Samuel Peña, Yvonne Montoya. "Deslengaudas," recorded April 2018 with excerpts of oral histories conducted by Yvonne Montoya in 2004.

17. Samuel Peña, Yvonne Montoya. "Deslengaudas," recorded April 2018 with excerpts of oral histories conducted by Yvonne Montoya in 2004.

18. For information on the impact of Americanization programs in Northern New Mexico on aesthetics as it pertains to body and dress, see Montoya, Yvonne Marie. "*'ASINA NOS CRIARON': Contesting the Narratives and Claiming Place in the Atomic Age: 1912-1955.*" Master's thesis. University of Arizona, 2005. For more information on Americanization programs in New Mexico see Deutsch, Sarah. *No Separate Refuge: Culture, Class, and Gender on an Anglo-Hispanic Frontier in the American Southwest, 1880-1940.* University of New Mexico Press, 1994.

WORKS CITED

Anonymous. "Notes from CRP Workshop." Tempe Annex. 21 May. 2017, Arizona State University, handwritten notes.

Anzaldúa, Gloria. *Borderlands/La Frontera: The New Mestiza.* Aunt Lute Books, 1987.

Bender, Steven W. *Greasers and Gringos: Latinos, Law, and the American Imagination.* New York University Press, 2003.

Bonccelli, Dominic. "La Troquita." 2015. Safos *Dance Theatre.* Photo Gallery. *Safos* Dance Theatre. 1 April 2015. http://safosdance.wixsite.com/safosdance/gallery

Dance Spirit, *The Age Equation,* 2012, www.dancespirit.com/the-age-equation-2326145152.html. Accessed 11 May 2018.

Delgado Bernal, Dolores. "Using a Chicana Feminist Epistemology in Educational Research." *Harvard Educational Review,* vol 68, no. 4, 1998: pp. 555-582.

Lerman, Liz. Borstel, John. *Critical Response Process: A Method for Giving Useful Feedback on Anything You Make, from Dance to Dessert.* The Dance Exchange, 2003.

McDowell, Linda. *Gender, Identity and Place: Understanding Feminist Geographies.* Blackwell Publishers Ltd., 2004.

Montoya, Yvonne Marie. "'ASINA NOS CRIARON': Contesting the Narratives and Claiming Place in the Atomic Age: 1912-1955." Master's Thesis. University of Arizona, 2005.

Montoya, Yvonne Marie. "La Troquita." *yvonnemontoya.co,* produced by *Safos* Dance Theatre. 1 April 2015. www.yvonnemontoya.co/choreography

New England Foundation for the Arts. *Moving Dance Forward: New England Foundation for the Arts' National Dance Project At 20 & Critical Field Trends,* 2016, https://www.nefa.org/sites/default/files/documents/Moving%20Dance%20Forward.pdf. Accessed 29 January 2019.

Negrón-Muntaner, Frances. "Jennifer's Butt." *Perspectives on Las Américas: A Reader in Culture, History, & Representation,* edited by Matthew C Gutmann, Félix V Matos Rodríguez, Lynn Stephen, Patricia Zavella, 2008, pp. 189.

Peña, Samuel. "Deslenguadas." AZ Beat Lab, 2018.

Said, Edward W. *Orientalism.* Pantheon Books, 1978.

Sheridan, Thomas E. *Los Tucsonenses: The Mexican Community in Tucson, 1854-1941.* University of Arizona Press, 1986.

"LET'S GET WEIRD"

EL MUNDO ZURDO AS A DESIGNER TOY

CLAUDIA ZAPATA

On November 11, 2017 in Austin, Texas, the Puro Chingón Collective released the designer toy *Mundo Zurdo* for public sale (see fig. 1).

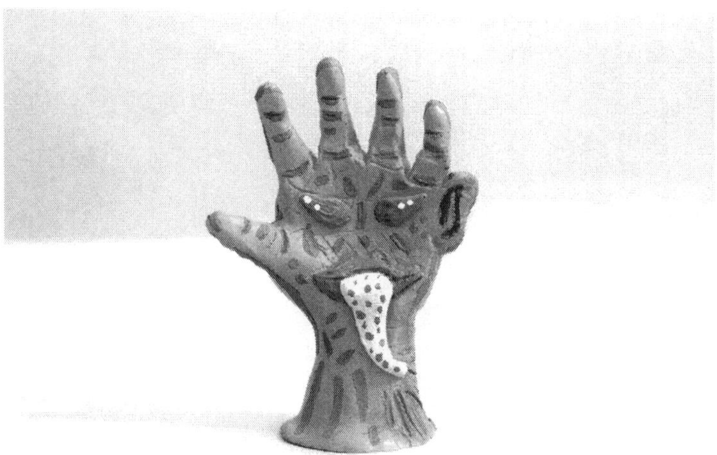

Fig. 1 *Mundo Zurdo*, Claudia Zapata, 2017; acrylic on resin, hand-casted and hand-painted; 4"; Edition of 10. Image courtesy of Whitney Devin.

Designed by me and developed by the Puro Chingón Collective members, this 4-inch art toy was part of an art merchandise line developed under the thematic rubric of "Let's Get Weird." This open-ended theme, intertwined with otherness and queerness, would act as the guiding thesis statement for the development of our new art toy line. The *Mundo Zurdo* designer toy references feminist solidarity, Mesoamerican quincunx patterns, Chicanx tattoo iconography, and Mexican artisan design patterns, but, most importantly, recalls Gloria Anzaldúa's left-handed-world concept of radical interconnectivity to fuse these concepts into one three-dimensional object. In this essay, I contextualize the Puro Chingón Collective's history of DIY art-making in Texas and my specific artistic influences and practices that informed this sculptural toy and its polyvalent visual influences. I argue that the *Mundo Zurdo* designer toy is a reimagined three-dimensional glyph form of Anzaldúa's original logograph defining *El Mundo Zurdo* as a concept of a communal otherness. The *Mundo Zurdo* sculptural form is informed by Anzaldúan consciousness and therefore acts as a spatial declaration and conduit for any toy owner's consciousness-raising. The visual outline of *El Mundo Zurdo* is replicated from an Anzaldúan drawing and, therefore, I suggest this outline form acts as a figurative substrate on which I then imprint my personal histories. This additive artistic overlay aligns my personal histories with the Anzaldúan theoretical concept in a form of transhistorical, transmedia fusion.

Puro Chingón Collective is a Latinx collective based out of Texas. Since 2012, I, along with Claudia Aparicio-Gamundi and James Huizar, have made up this creative trifecta. We originally started with only the development of our anthology zine named *ChingoZine* as an alternative exhibition format for local, regional, national, and international Latinx artists. This ongoing zine project is an artistic anthology that relies on the reader's ability to "read" images in a tangible paper object form. To commemorate the completion of each annual zine, we have a release party in Austin, Texas based on the zine's theme (see fig. 2).

Fig. 2 ***ChingoZine 7: Let's Get Weird*** **Release Party, 2017. Digital Photograph. Image courtesy of Whitney Devin.**

We want each of these events to be an interactive component of the zine itself, a sort of Latinx art Kaprowian “happening.” In addition to zines, Puro Chingón Collective develops murals, prints, interactive theater, installations, apparel, accessories, toys, and festival design. As workers at Mexic-Arte Museum, a Mexican and Mexican-American museum where we all met, we oversaw exhibition process and development and wanted to steer away from the formal white space of arts institutions for our own personal project. Instead, our artistic endeavors were about our collective desires to experiment in unknown media and creatively skillshare.[1] In 2014, we decided to develop a designer toy line within the larger Puro Chingón Collective orbit called Chingolandia.

Designer toys, or limited-edition artist toys, emerged internationally by the end of the 20th century from Asia, specifically Japan, through companies such as Kidrobot (Schmidt, nytimes.com). The independent toy artists movement exists in a hybrid space—part aesthetic object for popular culture consumption and part fine-art sculptures designed by fine artists. Artist Gary Basemen sums up the aims of designer toys when he describes the medium as a way to transcend limiting definitions of “fine art” or “commercial art” (Pasadena Museum 17).

Puro Chingón’s first foray into toymaking was guided by our previous public mural iconography. *Wonderful, Amazing, Stunning, Phenomenal, Fiesta* was a 1996 mural we completed in 2013 (see fig. 3).

Fig. 3 Puro Chingón Collective, ***Wonderful, Amazing, Stunning, Phenomenal, Fiesta*** **Public Mural, 2013. Funded by the Downtown Austin Alliance. Photo Courtesy of Whitney Devin.**

This public mural was funded by the Downtown Austin Alliance with the objective of referencing downtown Austin in some visual capacity. Nestled in the heart of

Austin's Red River district, this downtown-alley mural was predominately informed by Austin's history of segregation and the "1928 Master Plan" (Gregor, austin-chronicle.com). This plan sought to relocate and segregate "the negro population" east of East Avenue, where I-35 is today. Although the 1928 Austin City Plan was not directly created to remove the Mexican community from downtown, the discriminatory act unofficially displaced Mexican and Mexican American families to East Austin (Stensland).

Despite the inequities of Austin's past and, unfortunately, the effects of it today, the Puro Chingón Collective strived to symbolically relocate the Latinx population back to downtown Austin, replete with an allegorical parade to laud and celebrate the city's Black and Brown cultural makeup.

The figurative imagery we developed for this mural would inform our first Chingolandia line of toys known as the "Fiesta series," released in 2014. We developed six toys—three resin toys and three plush dolls with a steep DIY learning curve. The toy-making process is not an artistic medium found in art school curricula, and our toy-making literacy came entirely from YouTube videos and other toy makers' advice and suggestions.

After each of the Collective artists creates a three-dimensional figure with a material called Sculpey®, which has a texture similar to malleable clay, the resin casting process then begins by placing the figure in a conventional oven. Once this is hardened, we use this figure as a plug to develop a latex mold. With the mold available, we are then ready to cast multiple forms using a resin material. The resin casts are removed from the latex mold and then individually hand-painted by each of the collective artists. My distinct toys, such as 2014's *Mapache Bear*, a half-bear and half-racoon figure, are part of an ongoing artform I call "*alebrije* action figures" (see fig. 4).

Fig. 4 Claudia Zapata, *Mapache Bear*, 2014 acrylic on resin, hand-casted & hand-painted; 7" x 6" x 5". Photo Courtesy of Whitney Devin.

This is a term I developed for my specific design approach with our toys. The term *alebrije* originates from the Mexican papier-mâché artist Pedro Linares (1909-1992) and his dream-inspired three-dimensional sculptures (Brulotte 175). In present day, the the term *alebrije* is primarily associated with the tradition of Oaxacan wood carving in Mexico. The making of *alebrijes*, therefore, is a relatively new craft practice that recalls and reimagines modified ancient Mesoamerican iconography; the sculptures exist as three-dimensional experimentation of anthropomorphic figures and zoomorphism. Referencing this similar approach to form, color, and design theory, I often treat the resin substrate, as with the cast of *Mundo Zurdo*, with similar applications of repeated line work, bold colors, and abstract elements of design.

For Puro Chingón's newest Chingolandia series, we assigned each member a toy to create under the theme "Let's Get Weird." I decided to develop a toy based off Gloria Anzaldúa's transparencies from the Benson Latin American Collections at the University of Texas. Initially, I began reviewing Anzaldua's sketches to begin a paper on Gloria Anzaldúa as an artist, looking specifically for art journals or sketches, but in her papers, I kept coming across these recurring visual vocabularies on transparencies. Her use of pictographs—or what she referred to as "glyphs"—helped visually translate her larger conceptual discussions. Anzaldúa states in her later manuscript version of "Border Arte":

> Over twelve years ago I switched from using flow charts during my speaking engagements to using what I call pictograms or rough *glifos* (hieroglyphs) I sketch on transparencies. The images I place on overhead projectors 'illustrate' my ideas and theories. (Anzaldúa 217)

The transparency for El Mundo Zurdo was fairly striking primarily due to the eyes as a personified concept. In "The New Mestiza Nation: A Multicultural Movement," Anzaldúa states,

> [H]ieroglyph of a left hand on whose palm are pictured a pair of eyes, a mouth with a tongue hanging out and the writing tip of a pen at the tip of the tongue. *Los ojos* represent seeing and knowing which can lead to understanding or *conocimiento*. (Sharpe)

When viewing the glyphic qualities of the transparency and analyzing El Mundo Zurdo as a concept of a communal otherness, I wanted to engage with these historical visual writings in an equally glyphic undertaking via my preferred medium of three-dimensional toymaking. Puro Chingón's work is affordable artwork made for the general public. Often our toys end up in people's studios and on their desks and mantles due to their smaller size.

I wanted to develop an homage to Gloria Anzaldúa as an iconic person without the reductive qualities of simply making a likeness of her face. Using her glyph images as a visual jumping-off point, I developed an initial model recalling the linear qualities of the conceptualized left-hand. Designer toy writer Ivan Vartanian says, "Most figures represent characters that are meant to be life-size or creatures that are significantly larger than us," (Vartanian 15) and, in developing this toy, I wanted to encompass the breadth of Anzaldúan thought in a miniature form that would exist on the desks of its owners in a sort of talismanic quality. Unlike artwork that often sits so far removed from its viewers, encased in formality and protection, I wanted the owners of this toy to be able to see it on their desk or hold it as a visual reminder to incorporate Anzaldúan concepts into their work. Anzaldúa discusses the concept of the body's relationship to the imagination and the liminal experience with the inanimate:

> To me, everything is real. Fiction is as true as whatever happened literally to people…The body does not discern between different kinds of stimuli; the body doesn't distinguish between what happens in the imagination and what happens in the material world. (108)

Developing the toy involved reading Anzaldúa's work and analyzing the original transparencies. After designing the Sculpey® plug, I sent it to a fellow collective member to begin casting. For this iteration, we incorporated a dye process in the resin casting. At the time of this casting process there were several regional and national women's protests, and although I did not connect to the biological implications of the Pussyhat™ phenomenon, I decided to incorporate this concept of pink as a common shade in feminist solidarity (Pussyhat Project™). As a queer masculine-of-center person, often women's spaces are incredibly foreign to me; pink often reminds me of a childhood of forced gender conformity. While pink may have seemed like an innocuous Pantone choice, it was a major step for me personally to develop an artwork that relied on a predominately pink composition.

Utilizing the glyphic communication that Anzaldúa embraced, I incorporated a Mesoamerican quincunx design to the sculptural hand (see figs. 5-6).

Fig. 5 Maksim, "Quincunx." Digital image. WikiMedia Commons. 1 February 2018. https://commons.wikimedia.org/wiki/File:Quincunx.svg.

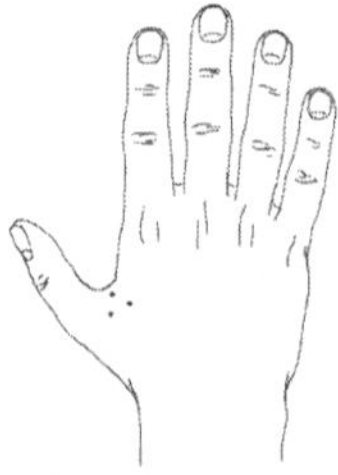

Fig. 6 Premeditated Chaos. "3 dots tattoo" Digital image. WikiMedia Commons. 21 February 2018. https://commons.wikimedia.org/wiki/File:3_dots_tattoo.GIF.

The quincunx is a quadripartite pattern consisting of four corners and a center. This commonly used spatial formation was meant to replicate the universe and its associated four directions (Foster 160). Meant to evoke a harnessing of the cosmos via a central figure's placement, the quincunx pattern relies on the central space to act as an *axis mundi* or connector of the heavens and the underworld, and, symbolically, the center of the universe. I also incorporated the three dots on the toy as the three dots reference a common tattoo design meaning "*Mi Vida Loca* [My Crazy Life]" (DeMello 485). Often associated with gang and prison culture, these three dots that make up one tattoo design have become a recurring tattoo choice among Chicanxs as an homage to this visual culture.

By placing these two heavily charged symbols amidst other *alebrije* line treatments on a three-dimensional visage of Anzaldúan-inspired form, I wielded a very heavy signature referencing the intersectional origins of my own consciousness and educational upbringing. As a Mayanist at the University of Texas at Austin, I studied pre-Columbian art, specifically Maya women and their elite marriages during the Classic era (300-900 CE). This particular field lacked a feminist and queer consciousness, and I eventually sought this consciousness as a Chicanx art specialist. This visual conflation of concepts and practices may be overlooked by those that pick up this designer toy. However, I see the toy's clandestine symbology regarding Mesoamerican space, Chicanx life, weirdness, and feminist consciousness as something that hides in plain sight. Like me, the toy is a rich amalgamation of information that—unless deciphered—remains unknown to the heteronormative world, but—if accepted, studied, and uncovered—reveals the answers to the universe, or at least my universe.

NOTES

1. Skill-sharing is an alternative form of education. Often groups organize to share their knowledge about a particular process and share these skills with less experienced group members. See Choudry, Hanley, and Shragge 166.

WORKS CITED

Anzaldúa, Gloria. *The Gloria Anzaldúa Reader.* Edited by AnaLouise Keating. Duke University Press, 2009.

Brulotte, Ronda L. *Between Art and Artifact: Archaeological Replicas and Cultural Production in Oaxaca, Mexico.* University of Texas Press, 2012.

Choudry, A. A., et al. *Organize!: Building from the Local for Global Justice.* PM, 2012.

DeMello, Margo. *Inked: Tattoos and Body Art Around the World.* ABC-CLIO, 2014.

Foster, Lynn V. *Handbook to Life in the Ancient Maya World.* Oxford University Press, 2005.

Gregor, Katherine. "Austin Comp Planning: Moving forward sometimes requires looking back." *Austin Chronicle,* 5 Feb. 2010, https://www.austinchronicle.com/news/2010-02-05/953471/. Accessed 3 February 2018.

Pasadena Museum of California Art and Los Angeles Toy, Doll, & Amusements Museum. *Beyond Ultraman: Seven Artists Explore the Vinyl Frontier.* Baby Tattoo Books, 2007.

Schmidt, Gregory. "Is It a Toy? Is It Art? Everyone Agrees It's a Collectible." *New York Times,* 29 Mar. 2017, https://www.nytimes.com/2017/03/29/business/smallbusiness/funko-kidrobot-designer-toys-collectibles.html. Accessed 12 January 2018.

Sharpe, Susanna. "Anzaldúa across Borders: A Traveling Thought Gallery." *LlILAS Benson Magazine,* 27 Aug. 2017, https://llilasbensonmagazine.org/2017/08/27/anzaldua-across-borders-a-traveling-thought-gallery/. Accessed 5 April 2018.

Stensland, Jeff. "Racism, Inequities Continue to Exist in Austin, Report Finds." *Spectrum Local News,* 5 Apr. 2017, http://spectrumlocalnews.com/tx/austin/news/2017/04/4/racism---inequities-continue-to-exist-in-austin--report-finds. Accessed 20 February 2018.

Vartanian, Ivan. "A pursuit of perfection." *Beyond Ultraman: Seven Artists Explore the Vinyl Frontier,* edited by Pasadena Museum of California Art and Los Angeles Toy, Doll, & Amusements Museum, Baby Tattoo Books, 2007, pp. 13-16.

LA FRONTERA RE-VISITED

CONSUELO JIMÉNEZ UNDERWOOD'S *BORDERLINES* SERIES

EWA ANTOSZEK

> 1,950 mile-long open wound
> dividing a *pueblo*, a culture,
> running down the length of my body,
> staking fence rods in my flesh,
> splits me splits me
> *me raja me raja*
> This is my home
> this thin edge of
> barbwire. (24–25)

So begins Anzaldúa's *Borderlands/La Frontera*, suggesting how important the border is for the author, as it plays a pivotal role in both parts of *Borderlands/La Frontera* and Anzaldúa's other works. Anzaldúa's border stories have been subsequently taken up by various Latinx writers and artists, who, inspired by the author of *Borderlands/La Frontera*, have contributed to the story of the palimpsestic space of the U.S.-Mexico border. The purpose of this analysis is to examine the history behind re-definitions of the border, its multiple representations, and the interplay between the nation-based or indigenous and immigrant paradigms as addressed in Consuelo Jiménez Underwood's *Borderlines* series. In addition, this essay will also address the question of how the artist's works contribute to the ongoing debate on the status of the U.S.-Mexico border and shed some light on the construction of borders all over the world.

Debra A. Castillo and María Socorro Tabuenca Córdoba, in *Border Women: Writing from La Frontera*, provide an analysis of the representations of the U.S.-Mexico border and recognize Anzaldúa's contribution to the debate on this complex space, giving her credit for opening this discussion in academia. They observe:

> Undoubtedly, the theoretical discussion on the metaphorical border owes its most enduring debts to Gloria Anzaldúa's much commented on and cited 1987 *Borderlands/La Frontera*. It is in part due to her influence that the idea of "the border" has become very prominent in a number of academic disciplines since the mid-1980s, especially in the United States, where this image has served as a popular locus for discussion on the breakdown of monolithic structures....In this sense, Anzaldúa's border...evokes the intellectual project of a discursively based alternative national culture while gesturing towards a more heterogeneous transnational space of identity formation. (2-3)

What may escape unnoticed in this acknowledgement of Anzaldúa's role of the popularization of the concept of the border in scholarship is the attribute "metaphorical" put together with "the border." A seemingly "innocent" adjective, it turns out to be of great significance, as it becomes part of the main argument of Castillo and Córdoba's book, namely the dual perspective on the concept of the border—a material vs. metaphorical reading of the border—related directly to the location/positionality of the author who writes a border story. In their categorization of border representations, the critics postulate, "[T]he border as perceived from the United States is more textual and theoretical than geographical, whereas from the Mexican side the geopolitical referent never entirely disappears" (16) and "[f]rom the Mexican side...the borderline itself retains a stronger materiality than is typical in U.S.-based commentary" (3). Therefore, Castillo and Córdoba argue that the different perceptions of the border, as seen from Mexican and American sides respectively, become reflected in literary and cultural productions from both sides of the border. The critics underscore the prevalence of the metaphorical character of border representations in Chicanx literature and claim that, in those works, "the border is an abstraction, an inexhaustible utopia, a 'Garden of Eden'" (28). In Mexican border literature, in turn, the image of the border is more diverse and it is "more than a trope or locus amoenus. It is part of a literary regional movement that, like the border itself, is in a state of constant development: dynamic and forever changing" (28).

Castillo and Córdoba apply this approach to their analysis of Anzaldúa's works, and they maintain that even though "critics have made Anzaldúa 'the representative' of 'the border'...[i]n Anzaldúa's work the border also functions primarily as a metaphor, in that the border space as a geopolitical region converges with discourses on ethnicity, class, gender/sex, and sexual preference" (15). Moreover, they add that Anzaldúa's "third country between the two nations, the borderlands, is still a metaphorical country defined and narrated from a First World perspective"

(15). Even if her border story is "less ludic than that of Gómez-Peña, and more anchored in real referents" (15), Castillo and Córdoba miss in her stories "many other othernesses related to a border existence" (15). The critics' arguments are in line with the postulates they include in their analysis of the representations of the U.S.-Mexico border: to add to those representations Mexican border literature in order to avoid one-sided approaches or "intellectual colonialism" (14).

However legitimate Castillo and Córdoba's remarks are, their resulting perspective on Anzaldúa's border narratives seems to disregard the complexity of her concept of the border and leads to a reductive reading of Anzaldúa's representation of the border and borderlands. In *Borderlands/La Frontera*, Anzaldúa does indeed evoke metaphorical border(s) crossed by Latinxs on a daily basis and challenges related to nepantilism. The very concept of "a new *mestiza* consciousness" as "a consciousness of the Borderlands" is grounded in a metaphorical reading of this space (Anzaldúa 99). Nevertheless, at the same time, the material aspect of this striated space is never forgotten, let alone excluded from Anzaldúa's discourse. The land, territory, *tierra* is as important for Anzaldúa as it is for other Latinxs who, in the course of history, have been dispossessed of this land and whose rights to this space have been questioned and denied. Already in the "Preface to the First Edition," Anzaldúa acknowledges the material aspect of the border with her declaration that "[t]he actual physical borderland I'm dealing with in this book is the Texas-U.S. Southwest/Mexican border" (19). She refers to various aspects of "[l]iving on borders and in margins" (Anzaldúa 19) throughout the whole text, emphasizing the divisive role of the political line, dubbing it the "Tortilla Curtain" (Anzaldúa 24) or using the most frequently quoted phrase, "*una herida abierta* where the Third World grates against the first and bleeds" (Anzaldúa 25), and explaining how this line prevents people from crossing to the other side of the river, where the other side can be either north or south of the border (Anzaldúa 161). She also acknowledges the problematic status of this territory and reminds the reader that "this land was Mexican once / was Indian always / and is. / And will be again" (Anzaldúa 113), referring directly to the historical legacy of the borderlands and the location of the border itself. In those references, Anzaldúa never forgets about people living on both sides of the border and the challenges they have to face due to the space they inhabit. She reflects on herself and other borderlands peoples she represents—those who are, as Sonia Saldívar-Hull notes in the introduction to *Borderlands/La Frontera*, "both native to the Americas and with a non-Western multiple identity" (2). Writing about Mexican borderlands dwellers in the poem "horse (*para la gente de* Hargill, Texas)," Anzaldúa notices the oppression and discrimination they face owing to their marginalization and exclusion, as a result of which "the *mexicanos* mumble if you're Mexican / you are born old" (Anzaldúa 129).

Consequently, the concept of La Frontera Anzaldúa deploys in *Borderlands/La Frontera* ranges from the demarcation line determined by political treaties to the more fluid and less fixed space of the borderlands. In their analysis of various definitions of the U.S.-Mexico border, Edward Casey and Mary Watkins delineate a sequence of concepts, from "boundary, borderland, border" (21) to "walls and fences, and borderline" (21), which allows them to a coin a more precise definition of La Frontera. They define the borderline as "a cartographic entity, a linear representation of a limit established by political negotiation" and they emphasize that "neither aspect of La Frontera is to be confused with the *borderline* between the United States and Mexico" (20). The term from the other end of the sequence they propose—borderland—is described as

> the area that flanks a recognized international border, usually on both sides. It is an area, a region, in the form of a band or strip that cannot be measured in so many meters or miles. In its indeterminacy of the exact extent, a borderland resembles a boundary, but a borderland is bound, conceptually and concretely, to the border it surrounds. (21)

Their definition of the borderland resembles the concept Anzaldúa proposes in *Borderlands/La Frontera*. Consequently, Casey and Watkins argue that La Frontera, or the border, escapes easy classification and combines elements of all the concepts in the sequence, as it "is closer to a borderline in terms of its putative precision but also integral to the very idea of a borderland" (21).[1] Their positioning of the border resonates with Monika Kaup's division of dominant paradigms in Chicanx literature, namely nation-based and immigrant paradigms (26), which have been determined based on the approach to the space of the border, since "[b]eneath the surface of these models lie two different concepts of the border" (Kaup 10). In the nation-based paradigm, this space is regarded as "home territory, as homeland, as viewed by the original occupants of the borderlands" (Kaup 10), whereas the immigrant paradigm assumes the border is "a line crossed in the northward migration from Mexico, as viewed by the new immigrants" (Kaup 10). This division mirrors Casey and Watkins' aforementioned attempt at the categorization of La Frontera, as the border, defined through the interplay of the nation-based or indigenous and immigrant paradigms, combines aspects of the demarcation line and homeland (i.e., Aztlán transformed into borderlands). Such is the case of Anzaldúa's *Borderlands/La Frontera*, although Anzaldúa complements the representation of La Frontera with the metaphorical reading of the border. Indubitably, she does speak from north of the border, yet she can be classified as the author who in fact writes not only *about* the border but *on/from* the border as well.

CONSUELO JIMÉNEZ UNDERWOOD'S *BORDERLINES* SERIES.

Consuelo Jiménez Underwood is one of the artists, who, motivated by Anzaldúa's groundbreaking work, attempts to represent the complex story of the border, weaving its intertwining tales with real barbed wire and unearthing the multiple layers and legacies of this conflicted space. In her *Borderlines* series, the artist departs from Anzaldúa's concept of the U.S.-Mexico border as "*una herida abierta*" (25), re-constructs this space, taking into account the transformations of border imagery in time, and writes back the indigenous part into the story of the U.S.-Mexico borderlands.

Underwood is a California-based artist, "the daughter of migrant agricultural workers, a Chicana mother and a father of Huichol Indian descent" (consuelojunderwood.com). She is trained as a painter, but during her career she became more of a fiber artist and weaver (consuelojunderwood.com). Underwood also worked as a professor at San Jose State University. In the artist's statement on her website, she refers to the importance of multiple borders in her life—she explains:

> Crossing borders and negotiating between three perspectives has always been a fundamental aspect of my persona and the basis of my creative process.... My work is a reflection of personal border experiences: the interconnectedness of societies, insisting on beauty in struggle, and celebrating the notion of "seeing" this world through my tri-cultural lens. (consuelojunderwood.com)

In some of her works, the artist makes use of the indigenous paradigm, emphasizing the rootedness of the ancestors of some Latinx groups in the U.S. with the technique she deploys—weaving, which "was the high art of Huichol (from whom the artist descends on her father's side), equivalent to painting" (Pérez 163). *Land Grabs. 500 Years* is a good example of the artist's focus on the indigenous aspect of Latinx life in the U.S., and therein she—similarly to Yreina D. Cervántez, another Latinx artist—calls attention to "the impermanence and unnaturalness of political boundaries...further underscored by the unfinished appearance of the weavings, which are seen suspended from their warps and woofs, in a way that visualizes them as unfinished processes" (Pérez 169).) Her other works address the immigrant paradigm; in a series of multimedia weavings, she treats the border as the demarcation line, weaving in "barbed and other wire into her meditations upon the U.S. Mexico border" (Pérez 164) or including the imagery often seen at or near the border (for example, road signs warning about migrants crossing the road) in order to indicate "its dangers for those crossing from Mexico into a militarized, vigilante-attracting, racially polarized U.S. 'frontier' culture" (Pérez 164).

This motif also prevails in a series of mixed-media installations collected in the artist's online portfolio under the category *Borderlines*, which gathers works with equally indicative titles, including *Undocumented Border Flowers*; *Undocumented Border Flowers: Día*; *Welcome to Border-landia*; *Flowers and Borders and Threads, Oh My!*; *Mountain Mama Borderline Blues*; *Borderline Premonitions. New York*; *Undocumented Border X-ings. Xewa (Flower Time)*; *Undocumented Border Tracks*; *We are Here Borderline*; and, simply, *La Borderline*. All of these works present the border as Anzaldúa's open wound—a dark line going across the image and often paralleled by scar-like stripes that divides the two states, cutting across formerly one environment/space, or, as it is in the case of *Flowers and Borders*, even continents. At the same time, they all refer to the nation-based paradigm, however complicated and paradoxical it may be, especially in its "reliance on the mythic" (Contreras 9),[2] which both points to the arbitrariness of the location of borders and reinforces Paul Ganster's statement that "the U.S.-Mexican border is the best known illustration of the paradoxical continued importance of borders in our globalizing world" (xvi).

What strikes the viewer immediately when we look at those installations is the aforementioned wound or scar that mars the otherwise almost idyllic representations of lands with colorful flowers, green lands, etc. Due to the specific framing, the border is visible from the distance, regardless of the size of the individual installations. Moreover, in all of the installations, the borderline is marked by a prominent color—red, brown, or purplish, which looks like a trail of blood, emphasized by two parallel white lines/spaces along the borderline, which make it even more visible. The artist often overlays the borderline with ropes and her "trademark," the barbed wire, the function of which can be both to stitch the two spaces on both sides of the border (in a hurtful way) and, at the same time, to separate them, which is a clear reference to the history of the region. In one of the interviews, Underwood emphasizes this latter function, maintaining that the barbed wire works "as a futile attempt of man to control life" (*Threads*). The double function of the barbed wire resembles that of safety pins—another of Underwood's trademarks. They are often present in her works as pendants, but in most cases they piece often unrelated fabrics or parts of her works together. For example, she uses them extensively in her rebozos, flags, or quilts. In *Borderlines* (series), they often pretend to link the two sides of the border, but this connection is very unstable, temporary, and fragile, just as is the idea of a quick fix that underscores a safety pin's role. The unity or wholeness the safety pin creates is very illusive and can be easily disrupted or broken.

The role of the border to simultaneously divide and link is also emphasized by the nails put in several spaces along the border where the wall has been already erected or "pendants" with names of border towns or twin cities on both sides of the border. The nails, as Underwood herself admits, represent the currency used "back in the day"—gold for dollars and silver for pesos (*Threads*). Therefore, for her, "all the border fight is about gold and silver" (*Threads*). Combined with the image of the bleeding border, the nails may also symbolize metaphorical crucifixion/striation of this space. Referring to the twinning of the cities, in turn, the artist shows how, for example, various foods and products are the same on both sides of the border, regardless of the political line dividing this space into two nation-states. To illustrate that correlation between the two sides of the border, Clara Román-Odio provides the example of "multiple iterations of the simple tortilla [the artist deploys], as a symbol of the pervasiveness of indigenous cultures, and of the immemorial eating habits they shared" (3). These images can be also interpreted as an allusion to the economic interdependence of the two sides of the border, visible particularly in border towns/cities but in fact present as far away from the border as in the most remote regions of the U.S. and Mexico to the north and south, respectively. Such an approach goes along with Oscar J. Martínez's typology of the borderlands where he defines the U.S.-Mexico borderlands as "interdependent borderlands," which suggests a symbiotic connection between border regions on both sides and implies "the existence of a favorable economic climate that permits borderlanders on both sides of the line to pursue growth and development projects that are tied to foreign capital, markets, and labor," which results in "a mutually beneficial economic system" (8). However, as he explains further in *Border People*, in the case of the U.S.-Mexico borderlands, they "are a good example of strong asymmetrical interdependence" (Martínez 9), where the profits of economic interdependence and the financial, social, and environmental costs of this relation are not distributed equally between the two neighbors.

Apart from the aforementioned features, the border in Underwood's works cuts across natural habitats of the plants that are indigenous to the region and appear on both sides, regardless of the political division line imposed on the region and the physical wall erected there. Therefore, the white space alongside the border can be interpreted as what the artist herself refers to as the "dead zone" (*Consuelo Jiménez Underwood Speaks*), or the "desert wasteland" (*Consuelo Jiménez Underwood Speaks*) that is being created by the newly constructed fragments of the wall (*Artist Talk: Consuelo Jiménez Underwood*).[3] Consequently, Underwood draws the viewer's attention once again both to the arbitrariness of borders and to the devastating effects the wall has on the environment in the region. She admits that through her "non-confrontational icons," she wants "to engage the viewer in a discussion about borderline issues" including "the ecological disaster...constructed in the southwest" combined with the question of immigration (consuelojunderwood.com). The artist not only presents images but also voices her concerns, asking rhetorical questions about the flowers' status and commenting, "The California poppy, Arizona saguaro, New Mexico yucca, and the Texas bluebonnet grow on both sides of the border. Will they require documentation as well? How? Yikes!" And, talking about *Undocumented Border X-ings*, she adds, "The flowers live on both sides of the US/MX border wall. All are undocumented, and are referred to as 'illegal aliens. Worse yet, their homelands are becoming wastelands" (consuelojunderwood.com).[4]

In addition to her commentary on environmental issues, Underwood hints here at a very important aspect of the border, namely its porosity. Even though some, especially politicians, would want the border to be fixed and impermeable, in reality, even the wall—the marker of the border—cannot completely prevent some kind of movement/exchange between two sides. Casey and Watkins also refer to this potential of the space and indicate the porosity of the border, identifying "many spontaneous transgressions of the wall at La Frontera" (18), which include "movements of the air, clouds, and weather over the wall; human voices that fly over the wall and can be heard on the other side; Internet communications between people in Tijuana and San Diego" (18). It also resonates with the later part in Anzaldúa's opening lines of *Borderlands/La Frontera*: "But the skin of the earth is seamless. / The sea cannot be fenced, / *el mar* does not stop at borders" (25). Those spontaneous crossings indicate the porosity of the border, which, even in the times of militarization of this space, resists the endeavors to keep it as fixed, rigid, and solid as the newly erected wall.

Finally, Underwood's installations illustrate the combination of Kaup's immigrant and nation-based paradigms deployed to represent the U.S.-Mexico border, since the artist often includes in them elements pertaining to the indigenous status of Chicanxs in America. *Undocumented Border X-ings. Xewa (Flower Time)* is a good example of this interplay between Kaup's nation-based and immigrant paradigms. On the one hand, we see the familiar images of the border and flowers on its both sides, which again implies its divisive role. However, the flowers have grown in the area for centuries, "disregarding" the divisions imposed on them, just as people indigenous to this region have endeavored to do it, moving across the borderline in both directions, in spite of the increasing challenges they have had to face. Moreover, at the bottom of this work, the artist lists "[t]he numerous languages that were spoken when John Smith first entered the Washington, DC region…" (consuelojunderwood.com). Apart from that, "Meso-America is represented with an architectural presence" (consuelojunderwood.com). Superimposed on the picture is a sketch of "the mighty sturgeons" (consuelojunderwood.com) that "up until the 1970s, swam…freely, from continent to continent, undocumented, up and down the great Potomac and Anacostia Rivers" (consuelojunderwood.com), implying naturalness of movement and mobility that lay at the core of the Americas. The image of native and, at the same time, migrant species is combined with the drawing of the "Caution" sign warning the drivers near the border of the immigrants crossing the roads—another Underwood trademark that reappears in her works in different forms.[5] This combination of symbols pertaining to native and migrant status of people, plants, and animals of La Frontera illustrates greatly the interplay of the immigrant and nation-based paradigms in representations of the border.

Lastly, I would like to discuss the techniques Underwood uses in the works I have examined in this paper, as these techniques are also subversive and transgressive. In most of her works, including the *Borderlines* series, the artist mixes various media such as painting, weaving, or cut-outs. The textiles and other materials that she uses for her mixed-media installations are also diverse, of different origins, including such disparate paraphernalia as silk thread and the aforementioned barbed wire or safety pins and photos. According to Clara Román Odio, in this way, the artist's aesthetics are influenced by "what Amalia Mesa-Bains named 'Domesticana,' or the 'Sensibility of the Chicana Rasquachismo'" (3). Grounding it in Ybarra-Frausto's concept of Rasquache,[6] Mesa-Bains defines "domesticana" as "a Chicana feminist art theory that situates Chicana art production in the domestic sphere" (in Román Odio 4) and which results in works that are "the product of resistance to the majority culture…and an aesthetic of survival" (in Román Odio 4). Therefore, as Román Odio maintains, "[T]he use of the domestic…serves paradoxically as both affirmation and a powerful critique of this social sphere. By engaging with materials from the domestic realm, Chicana artists not only legitimize textile art as fine art, but also weave visual narratives that speak for social justice" (4). Moreover, Underwood's works combine art with functionality—the feature that is also mentioned by Anzaldúa when she talks about the indigenous people who "did not split the artistic form from the functional, the sacred from the secular, art from everyday life" (88). Consequently, Underwood, in her works, challenges the art-craft dichotomy, which the artist emphasizes on numerous occasions in different interviews. In this way, *Borderlines* works like Paulo Freire's "limit acts," evoked by Casey and Watkins and defined by them as "an act that both resists the imposition of destructive limits and creates anew in the face of them" (206).[7] In the case of Underwood's art, its role is to undermine the colonial legacy haunting the borderlands and to re-write or re-weave the history of the border, taking into account the complexities and intricacies of that space.

In both Anzaldúa's and Underwood's border tales, the U.S.-Mexico border is presented as a palimpsest with multiple tales, legacies, and histories that lie beneath the surface of this already complex space, making this concept even more evasive. *Borderlands/La Frontera* and the *Borderlines* series address the complexity of this spatial construct and attempt to tell at least some of its stories, thus contributing to the plethora of accounts about the U.S.-Mexico border. Both Anzaldúa s text and Underwood's *Borderlines* are the example of works created *on*, *about*, *of*, and *from* the border(lands). They are also works that "refuse to essentialize Indigenous origins [and to rely solely on the immigrant paradigm], instead deploying self-conscious, unsettled performances of conflicted mestiza/o identities" (Contreras 40). As such, these works have a great potential to defuse common stereotypes and myths regarding the border and encourage a more profound analysis of this space. Gloria Anzaldúa's *Borderlands/La Frontera* began the ongoing debate on the U.S.-Mexico border in 1987, and Consuelo Jiménez Underwood's works undertake the issues Anzaldúa raised back then and continue the discussion in the 21st century, which, in the light of the current situation on the U.S.-Mexico border, is a significant and important act.

NOTES

1. I use their conceptual analysis of the border in "The U.S.-Mexico Border as a Palimpsest in Ana Teresa Fernández's Art."

2. Sheila M. Contreras analyzes the question of Chicana/o indigenism in *Blood Lines: Myth, Indigenism, and Chicana/o Literature* and she indicates the problematic use of the Indigenous by Chicanas/os. Enumerating the challenges she "see[s] with regard to Chicana/o Indigenous history" (40), she nevertheless admits that it can also be deployed as an instrument to counter Anglo-American discourse relegating Chicanxs to the margin. She argues: "My argument is that Chicana/o indigenism creates cultural narratives of Indianness that rely most prominently on mythic accounts drawn from anthropology and archeology, and as it most often does, myth here supplants history. Nevertheless, through indigenism, Chicanas/os have been able to place themselves in an oppositional historical context and to generate discourses of social change because of that positioning" (40).

3. Underwood talks about it when discussing the project with a giant tortilla that was thrown into the ocean by the artist and a group of students/activists. A few years after the project took place, she was not able to get to the same spot she threw the tortilla in, even though, technically, the place it is located is still American land, and she should be able to go in there (*Artist Talk: Consuelo Jiménez Underwood*).

4. As the artist explains, the flowers in *Undocumented Border X-ings* visit the American Beauty Rose (the official flower of the District of Columbia) in Washington, D.C. and try to influence the transformation of policies regarding migrants and immigrants: "The American Beauty is hosting her state flower cousins from the borderlands: California poppy, Arizona saguaro, New Mexico yucca, and the Texas bluebonnet. The visiting state flowers have come to Washington, DC, hoping the American Beauty can influence the policy makers that reside in her region" (www.consuelojunderwood.com).

5. The sign pertains particularly to her personal experience of smuggling her father back to the United States (since he did not obtain papers until she was 9 or 10). She also recollects this chilling thought that she had the first time she saw the sign: "[T]hey are treating us like animals," she thinks, since this type of sign is usually used to warn motorists about wild animals (*Threads*).

6. "In the realm of taste, to be rasquache is to be unfettered and unrestrained, to favor the elaborate over the simple, the flamboyant over the severe. Bright colors are preferred to sombre, high intensity to low, the shimmering and pattern filling all available space with bold display" (Ybarra Frausto in Calvo 219).

7. I also use Freire's concept to talk about Ana Teresa Fernández's work, *Borrando La Frontera* in "The U.S.-Mexico Border as a Palimpsest in Ana Teresa Fernández's Art."

WORKS CITED

Antoszek, Ewa. "The U.S.-Mexico Border as a Palimpsest in Ana Teresa Fernández's Art." *Polish Journal for American Studies*, vol. 12, Spring 2018, pp.197-210.

Anzaldúa, Gloria. *Borderlands/La Frontera*. 2nd edition. Aunt Lute Books, 1999.

Artist Talk: Consuelo Jiménez Underwood. The UCLA Chicano Studies Research Center, YouTube. Accessed 5 September 2018.

Calvo, Luz. "Art Comes for the Archbishop: The Semiotics of Contemporary Chicana Feminism and the Work of Alma Lopez," *Meridians: feminism, race, transnationalism*, vol. 5, no. 1, 2004, pp. 201-224.

Casey, Edward S. and Mary Watkins. *Up Against the Wall: Re-imagining the U.S.-Mexico Border.* University of Texas Press, 2014.

Castillo, Debra A. and María-Socorro Tabuenca Córdoba. *Border Women: Writing from La Frontera.* Minneapolis/London: University of Minnesota Press, 2002.

Consuelo Jiménez Underwood Speaks on Her Piece "Undocumented Flowers." www.consuelojunderwood.com. Accessed 5 September 2018.

Contreras, Sheila M. *Blood Lines: Myth, Indigenism, and Chicana/o Culture*. Austin: University of Texas Press, 2008.

Ganster, Paul. *The U.S.-Mexican Border Today: Conflict and Cooperation in Historical Perspective.* Rowman & Littlefield, 2016.

Jiménez Underwood, Consuelo. www.consuelojunderwood.com. Accessed 20 March, 2018.

Kaup, Monika. *Rewriting North American Borders in Chicano and Chicana Narrative.* Peter Lang, 2001.

Martínez, Oscar J. *Border People: Life and Society in the U.S.-Mexico Borderlands.* University of Arizona Press, 1994.

Pérez, Laura E. *Chicana Art: The Politics of Spiritual and Aesthetic Altarities*. Duke University Press, 2007.

Román Odio, Clara. "Colonial Legacies and the Politics of Weaving in Consuelo Jiménez Underwood's Fiber Art." *Textile Society of America's 13th Biennial Symposium*, 2012, http://works.bepress.com/clara_roman-odio/31/. Accessed 25 March 2018.

Threads. PBS, May 11, 2012. http://www.craftinamerica.org/episodes/threads/. Accessed 6 September 2018.

TESTIMONIOS OF HEALING, PERSISTENCE, AND FEMINIST PRAXIS

CHICANA/LATINA STUDIES: THE JOURNAL OF MUJERES ACTIVAS EN LETRAS Y CAMBIO SOCIAL

AN ANZALDÚAN APPROACH TO CHICANA FEMINISTA EDITORIAL PRAXIS

LILLIANA P. SALDAÑA & SONYA M. ALEMÁN

In 2018, *Chicana/Latina Studies: The Journal of Mujeres Activas en Letras y Cambio Social* (MALCS)—the only peer-reviewed, bilingual journal publishing groundbreaking interdisciplinary scholarship and creative works by and about Chicanas, Latinas, and Indigenous women—celebrated its 15th year of publication. A collective effort of the members of MALCS, *Chicana/Latina Studies* has cultivated a Chicana feminista editorial praxis grounded in the production of knowledge and the activism of its members. As noted by Davalos and Partnoy, *Chicana/Latina Studies* can be regarded as "the fruit of a feminist publishing practice that has its roots in the many years of MALCS meetings, e-mail discussions, and sharing of our experiences as Chicanas and Latinas in academia" (11).

It is the implementation of this Chicana feminista editorial praxis that we—the current editors of *Chicana/Latina Studies*—focus on here. As the most recent initiates of the journal's editorial management style, we benefit from the conocimientos and spiritual activism of the mujeres who preceded us—Gloria H. Cuádraz, Karen Mary Davalos, C. Alejandra Elenes, Tiffany Ana López, Josie Méndez-Negrete, Alicia Partnoy, Eliza Rodriguez y Gibson, and Adaljiza Sosa-Riddell—as well as the canonical work of Gloria Anzaldúa. Together, conversations with former editors, journal archives, and reports[1] have coalesced with Anzaldúan theories to provide a map of five core commitments that currently shape our Chicana feminista editorial praxis. These are a commitment to: 1) cultivating Chicana/Latina scholarship;

2) shifting the paradigm of academic writing; 3) collaboration and collectivity; 4) providing feminist editorial feedback; and 5) balancing feminist principles and professionalism. Drawing from our initial years as editors, we deconstruct the ways these principles manifest in the daily operation of the journal. In this essay, we treat each commitment separately, indicating how we draw from Anzaldúan onto-epistemology and ethics regarding the production of knowledge (*Light in the Dark*). We apply Anzaldúa's concepts/theories of nepantla, spiritual activism, conocimiento, and the Coyolxauhqui imperative to describe and make sense of our work, particularly by positioning ourselves as nepantla editors. We conclude by drawing parallels between our Chicana feminista editorial praxis to Anzaldúa's Coyolxauhqui theory of writing.

SEMBRANDO CHICANA/LATINA SCHOLARSHIP

Editors of *Chicana/Latina Studies* act as stewards for Chicana/Latina scholarship, an enterprise Anzaldúa launched as one of two Chicana students in her graduate program. Her work sought to change and heal "colonialism's wounds" (*Light in the Dark* 44) by using Chicana and Indigenous "mythical heritage and spiritual traditions" to "shift the understanding of what knowledge consists of how we come to know" (*Light in the Dark* 119). She shaped a field of study pivoted on the unmaking and remaking of feminized knowledge and mestiza spirituality, a journey she named conocimiento (*Light in the Dark* 19). As caretakers of this school of thought, we recognize every submission provides an opportunity to acquire additional understanding on the methodological and theoretical contributions of Chicana/Latina/Indigenous frameworks in theorizing and transforming the experiences of brown and native women. Importantly, the writing that constitutes the field of Chicana feminism mirrors Anzaldúa's Coyolxauhqui imperative, a type of writing that evokes "healing and transformation ... by using words, images, and theories that stimulate, create and in other ways facilitate radical physical-psychic change in ... the various worlds in which we exist and to which we aspire" (*Light in the Dark* xxiii). Thus, scholars who contribute to this area of study "... want to change the reader's sense of what the world is like" (*Light in the Dark* 96). Moreover, these knowledge producers make "a commitment to add to the field of literature and not just duplicate what's already there" (*Light in the Dark* 97). In pursuit of this revolutionary charge, we extend the work of former editors and envision new ways to foster this field of study in the following ways.

Four criteria designated by former editors provide benchmarks for the evaluation of new submissions, namely asking if the manuscript 1) makes a contribution to the field of Chicana/Latina studies; 2) contains cogent argumentation; 3) meets the criteria for high-quality writing; and 4) acknowledges literature relevant to the topic. For example, in determining how a submission might make a contribution to the field of Chicana/Latina studies, we consider whether a new concept, methodology, theoretical framework is outlined in the text; whether a fusion of two or more concepts, methodological approaches, theoretical frameworks is explicated or employed; or if a previously unexplored or under-researched area is being studied via a Chicana/Latina/Indigenous lens. We rate the impact of the contribution, using a range of "1"—a contribution whose value is not fully articulated—to "3"—extends previous work in interesting and important ways—to "5"—innovative, groundbreaking, pioneering work. While calibrating each manuscript may seem antithetical to feminist principles, we find it provides consistency and focus to our assessments, allowing us to pinpoint opportunities the author(s) can capitalize to strengthen the manuscript.

Expanding our pool of reviewers also allows us to bolster the field of Chicana/Latina studies. The journal's foremothers assembled scholars from a variety of disciplines to function in a collaborative, interactive, and interdisciplinary way to review manuscripts. The current online submission platform limits interactions between reviewers, but it allows us to steadily build up this group, enabling us to connect with identifiable scholars knowledgeable in Chicana/Latina/Indigenous studies. We do this by searching online to learn about scholars cited in submitted work, by reaching out to our own professional networks, and by requesting recommendations from our existing reviewers.

We also promote the field of Chicana/Latina studies by attending various feminist and Latina/o studies academic conferences to recruit contributors and provide information about the journal. Attending and tabling at the National Association of Chicana and Chicano Studies has been a standing practice of *Chicana/Latina Studies* for over a decade. More recently, editors also began attending other national conferences like the National Women's Studies Association and Latino Studies Association to increase the visibility of Chicana/Latina/Indigenous scholarship.

Some newer initiatives take advantage of social media platforms and digital technologies to raise awareness about the journal and tout its prestige as the only bilingual, peer-reviewed academic journal dedicated to Chicana/Latina scholarship. We established a Facebook page for the journal where we feature excerpts from the published content, interview segments with the authors, and detail the publication process of *Chicana/Latina Studies*. We created a social media presence on Instagram and Twitter, cultivating a new generation of Chicana/Latina/Indigenous feminist scholars in order to ensure the journal not only maintains a steady readership but grows it as well. In addition, these platforms allow us to distribute calls for submissions to cultivate a steady pipeline of manuscripts. As a result of this social media presence, we have coined the hashtag, #citeaMALCSista, to anchor an ongoing campaign that promotes the research published in the journal. By incorporating this phrase in our online posts and other marketing material, we build the brand and mission of the journal, while providing a feminist response to the trend towards metrics that quantify scholarly impact. The #citeaMALCSista message reminds *Chicana/Latina Studies* readers and MALCS members of the importance of leaving citational footprints by citing fellow Chicana/Latina/Indigenous feminist scholars.

We have also instituted a yearly letter-writing campaign to increase the number of institutional subscriptions. Using the MALCS membership database, we identify institutions of our members who do not subscribe to the journal. We distribute a template letter requesting an annual subscription and ask our targeted members to forward it to the responsible parties at their campuses. This project seeks to increase the presence and availability of Chicana/Latina feminist scholarship in academic spaces so students and scholars can be informed by, inspired by, and connected to this vital area of study. Lastly, we created a MALCS chapter at our current institution to form a community of Chicana/Latina/Indigenous woman-identified scholars who can build a relationship to both MALCS and the journal. By building this pipeline at our home campus, we embrace the type of grassroots and micro-level organizing that defined the Chicana feminist movement.

NEW CONOCIMIENTOS: CULTIVATING A PARADIGM SHIFT IN ACADEMIC WRITING AND PUBLISHING

With all but dissertation, Anzaldúa left the academy to produce new ways of thinking and writing, opening a path for Chicana feminist scholars to shift the paradigm of academic writing. An interdisciplinary scholar who was grounded in fields like philosophy, psychology, and anthropology, Anzaldúa tapped into non-Western, forbidden, and oftentimes illegitimate forms of knowledge like dreams, tarot card readings, curanderismo, fantasies, and yoga to produce concepts, theories, and methodologies for personal and transformative social change. Anzaldúa believed the academy produced "dependent scholars" (*Interviews/Entrevistas* 18)—scholars reliant on the institutional standards and expectations of their discipline to validate and publish them. Instead, she challenged institutionalized forms of writing and thinking by producing one of the most intellectually groundbreaking archives of this century—an extraordinary and expansive body of pensamiento crítico feminista y descolonial—that grounds this journal's Chicana feminista editorial praxis.

For Anzaldúa, part of what made academia so foreign, impersonal, and constraining was its dominant Western viewpoint that split the personal and the academic. Rather, she included "the spiritual and the intellectual, or the emotions and body" to inform knowledge-making (Keating 114). Anzaldúa's body of work serves as a cornerstone for corporeal-based, political, and spiritually-inflected scholarship. As an autohistoriadora, Anzaldúa encourages us to be vulnerable (to enter the wound) and to integrate our own biographies in our quest to generate new conocimientos in our scholarship, particularly around issues of sexuality, spirituality, ethnicity, racialization, identity, and consciousness. As such, many of the journal's contributors weave the personal with the collective/historical experience, bridging their testimonios and scholarly analyses with recurring political issues like U.S. colonialism, intergenerational trauma, racism, sexism, and other forms of oppression. Poised on the threshold between the academy and the communities we serve, *Chicana/Latina Studies* cultivates this paradigm shift in academic writing by supporting submissions that center personal testimonios—a practice that is largely discouraged in certain academic disciplines. As editors of a feminist women of color journal, we recognize that it takes tremendous courage to challenge academic norms and to create new theories and perspectives. As a space for counterhegemonic scholarship, the journal publishes the work of mujeres who access ways of knowing that are outside the conventions of their disciplines. These conocimientos bridge the academy with marginalized communities.

As editors, we recognize that our Chicana/Latina feminist scholar contributors write in nepantla—the "liminal state between worlds, between realities, between systems of knowledge" (*Interviews/Entrevistas* 268). Anzaldúa noted in her preface to *Light in the Dark/Luz en el oscuro*, her dilemma "and that of other Chicana and women-of-color writers, is twofold: how to write (produce) without being inscribed (re-produced) in the dominant white structure and how to write without reinscribing and reproducing what we rebel against" (7-8). Often, the Chicana/Latina feminist scholars who live on the threshold of multiple epistemic worlds center their lived experience in their scholarly work. Anzaldúa's construct of the Coyolxauhqui imperative articulates the complex emotional, psychical, corporeal, and spiritual process of re-visioning ourselves and the world via these artistic-intellectual creations. Since its inception, the journal has featured creative writing pieces, artwork, and scholarly manuscripts of Chicana, Latina, and Indigenous women who seek to transform and heal through their work to "blur and transcend customary frameworks and conceptual categories reinforced by language and consensual reality" (*Light in the Dark* 45). As chamanas, curanderas, visionaries, and nepantleras, these creative writers, artists, and activist scholars tap into their imagination to offer liminal perspectives and create "'other' epistemologies—those of the body, dreams, intuitions, and sense other than the five physical senses" that are often disregarded as legitimate sources of knowledge (44). These expressions jolt an awareness to "repair el daño" (*Light in the Dark* 10), as necessitated by a field of study born of activism.

Guided by the Anzaldúan spirit of rejecting imposed borders and bifurcating spaces, the journal "reject[s] the separation of academic scholarship and community involvement," and encourages mujeres to produce scholarship that "strives to bridge the gap between intellectual work and active commitment to our communities" (Declaración June, 1083, cited in Davalos). As such, we publish MALCSistas who write about their community's struggles for dignity and respect, from writing about Latina trans women, DREAMers and undocumented immigrants, to scholarly work that unearths the narratives of Chicana/Latina and Indigenous women buried in Eurocentric and Chicano nationalist histories.

NEPANTLERA PRAXIS: INTENTIONALLY COLLABORATIVE AND COLLECTIVE

In the spirit of Anzaldúa's feminista vision of interconnectedness, *Chicana/Latina Studies* cultivates collaborative writing and editing processes and feminist mentorship (femtorship), challenging the Euro-centric, male, capitalist assumption that competition and individualism yield scholarly excellence. We are cognizant that our Chicana feminista editorial praxis is increasingly rare in academia, as noted by Douglas Dowland and Annemarie Pérez in their article in the *Chronicle of Higher Education*. Indeed, Anzaldúa's framework of "writing comadres" (*Light in the Dark* 95) describes the journal's collaborative writing process; namely, through a writing workshop and a mentorship program.

As a feminista journal, we attempt to demystify the process of academic publishing through mentoring that enhances new conocimientos and nepantlera solidarities. Our vision is to support emerging and established scholars who are moving from assistant to associate or from associate to full professors through mentorship. This is particularly important since, as of 2010, only three percent of all assistant professors and 0.06 percent of all full professors are Latina (Machado-Casas, Ruiz, and Cantú 4). As Davalos noted, we believe "feminist editorial practices [would] increase the number of quality publications for and by Chicanas, Latinas, and Native women in academia, … and transform academia" (Davalos 2003, 5).

Over the past 15 years, the annual writing workshop has become the journal's primary method of manifesting this transformation. Modeled after the Tomas Rivera Center Dissertation Workshops at the University of California, Riverside, the writing workshop provides both peer and editor feedback for accepted applicants. Led by former editors, participants share a completed manuscript with all participants. The facilitator and participants review and provide feedback on all essays prior to the face-to-face workshop held during the annual MALCS Summer Institute. Participants include independent scholars, recently minted PhD's, and tenure-track assistant professors who gather for a pre-institute meeting and during the institute. Participants who apply, participate, and complete the workshop leave "with clear recommendations for meeting internal criteria of *Chicana/Latina Studies*, specific directions from the Editors, and first-hand knowledge about our feminist editorial process" (Davalos 2003, 7). As Davalos notes, while participation does not guarantee publication in the journal, "the information and experience will facilitate the submission and double-blind-review process" (7)—the latter of which goes above and beyond many journals' rigorous standards for publishing quality work.

At a recent writing workshop, a young scholar shared that her faculty advisor/mentor discouraged her from submitting to *Chicana/Latina Studies* because she believed it was not competitive, reputable, or high caliber. Unlike whitestream top journals that pride themselves in rejecting 90% of their submissions, *Chicana/Latina Studies* does not value rejection as a standard of excellence. On the contrary, we leverage alternate standards of excellence—ones that are based on interconnection, generosity, solidarity, and compassionate feedback. Rather than touting exclusionary statistics as a sign of quality, *Chicana/Latina Studies* extends solidarity with contributors—some who are dissertating, others who are newly hired junior faculty, and others who are senior scholars in their fields—as they move through the revision process.

The *Chicana/Latina Studies* mentoring program is a second way of enacting a nepantlera praxis that is collective and collaborative. It pairs an emergent scholar/ author who has submitted a manuscript that falls short of meeting all four previously discussed standards with a senior mentor who helps polish their work. The senior mentor is required to comment on their mentee's paper at least three times over the nine-month period, and in a timely manner. Ideally, the faculty mentor and mentee meet face-to-face at the MALCS Summer Institute where mentees can ask questions and mentors can offer more extensive editorial consejos. Reflecting Anzaldúan ethics of honesty, collaboration, and compassion, Davalos describes the mentoring component as one in which the labor of women of color scholars is valued within the exploitative and demanding structures inside and outside of the academy. A Chicana feminist editorial praxis is thus "based on the premise that we are all intelligent scholars—the faults in our writing are due to our workloads" (Davalos 2003, 6). We frame such collaboration and collectivity as nepantla solidarities—modes of supportive mentoring that represent what a feminist academic culture can look like outside of the male-dominated neo-liberal model that privileges competition, exclusivity, and individualism as standards of professionalism. Additionally, we model feminist editorial review practices for authors who may one day serve as reviewers.

Building on the legacy of past editors and las sabias de MALCS, another way we foster these collaborations is via the Editorial Board and National Advisory Board, the governing and institutional bridges that sustain this Chicana feminist editorial praxis. The Editorial Board, which reviews content, consists of a group of 15 to 20 senior, pre-tenure, and independent scholars who are active and current members of MALCS. In alignment with Chicana feminist epistemologies, rank is not used as a criterion for invitation to serve on the Editorial Board. The organization recognizes "that our best and brightest scholars may not be employed or holding tenure-track lines due to institutionalized racism, racism, and homophobia, or due to life stages associated with mothering, families, and race- and gender-specific expectations" (Davalos 2013, 10). We also work with the National Advisory Board, a group of 10 to 12 senior scholars that provides "the editorial team with advice, recommendations, and advocacy related to scholarly, creative productions, or academic matters of the journal" (*Chicana/Latina Studies* 2019). As sabias, members of the National Advisory Board recommend new areas for development, research and publications, funding, and identify potential contributors and Editorial Board members. The conocimientos of National Advisory Board members "help us make the crossings, and guide us through the transformation process" (*Light in the Dark* 17).

CON RAZÓN Y CORAZÓN EN LAS MANOS: QUALITIES OF FEMINISTA FEEDBACK

At the 2002 MALCS Coordinating Committee midyear meeting, Davalos emphasized that "the content alone does not make a journal feminist. Feminist editorial practices are inclusive, collaborative, honest, environmentally-friendly, economically and fiscally efficient and responsible, and supportive of authors and journal staff" ("Guiding Principles" 1). Anzaldúa's work highlights the importance of being in conocimiento with journal contributors—to engage in raw listening while reading scholars' carefully crafted words, provide constructive feedback, and offer words of encouragement throughout the revision process. This aspect of our Chicana feminist editorial praxis requires enormous amount of time and energy. It is not unusual for submissions to go through dozens of hours of editing, first by our reviewers and then by the editorial team consisting of the editors and undergraduate and graduate assistants to the journal. Because Chicana/Latina faculty are still largely underrepresented in the academy, editors and reviewers of *Chicana/Latina Studies* play a vital role in demystifying the academic publishing process. With the support of our feminista reviewers, we are able to model a professional generosity (Dowland and Pérez 2018) that is becoming rare in academic whitestream professional organizations that do not incentivize this kind of service. This kind of professional generosity is evidenced in the words of one reviewer who wrote: "I want this article to be published by *Chicana/Latina Studies* and therefore I hope the author strongly considers revising and resubmitting it ... I would be happy to review a subsequent version of this important essay." Such generosity is rare in the academy as most reviewers assess a manuscript once. Another reviewer stated: "I also want to underscore that this essay is extremely promising and my comments are sincerely aimed at encouraging the writer to resubmit as soon as possible—which, as I explain below, will be a very manageable task." This reviewer provided meticulous feedback, from minor edits to more extensive conceptual and organizational recommendations.

Chicana/Latina Studies reviewers bring a unique sensibility to the review process. As experts in their fields, they bring knowledge of foundational theories, research methodologies, and emergent epistemologies; as women of color scholars, they bring embodied knowledge of the structural and systemic barriers first-generation Chicana/Latina scholars experience in publishing their scholarship. Like reviewers for other journals, reviewers for *Chicana/Latina Studies* are tasked with the responsibility of assessing manuscripts for publication based on the quality of writing, conceptual framework, research design, organization, analytical strength, and fit. However, they also extend professional generosity by attaching extensive notes with their rubric, outlining in great detail consejos y palabras alentadoras—recommendations and words of encouragement—that provide direction and support to contributors who will then return to the artistic-intellectual process of componiendo y descomponiendo (Anzaldúa 2015) until they finalize their manuscript.

Chicana/Latina Studies reviewers play an anonymous but very active role in the journal, serving as bridges between the contributors and the editors and ensuring that work gets through the pipeline and into production and, finally, in print. Because of the varied ways they are intermediaries in the knowledge production process, we see them as nepantlera reviewers who help in the passage of ideas, writings, and publication. One of our goals as current editors of *Chicana/Latina Studies* is to continue to cultivate additional nepantlera reviewers with this feminist sensibility. To do so, we have created a set of guidelines, a conocimiento of what it means to enact a Chicana feminista editorial praxis. In particular, we want our reviewers to recall Anzaldúa's consejo of being receptive rather than adversarial when reviewing manuscripts.

For new reviewers, these guidelines "provide suggestions for constructive criticism, phrasing of feedback, and supportive language while upholding a higher caliber of standards" (*Chicana/Latina Studies* 3). Central to this Chicana feminist editorial praxis is "a feminist language in all communications with potential authors" that "[allows] for alignment between theory and praxis" (*Chicana/Latina Studies* 3). The journal thus practices an Anzaldúan ethics of solidarity that supports the intellectual and professional development of Chicana/Latina feminist scholars.

As editors, we are also attentive to the writer's mindset. Writing-in-process is a liminal stage, much like nepantla—a Nahuatl word that means "el lugar entre medio" or the space in-between. Nepantla can help articulate the space between ideas in process and the space of final publication. We envision the revision and resubmission process as a place of inner struggle to commit ideas, visualizations, and feelings onto paper in ways that communicate and build bridges with others. Indeed, some of our reviewers' feedback necessitates re(opening) a wound, returning to primary resources, or reading new material in the hope that it will open up new conocimientos and perspectives. This type of writing can create ansiedad, but because writing is a necessity in the academy, we seek to nurture it is as a form of healing (Anzaldúa 2015).

Moreover, as Anzaldúan-inspired editors, we bring our entire bodyspiritminds to the creative and intellectual processes of our Chicana feminista editorial praxis. We work with contributors before, during, and after the review process, assisting contributors as they engage the iterative process of "rearranging individual words, entire sentences, and paragraphs; adding or deleting large chunks of material; copying and repeating especially significant phrases; and inserting material from other works in progress" (*Light in the Dark* xii). Drawing from Anzaldúa, we recognize that writing entails "your creative process and touching on your writing habits, rituals, and emotional upheavals, your beliefs about writing, your relationship to it, and the support you get from your writing comadres, the 'godmothers' who read and encourage your work" (*Light in the Dark* 95). Our work, then, positions us as writing comadres of sorts who nurture the production of knowledge in its many manifestations, through its various iterations of creation, evolution and presentation.

As a writer/theorist who invites us to be vulnerable to other people's trauma and perspectives, Anzaldúa invites us to be open to creating new forms of connection among our MALCSistas. Estar en conocimiento means to place oneself in a state of resonance with others, which requires empathy, generosity, and the act of listening con el corazón y la razón en la mano. In an academic culture where Chicana/Latina faculty are still largely underrepresented, MALCSistas play a vital role in demystifying the academic publishing process. Some submissions read as working drafts that require dedicated one-on-one support from reviewers and editors; others read as more polished pieces. Anzaldúa also invites us to be intentional about receptivity rather than engaging in an adversarial approach to reviewing and editing pieces. As a community of Chicana/Latina feminist activist scholars who merge social justice ethics in our personal and professional lives, we are almas afines or "kindred spirits" doing this "work that matters." Anzaldúa invites us to share an interconnectedness that is grounded in an "ethics of reciprocity" (Keating 10) that is visible in the journal's Chicana feminista editorial praxis.

BALANCE CHICANA FEMINISM AND PROFESSIONALISM

We often sit at a crossroads between Chicana feminista editorial praxis and the norms of professionalism. In "Putting Coyolxauqui Together," Anzaldúa noted that she herself struggled with these competing demands, writing that she would often construct a writing plan that allowed her to freewrite, revise, and reflect in order to meet her deadlines. Inevitably, life would disrupt her carefully laid stages and she would have to create another schedule. Our Chicana feminista editorial praxis operates with the same intentionality. As nepantleras, we balance the obligations of the journal with the needs of our contributors. Specifically, these competing needs surface in the interactions with fellow editors and student staff, the imposition of deadlines, and the timeliness of communication with all stakeholders affiliated with the journal.

Currently, the *Chicana/Latina Studies* editorial team consists of two editors at the same institution who oversee the academic content and administrative responsibilities of the journal, as well as a creative writing editor and a book review editor, each of whom is from a different institution. The first year of publishing *Chicana/Latina Studies*, the four of us tended to our respective sections, with communication limited to email. However, after the steep learning curve of the first year, we realized that while our interactions led to the successful publication of two issues, they did not embody feminist practices. We now use a virtual conferencing service to meet monthly, allowing us to stay current on production issues and build relationships with each other. We invest a few minutes asking about each other's well-being, sharing about our families, our professional lives, and recreational activities. Although not tied to the production of the journal, these exchanges have allowed us to envision opportunities for growth, such as overarching section themes for upcoming issues; journal policies regarding the use of racial or ethnic terms; and a review process for creative writing. By building rapport, we have coalesced our expertise and imagination.

Similar tensions arise when taking time to build relationships with each other and our student staff. Fortunately, support from our home institution includes an undergraduate work-study and a graduate student research assistant. Much of our communication happens primarily over email, which makes relationship building harder. In addition, our weekly meetings are labor-intensive, without pausing to account for each other's body/mind/spirit. We thus struggle to balance working efficiently within recognizing our whole humanity. Some weeks, we are better at striking this balance, and when we are not, we remind ourselves of this commitment and its importance to a Chicana feminista editorial praxis.

Another instance of this conflict is in implementing and enforcing deadlines. For example, when a reviewer misses a deadline for submitting a review, our online submission system generates an email reminder. As feminista editors, we are mindful of all the work our Chicana/Latina/Indigenous scholar-activist reviewers are juggling, while advising them to provide expedient feedback to move contributors' manuscripts towards publication. There is no universal way we address these situations, but we use personal communication to navigate them.

The speed with which we convey feedback or decisions to contributors intersects conventional edicts of professionalism and values of feminist practices. For a typical academic journal, it can take a year and a half to two years before a submitted manuscript is in print. *Chicana/Latina Studies* attempts to shorten that process so emerging scholars can establish their publication record. With such a dismal number of Chicana/Latina/Indigenous scholars in academia, playing a role in securing these mujeres a job offer, tenure, or promotion is an aspiration grounded in the commitments of the journal's Chicana feminista editorial praxis. While traditional norms of professionalism also encourage prompt attention and action, the commitments of a Chicana feminista editorial praxis necessitate feedback that is judicious, thorough, and uplifting—a time-consuming process. Balancing a quick turnaround time while offering mentorship is a demanding pressure point of a Chicana feminista editorial praxis.

CONCLUSION: CHICANA FEMINISTA EDITORIAL PRAXIS AS COYOLXAUHQUI IMPERATIVE

For the past 15 years, *Chicana/Latina Studies* has cultivated a Chicana feminista editorial praxis that challenges Eurocentric, patriarchal, and capitalist practices in the publication of new conocimientos in the academic borderlands. Anzaldúa understood the transformational power of the written word and the role of the imagination in creating—writing that world into reality (*Light in the Dark* xiv). As nepantlera editors building on the work of past editors and MALCSistas, we are present to the importance of implementing the journal's Chicana feminista editorial praxis in order to foster Chicana/Latina feminist scholarship, creative writing, and visual artwork. We also value our nepantlera reviewers, and accept the multiple states of nepantla the writing, reviewing, and publishing process demands.

To guide us in these in-between spaces, we ground our praxis in five core commitments that reflect Anzaldúa's onto-epistemology and ethics: 1) cultivating Chicana/Latina scholarship; 2) shifting the paradigm of academic writing; 3) collaboration and collectivity; 4) providing feminist feedback; and 5) balancing feminist principles and professionalism. These principles frame our Chicana feminista editorial praxis—one that parallels Anzaldúa's Coyolxauhqui theory of writing as an "epistemological, intuitive, and communal" (Keating xii) process.

In short, "our journal is a gathering of wild tongues," (Davalos and Partnoy 16) necessitating a Chicana feminista editorial praxis that honors a commitment to interconnectivity and embraces "contradictions and ambiguity as sites of possibilities and creativity" (Davalos and Partnoy 7). Because of our positions in the academy, we are aware that we can be "complicit in the existing power structures, that we must deal with conflictive as well as connectionist relations within and among various groups" (83). To guarantee that our acts as nepantlera editors do "not mirror or replicate the oppression and dominant power structures we seek to dismantle" (*Light in the Dark* 83), we employ a Chicana feminista editorial praxis in communal and anti-patriarchal processes that decolonize the academy.

NOTES

1. See Davalos 2003; Davalos 2009; Davalos and Partnoy 2004; Elenes and Cuádraz 2017; Lopez and Davalos 2009; Maiz-Peña 2009; Méndez-Negrete 2009; Partnoy 2006.

WORKS CITED

Anzaldúa, Gloria E. *Interviews/Entrevistas*. Edited by AnaLouise Keating, Routledge, 2000.

---. *Light in the Dark/Luz en lo oscuro: Rewriting Identity, Spirituality, Reality.* Edited by AnaLouise Keating, Duke UP, 2015.

Chicana/Latina Studies: The Journal of MALCS (Mujeres Activas en Letras y Cambio Social). "Proposed By-laws." 2019.

Davalos, Karen Mary. "Journal Report, 2003-2009." *Chicana/Latina Studies*, Fall 2009, vol. 9 no. 1, pp. 14-22.

Davalos, Mary K. Guiding Principles, Procedures and Policies of *Chicana/Latina Studies: The Journal of MALCS*. 2003.

Davalos, Karen Mary and Alicia Partnoy. "Editors' Commentary: Translating the Backslash," *Chicana/ Latina Studies*, vol. 4, no. 1, Fall 2004, pp. 6-18.

Dowland, Douglas and Annemarie Pérez. "How to be a Generous Professor in Precarious Times." *Chronicle of Higher Education*, 23 Sept. 2018. https://www.chronicle.com/article/How-to-Be-a-Generous-Professor/244581.

Elenes, C. Alejandra and Gloria H. Cuádraz."Speaking to the Times. Chicana/Latina Studies." *Chicana/ Latina Studies*, Spring 2017, vol. 9 no. 1, pp. 22-40.

Keating, AnaLouise. "Risking the Personal: An Introduction." *Gloria E. Anzaldúa: Interviews/Entrevistas*. Edited by AnaLouise Keating, New York, Routledge, 2000, pp. 1-16.

---. "Re-envisioning Coyolxauhqui, decolonizing reality: Anzaldúa's twenty-first century imperative." *Light in the Dark/Luz en el oscuro: Rewriting identity, spirituality, reality*. Edited by AnaLouise Keating, New York, Duke University Press.

López, Tiffany Ana and Karen Mary Davalos. "Knowing, Feeling, Doing: The Epistemology of *Chicana/ Latina Studies*." *Chicana/Latina Studies*, Spring 2009, vol. 8 no. 1, pp. 10-22.

Machado-Casas, Margarita, Elsa Cantú Ruiz, and Norma E. Cantú. "Laberintos y testimonios: Latina Faculty in the Academy." *Educational Foundations*, Winter-Spring, 2013, pp. 3-14.

Maiz-Peña, Magdalena. "Nopalito Words and MALCS Feminist Editorial Practice." *Chicana/Latina Studies*, Spring 2009, vol. 8 no. 1, pp. 24-26.

Méndez-Negrete, Josie. "Dreaming and Scaffolding." *Chicana/Latina Studies*, Fall 2009, vol. 9 no. 1, pp. 32-34.

National Center for Education Statistics. "The Condition of Education." May 2018. https://nces.ed.gov/programs/coe/commissioner.asp.

Partnoy, Alicia. "Prefacio y Despedida." *Chicana/Latina Studies*, Fall 2006, vol. 6 no. 1, pp. 10-12.

Pérez, Annemarie. "Practice and Praxis: Chicana Feminism and the History of the *Chicana/Latina Studies* Journal." *Diálogo*, vol. 20, no.2, Fall 2017, pp. 55-66.

Pérez, Emma. *The Decolonial Imaginary: Writing Chicanas into History*. Indiana UP, 1999.

TESTIMONIAL OF HEALING

WRITING FOR TRANSFORMATIVE CHANGE THROUGH SELF-EXPRESSION AND SELF-REFLECTION

VICTORRIA SIMPSON-GERVIN

I define healing as taking back the scattered energy and soul loss wrought by woundings. Healing means using the life force and strength that comes with el ánimo to act positively on one's own behalf and on others. Often a wound provokes an urgent yearning for wholeness and provides the ground to achieve it. In shadow work, the problem is part of the cure—you don't heal the wound, the wound heals you (Anzaldúa, *Light in the Dark* 89).

Gloria Anzaldúa's *autohistoria-teoría* has given voice to women of color by acknowledging the importance of self-expression, which allows others to seek transformative change through writing as they highlight their experiences of trauma, oppression, and resistance in their everyday lives. This form of self-expression, self-writing, allows you to interrogate your feelings as a means of understanding the self. *Autohistoria-teoría* allows us not only to demonstrate self-knowledge, but also to put this knowledge to practice. Through demonstration and practice, I employ Anzaldúa's concept of *autohistoria-teoría* as I attempt to process the trauma of loss and caring for two siblings who succumbed to cancer at an early age. My journaling and writing became approaches to healing. Storytelling provided me with a form of narrative medicine, which opened up a multitude of possibilities for promoting my own health and healing. In *Light in the Dark*, AnaLouise Keating refers to this Anzaldúan medicine and state of awareness as "Coyolxauhqui consciousness," defined as "both the process of emotional psychical dismemberment, splitting body/mind/spirit/soul, and the creative work of putting all the pieces together in a new form" (Introduction). It is through this fragmented pain and self-expression that we find transformative healing.

Below is a testimonial of an eleven-year-old girl who creates her own story about healing, a story she can revisit and retell as often as need be. A story of hope that includes light in the darkness. Certain the journey through the Coyolxauhqui would claim her life, she seeks ways of overcoming the silence through journaling her emotions, which she considered too visceral to speak. She attempted to convey the pain through the act of writing, in hopes of finding healing and meaning for her brokenness. In desperation to move forward out of this liminal space, she was confronted with several questions. If this series of events were not meant to kill her, which she was certain it would, then what was it she would learn from all of the pain and brokenness? How would she begin to deconstruct/construct her new identity, the transformation of the self? And how would she move past it all, to see light in the darkness?

Her story begins in the year 1970. The young girl remembers being told by her older sister why her mother was sobbing uncontrollably, and why the priest was in their home. Her mother had just received the news of her 54-year-old husband's passing. He died of a brain aneurysm while at work. The young girl remembers questioning her older sister as to how her father could have died on the hospital floor where he worked for twenty-five years not ever being sick or missing a day of work. He went to work one day and collapsed and died instantaneously. The little girl was not sure how to process all of the events. What would they do now without her dad around? How would her mother survive? How would they survive without their father's love and support? The young girl missed her father terribly; they were extremely close. Her mother kept her father's memories alive by telling her stories of him and how much he loved each and every one of them.

Five years after the passing of her father, this same girl stared death in the face again with the passing of her mother. Her mother passed away two weeks before her sixteenth birthday. Instead of planning a Sweet Sixteen party, she was instead helping her older siblings plan the funeral arrangements for her 54-year-old mother. Yes, her parents died five years apart and both at age 54. The young girl decided to keep a journal to keep track of what she was feeling and to try to make sense of the tragedy of her mother's death. She did not know it at the time, but she would journal the loss of three of her siblings before she understood the relevance of the journal. As a further component of this girl's history of loss, she was a triplet, though one triplet did not survive in birth. In 1993, she was informed that her twin brother had stage 3 metastatic lung cancer; this struck her to the core. Like many people diagnosed with a chronic or life-ending illness, she was struck with disbelief, denial, and anger. However, for her, these emotions did not come in stages, she experienced all of these emotions simultaneously. She didn't stop to think how her brother was processing the news, because she could feel his hurt and his pain as well. They were very much in tune with each other's emotions. They had not only been connected in the womb; that connection remained throughout the remainder of their lives. They were so close, so much so, they would finish each other's sentences. At one point, her twin brother lived on the West Coast, and she on the East Coast, yet they still could sense if one was ill or in need of the other.

The sister came home to help care for her twin brother, a task she thought would certainly send her over the edge. She was wracked with grief, yet she still continued to write in her journal. She and her twin brother would sit for hours as she listened to him talk about his life, past and present. As they talked, she began to see things through his eyes. She had the ability to see what he could see. Perhaps it was due to their being twins; she was not really sure. As the brother's health quickly deteriorated, their talks decreased. However, the sister still had her journal to revisit and cherish those memorable moments. Two years after her twin brother's diagnosis, he passed away. The year was 1995. Oh, how she missed him and their talks. How she missed seeing things through the lens of her beloved brother.

In 2008, death came to knock on the family's door again; her older sister was stricken this time. In this case, there was no time for preparation—not that this woman could ever prepare herself for the death of another loved one. Her older sister was more like a mother to her. They were eleven years apart, but it was not the age difference that made her sister a mother figure; the older sister had taken the twins in after the loss of both parents. Figuratively speaking, the older sister was a second mother to the twins. The pain of losing a mother for the second time was almost unbearable for the young woman. She wondered how many more of her family members must succumb to death. The answer to her question came swiftly. In three months, one of her older brothers was also diagnosed with metastatic prostate cancer.

The young woman remembers the day as if it were yesterday, as she sat in the doctor's office with her brother awaiting the test results, only to be told the diagnosis was cancer. She thought this couldn't be so. To both her brother and herself, the moment seemed so surreal. While sitting in the doctor's office, she promised her brother that she would be there with him every step of the way. She made good on her promise, as she became his primary caregiver—all while she was working and going to school. She attended all of his treatments and medical appointments. Her brother gave her medical power of attorney in order to make medical decisions for him should he become incapacitated.

The brother suffered a long and painful death, with many hospital stays and near-death experiences. She remembered how it felt to be sitting in class, waiting for her phone to ring with a nurse on the other end telling her she needed to rush to the hospital right away. She confesses this was the most difficult time of her life. There were many occasions when she just wanted to throw her hands up in the air and give up, but she could not; she remembered the promise she made to her older brother, vowing to be there for him every step of the way. The only thing that kept her sane was journaling her thoughts and conversations with her brother.

After fighting the battle against cancer for five years, the brother was no longer able to breathe on his own; at this point, he was placed on a ventilator. After struggling with the decision to do what was best for her brother, she decided to let him die with dignity. She decided to have the ventilator disconnected. It was what he wanted, which is why he trusted her to make the right decision on his behalf. This was the hardest decision she has ever had to make.

THE REDEEMING POWER OF NARRATIVE LANGUAGE

As someone seeking to transform her silence into language, and as a caregiver of two brothers whose lives were cut short due to cancer, she was fully aware of the power of narrative medicine. She used her journal to channel all of her emotions and fond memories of her loved ones, and she visits it often. She even sometimes re-visits the not-so-fond memories in her journal, the entries that are filled with pain and sorrow. Her journal helps her to compartmentalize the stories, so she can take as much as she needs, or as little as she needs, depending on the circumstances. Her journal also provides her with a space to navigate through the stories in whatever manner best serves her, and perhaps others with whom she has shared her story. Her hope is that by sharing her story, others may be able to create their own stories in order to make sense of a traumatic experience with which they too may have been unexpectedly confronted.

Now, in 2019, although she felt the chain of events in her life would be her demise, she was indeed made stronger. I am the eleven-year-old girl, now grown up into a 61-year-old woman. I am that girl; this is my story. I understand the power of narrative medicine and storytelling, and how it can be used as a source of healing and coping with traumatic experiences; I am a living testament to Gloria Anzaldúa's *autohistoria-teoría*. It is from that place of self-knowledge through reconstructing the traumas that I was able to make sense and bring meaning to my suffering. From multiple knowledges of knowing, I am able write about transformation and healing. My personal narrative focuses on the benefits of allowing caregivers to express their fears and concerns through the use of storytelling as a way to come to terms with their loved ones' illnesses. My hope is that by sharing my personal testimonial of healing, others may find ways to navigate through trauma, oppression, and resistance through the use of storytelling.

WORK CITED

Anzaldúa, Gloria. *Light in the Dark/Luz en lo Oscuro: Rewriting Identity, Spirituality, Reality.* Edited by AnaLouise Keating, Duke University Press, 2015.

ROMPECABEZAS

PIECING TOGETHER MY BORDERLAND ROOTS

SAMANTHA CEBALLOS

I FORGOT

I forgot mental illness does not exist in my family
I forgot that my grandmothers were not anxious
I forgot my mother was not depressed
I forgot my uncle was not bipolar
I forgot my cousin didn't commit suicide
I forgot that I was not anxious, depressed, or suicidal
I guess it just slipped my mind

LALA

I saw her when I was little.
She stood there calling for my abuela.
Her dark hair filled me with comfort.
She kept calling for her. She stood behind the fence, but never crossed.
I looked at her from the old porch of the ratty white house with green trim.
The distance between us was great, but I knew it was her.
I knew who she was.
"Lala, Abuelita. Lala!"
I called to her with a smile. Abuelita looked upset as she walked out onto the porch,
Cigarette in hand.
When I turned back to look for Lala,
She was gone.
"Lala, Abuelita she was your best friend. Era Lala!"
Abuelita shook her head
I couldn't go outside the rest of the afternoon.

It took years for me to find out
Lala had died before I was even born.
I found her picture in a pile my abuela had.
It was my dad who told me.
I never mentioned Lala to anyone,
But when I saw the photo of her with my abuela
The black hair was the same
And I found comfort in it.

"You Bring Out the Writer in Me" pays homage to Cisneros's "You Bring Out the Mexican in Me." I wrote this poem as a way to claim my title as a writer. It talks about my inspirations for writing and shows the contradictions I enact/embrace as a writer.

YOU BRING OUT THE WRITER IN ME

—After Sandra Cisneros's "You Bring Out the Mexican In Me"

You bring out the writer in me.
The silent, patient dark mind.
The reason behind my beating heart.
The darkest ink
The whiskey-induced days
Through next month.
You are the one I lift my pen for
Scratch, scratch, scratching my emotions.
Alleviating everything bottled in,
Even the most violent of thoughts
Yes. Yes

Because of you.

You bring out the Sylvia Plath in me
The dark Mexican-American in me
The non-apologetic, dance with el diablo spirit in me
The paper cuts on me
The pens running out of ink in me
The iambic pentameter of creativity in me.
The beatnik love of chaos in me.
The fierce words not said with the tongue in me.
The rebel in me, bien rebelde, in me
The Lewis Carroll curiosities in me
The post-Edgar Allan Poe death and dying in me
The killing trees, and losing steam in me.
The fear of censorship in me.

Yes, you. Always, you.
You force out the editor in me
The grammar checking desire in me
The unknown beginning of Chicanx literature in me.
The malinche in me
The never-ending wave of depression in me.
The Emily Dickinson romanticism in me.

The hot coffee and conchas on a rainy day in me.
The hiding my writing from everyone in me.

Sweet girl. My other self
I am the thought haunting you
Tugging at your brain as the ink flows free.
I hold you prisoner
Until you reach manuscript destiny.
I want to split and spoil you.
I want to destroy you and make you new.
I want to yank every emotion—
Light and dark—and push them on paper.

You bring out the Gloria Anzaldúa in me.
The write-for-what-I-believe-in me.
The notebook at the ready in me.
The palm trees drive down 77 in me.
The Hurricane Harvey anxiety in me.
The writer's block in me.
The guiltfree poetess in me.
I have killed characters relentlessly
And found it worth it. Quick—painless or humble— deaths.
Even if they aren't always needed.

Oh, how evil. I am a guiltless goddess
The teller of tales
The truth of myself on the page.
The satisfying scribbles. You bring out
The creative soul in me.
The obsessive, loud typing in me.
The realistic, made-up sin in me
The original intent in me.

Tinta negra, red ink, navy blue.
Lavender. Chamomile. Amber. Eucalyptus.
All the scents, focused and relaxed.
Sandra Cisneros, Oscar Cásares
I call on you

Todo lo que soy, enseñas tú. Only you.
You broke my silence, their silence, our silence.
I write the way I know how to write. Let me
Show you. Write the way only I know how.

THE CALMÉCAC COLLECTIVE, OR, CONOCIMIENTO AND THE PATH OF REVOLUTIONARY SCHOLARSHIP

THE CALMÉCAC COLLECTIVE

Catalina Bartlett, Casie C. Cobos, Amanda E. Cuellar, Qwo-Li Driskill, Andrés C. López, Gabriela Raquel Ríos, Stephanie K. Wheeler

STEPHANIE: "El arrebato, the first stage: Rupture, fragmentation, woundings, and endings.
A beginning" ("now let us shift" 540).

QWO-LI: [Singing in Cherokee]
Naiqwo sunale nigalsda
Naiqwo sunale nigalsda
Ayvno, ayvno Yihowa
Gvyalihelitse Yihowa
Gvyalihelitse Yihowa

STEPHANIE: It's the day of my wedding, and I'm watching a tiny dress with watermelons float past the wedding cake, little giggles overpowering the rushing sound in my ears, and I can't help but smile.

ANDRÉS: I'm sitting at my kitchen table reading "The Calmécac Collective, or, How to Survive the Academic Industrial Complex through Radical Indigenous Practices" from *El Mundo Zurdo 3*, and I start to cry (Bartlett et al.).

STEPHANIE: This is where my rupture begins, I think.

ANDRÉS: I cry for what feels like hours.

STEPHANIE: Where all my biggest accomplishments, hopes, fears, and dread meet.

ANDRÉS: I cry for microaggressions that feel as if they were done to my own mind and body.

STEPHANIE: Right here, with little feet standing in teal shoes, the white birds on them looking outwards, away from the here and now, directing me with their gazes to the path of conocimiento.

ANDRÉS: I cry because I haven't cried about this enough.

STEPHANIE: This is where the echoes of seven years' worth of graduate school expectations swell to nothing, and where a pair of tiny, chocolate-covered hands reach up to give me one last abrazo.

ANDRÉS: I cry because even though I don't know most of my older intellectual siblings in the Calmécac Collective, I know the pain of the words that they share.

STEPHANIE: When we talk about the Calmécac Collective, we talk about the stories. I've said before that we're all just a story away from each other.

QWO-LI: The Calmécac Collective, a group of Indigenous and allied scholars, coalesced within a context of surviving and resisting an often hostile academic system through intentional use of what Daniel Heath Justice calls "critical kinship" (Bartlett et al. 300). Since the Calmécac Collective's original formation, members have followed new paths in academic and political trajectories.

GABI: As we attempt to understand how racism materializes in people's everyday lives, I think we struggle with how to address them. We have used terms like "microaggressions" to consider how seemingly innocuous practices reify and recapitulate racism. I want instead to consider how indigenous theories of stories can offer a more salient approach to understand and theorize my own experiences with race and racism as a Chicana in the academy.

QWO-LI: The name of our collective—from the Nahua educational institutions that existed both before and after Spanish invasion of central Mexico—remembers that settler universities are not the first formal systems of education in the hemisphere, that we come from memories and stories that are deeper and older than what Walter Mignolo, drawing on Anzaldúa, calls the "colonial wound" (74).

ANDRÉS: What happens to those of us who don't fit into the machine?

CASIE: My daughter was the undoing of me.

AMANDA: My maternal great-grandparents immigrated to El Paso, Texas from Chihuahua, Chihuahua, at the turn of the 20th century and planted their roots in south El Paso.

ANDRÉS: We survived because of the many kin who imagined us into the future centuries ago.

CASIE: My daughter was the breaking open of me.

AMANDA: They purchased a piece of land five miles north of the Rio Bravo and built their home there. Since then, four generations of la familia Cordova have lived on that land.

CASIE: My daughter was the teaching and being taught of me. My daughter is the difficult putting theory and words and research into practice away from the university and home places and big family and "familia from scratch" (Moraga 35).

AMANDA: I lived there for 30 years before deciding to leave the home, family, and community I dearly love and to pursue a PhD at the University of Oklahoma.

CASIE: My daughter is the continual questions of how to take what I have learned from this Collective-—from the theories and words and familia from scratch—and put that into practice. Or she is the not-knowing-how-to-at-all. My daughter is the current moment of my being outside and the feeling of confusion as I teach her things that used to seem so much easier among this Collective but were always so easily part of the family we don't currently live among.

CATALINA: My first year in Michigan, I watched 30 television series in their entirety.

CASIE: Just this week, my almost-five-year-old daughter asked for Cherokee words. I can teach her "hello" and "thank you." I can teach her "I love you" and "baby." I can teach her "water" and "dogwood." Siyo. Wado. Gvgeyu. Usdi. Ama. Kanvsita. Just the few words falling through my cupped hands reaching for the water of the forest mountains.

CATALINA: This tally doesn't include the fifteen I started but didn't finish and the thirty-plus films I watched on Netflix or Amazon Prime.

CASIE: My daughter tells strangers, "Hola. I can speak Spanish." And she lets just some of the words go from her mouth, words that she learns in school from her teacher, at home from me, at home from my mother. Morado. Amarillo. Rosa. Cuchillo. Haz tú trabajo. Rattling words and phrases off to strangers like a desert snake.

CATALINA: My first year in Michigan, I couldn't write. I don't mean emails, syllabi, assignment prompts, responses to student writing, and other writing that pertains to teaching. I'm referring to the novel that had been my dissertation, a coming-of-age story about a young mixed-race woman who becomes an activist in the midst of the 1979 uranium tailings spill near Gallup, New Mexico.

GABI: Maybe I am crazy. But, there are experiences I've had that cannot be explained rationally. They conflict with others' experiences. They contradict themselves, even. And, yet they are experiences shared by many women of color who do not neatly fall into categories defined in conjunction with whiteness. Categories like "normal," "non-threatening," "professional," "competent." By that I mean to say that in many cases, what gets defined as "normal," "non-threatening," "professional," and "competent" is also racialized differently across bodies and experiences.

STEPHANIE: This isn't what it was supposed to be like.

AMANDA: As a lifelong El Pasoan, I savored everything El Paso and Juárez had to offer. I enjoyed living in a community of immigrants, but I also witnessed their pain in adjusting to a new life in the United States as I learned about the lives they left behind in Mexico. Living in la vecindad that my great-grandparents built helped me learn about the importance of community. My perspective in high school expanded a bit more. Not only did I continue forming relationships with people who had immigrated to the United States from Mexico, but I befriended a few people who lived in Cd. Juárez. These friends introduced me to everything Juárez has to offer—los mercados, el fútbol (no el fútbol americano), los mejores puestos de tacos y tortas, y las fiestas. So when the time came to decide on where to I would go to college, I made the choice that many El Pasoans and Juarenses make; I decided to stay home and attend UTEP (the University of Texas at El Paso).

GABI: Maybe I'm crazy. But I do not know how to navigate the tension between racialized and gendered experiences in ways that actually account for stories my students sometimes bring me. Stories where they are coming to consciousness about race and gender and where that growing consciousness has made them hyper-sensitive to "microaggressions"—or, to the stories that are constantly making and unmaking them. I see their emotional responses and recognize some of them, but also know deep down that they are not allowed to have them. That when they have these human responses to growing consciousness of oppression they will be labeled: "Crazy." "Difficult." "Dramatic." "*Exajeradas.*" Or worse— "liars." Or worse still— "misguided."

AMANDA: I was not ready to leave the two cities I had grown to love.

GABI: The "aggressors?" They will be coddled, most likely. Their humanity will be reiterated over and over again. The problem is that some of us are "allowed" to have genuine emotional experiences and be seen as victims, or at the very least be seen as human and given the space they need to have and deal with these intense emotions. But, these students of color will not. Having and working through these feelings—feelings connected to textbook microaggressions, mind you—will lead them to be judged. Harshly.

CATALINA: During fall semester 2016, beginning in September, I was going to finish the novel, get a contract, get published. I thought I could do it even though I had a new home, a new job, a new department, a new institution, a new curriculum, a new post-graduate-student life. Such is the delusion of academia and the workaholism that defines my life. I called Qwo-Li Driskill, my dissertation co-chair, in the middle of October and said that I needed a break, that I was emotionally exhausted, that I didn't think I could go back on the market that fall. The trauma of the PhD program had finally caught up to me. Ironically, I needed permission to let myself rest after eight years in school, even though three had been in a nourishing MFA program. Qwo-Li granted what I could not give myself. Thankfully.

GABI: The problem, I have learned, is that despite myself, I have tried to appease the contradictory *perceptions* of others. Perceptions that do not allow women of color to exist outside of binaries or stereotypes. There are multiple times I can recount when my body was perceived to be not necessarily *inferior* to a white woman's but more *demonic* and more *pathologized.* What's needed, as Anzaldúa has said, is a "new description of what's perceived—in other words [the creation of] a new reality" (*Luz* 43).

ANDRÉS: I had just started a PhD program at a prestigious university. It was my first semester there. They offered me what seemed like a decent funding package. Told me about the types of community building that they encouraged in their program. Told me how excited they were about my work. Told me I would be so lucky to work with them on it. Told me I would have a better chance at getting any job with a degree from their prestigious school. Said their program was "like a well-oiled machine" that knew how to get students through and into jobs. I should have heard the warning in those words.

STEPHANIE: As I write this, I'm sitting in my office—in the very office and the very chair of another best friend who worked in this department before I came. The air in here feels heavy. If I look deep enough in the desk drawers, I will find stray business cards, pens, and candy wrappers that are not mine. If I turn around, I'll see a pile of her mail that continues to be sent here. I keep it all as a reminder of something I don't know how to articulate yet.

People ask me about her all of the time. Especially those who sought me out because they know I know her. Whenever I see them, they lovingly warn me of doing too much that won't get me tenure. They tell me they appreciate my work, but they don't want me to take on too much of it.

AMANDA: Although undergraduate studies had its challenges, I survived because of the support I continued to receive from my family and my community. After I made the decision to pursue an MA at UTEP, I found it difficult to juggle working full-time as a high school English teacher and attending school part-time, but I still found coursework incredibly rewarding.

QWO-LI: Anzaldúa writes, "A form of spiritual inquiry, conocimiento is reached via creative acts—writing, art-making, dancing, healing, teaching, meditation, and spiritual activism—both mental and somatic (the body, too, is a form as well as a site of creativity)" ("now let us shift" 542).

AMANDA: I first read Gloria Anzaldúa in my literary criticism and theory course. Most students used the process of autohistoria that Anzaldúa describes in "now let us shift...the path of conocimiento...inner work, public acts" as we connected experiences of living in our own literal and metaphysical borderlands to those of Anzaldúa and our extended communities (557). Instead of interrogating any problems we located in her ideas, most of us were struck by her ability to capture the realities of living in the El Paso/Juárez border.

GABI: Anzaldúa's theory of conocimiento as an epistemology is connected to an ontological condition in the same ways that many new materialists are now arguing: Anzaldúa's path to conocimiento as a journey that shows how liberating yourself from painful experiences allows you to share them with others in ways that transform realities (*Luz* 87-93).

QWO-LI: I try to remember to follow my teachings: put tobacco down, smoke myself off with cedar, sing a song to the rising sun. I don't always succeed: I forget our original instructions, I'm often in too much pain and too tired to do anything but get through a flare-up. The path of conocimiento isn't easy work, particularly now.

ANDRÉS: I was already part of the Calmécac Collective, even though I didn't know it.

STEPHANIE: Reeling off the pain from the first rupture, six months after I started my new job, I faced another.

QWO-LI: Since the election of 45, I've been exhausted. What is traumatizing for me is not the surprise of it, but the familiarity. I know this story. We know this story. I try to remember we've been through this, that my ancestors have been through worse. But it feels like queer and trans organizing in rural Colorado in the '90s, an experience I almost didn't survive, and it's hard to separate the then-and-now of it all.

ANDRÉS: I don't quite remember when I started to realize that things were not going well. I think it started out slowly, like any good trauma does.

STEPHANIE: I'm convinced that if I find the scattered, missing, and unrecoverable parts of myself, I can put them back together.

GABI: One consequence, I think, of the structures that bind us in the academy, is that it becomes difficult to walk the path of conocimiento because doing so will often mean having to recognize ourselves in others, others we have deemed fundamentally unlike us.

ANDRÉS: I was in a meeting with a faculty member who heard a rumor I was thinking about leaving the program.

"I hear you're thinking about dropping out?" she asked.

I corrected her and said, "No, I'm thinking about leaving *this* program." There is a difference, I thought to myself.

She proceeds to tell me about her own horrible experiences in graduate school. Talks to me about her own struggle to maintain her humanity within the academic system that was her intellectual upbringing. She assumes I have the same struggles because we share some identities. Gives me unsolicited advice on how I need to practice self-care, how I need to build community. She never bothers to learn or even ask how I've done this in the past. And then says the line that I'll remember never to mention to my own students seriously or in such a condescending manner.

"Grad school is supposed to be dehumanizing." You just suck it up, get through it, and then become faculty.

The problem with this trajectory, though, is that then you have a bunch of non-human faculty running programs and teaching other people the fastest way to not be human. This also assumes that faculty are not asked to renounce their humanity in other ways that benefit the university. And I'm not talking about the humanness we all spend time deconstructing and debating about through discourse. I'm not talking about the humanness of whiteness that assumes only specific bodies can be real people. I'm talking about a humanness that, as Daniel Heath Justice posits, acknowledges our relationships to one another. I'm talking about a humanness that answers Justice's questions: "*How do we learn to be human?* What are the experiences, customs, traditions, and ceremonies that define our humanity? How do we realize the full potential of our physical and imaginative human embodiment with healthy bodies, hearts, and minds" with integrity (28)? I'm talking about not losing *that* humanity.

STEPHANIE: You might say I'm in between stories now.

AMANDA: After I received my MA and took a few years to decide if I wanted to take the PhD route, I applied to a few programs. I was ecstatic when I learned that I had been accepted to the University of Oklahoma. Plus, my partner had been living and working in Oklahoma for the past year; I anticipated having similar support to the family and community support system I had in El Paso. I was determined to develop a strong learning community at OU, which was something I did not cultivate in El Paso because I already had a such a strong community outside of UTEP.

ANDRÉS: I stopped writing at some point during my four months in that program. I just couldn't get the words out. I couldn't bring myself to write what they wanted me to write. I couldn't bring myself to write how they thought I should. I couldn't find the words I wanted or needed to talk about what I was experiencing. It reminded me of how inadequate and incompetent my undergraduate program made me feel. It reminded me of learning how to say really big words without really knowing what I was actually saying just like my peers around me did. It reminded me of how depressed I was during my undergrad years. It reminded me of the many times I ran away to keep some form of my own humanity intact. It took me three years to recover some of my humanity after completing my undergraduate degree. It took me three years to feel like I could come back to do this work again. This program undid a lot of this work in months and brought me right back to the depression I learned to live with as an undergrad.

CATALINA: Notice the verb: "couldn't write," not "didn't write." Which means that I sat at my desk and tried to conjure words, scenes, rhythms. Short scenes, fragments of stories, and prose poems came and were just as quickly abandoned. The novel languished. I believed I had lost all creativity.

That first year in Michigan, I had never felt more alone.

ANDRÉS: I wanted to get my voice back. I wanted to write about the anger I felt. I wanted to write about all the microaggressions and gaslighting I experienced from faculty and peers alike. I wanted to write about how lonely I felt. I wanted to write about the isolation of not feeling like you're a good fit.

CATALINA: Physics Lesson: September 2016

This is a prose poem about the stairs in my new apartment. About how I sometimes stand on the landing and throw empty boxes down the stairs because I am fascinated by the physics of falling. I am not a thrill-seeker or a murderer-in-training. I do, however, appreciate the symmetry of stairs. The stairs bisect the place, and the feng shui article says that the old rules about stairs cutting someone in half, metaphorically, are untrue. This would be a good place to say that I am mixed race and that I feel cut in half everywhere I go. I breathed more easily after reading that article. Still, I feel cut in half in this house, and I choose to live upstairs more than downstairs because downstairs is a sad place. And I am sad already. And since I won't throw myself down the stairs, and I'm afraid of tripping on carpet and careening, head over heels, like an empty box, down fourteen stairs, I pretend that this is my home and that I'm as happy here as I would be anywhere.

ANDRÉS: What happens to those of us who, like water, create rust on oiled machine parts that are used to running without pause? I wanted to write about so many things, but I knew that if I did, I would never stop. I wanted to write all these things down, so I wouldn't forget. But I couldn't pull the words out without bursting into tears. And at that moment, what I needed more than writing was to get out.

GABI: As someone who has moved through the academy as a racially ambiguous body, I have been confused for many races and ethnicities, sans white or Black. I have come to recognize the signs of discomfort connected to my racial ambiguity well.

The end result is what all of us might expect, given that we are all well versed in Anzaldúan thought: I am perceived, interpreted, and *interpellated* in contradicting ways.

ANDRÉS: I met with so many faculty that I lost count. Some suggested I break my new lease and move closer to the university. Some said that no one has ever left their program before. Let's not count the cohort of one several years ahead of mine. Or the student a former mentor said had finished their coursework but never finished the program. I told them in October I was leaving at the end of the semester. They didn't believe me. I had to constantly remind them that I was not coming back.

A different faculty in particular asked me, in dismay, whom I could possibly work with once I left. She asked me about my ethnographic work without realizing that this is not the work I do. She asked me how I saw my work contributing to the field. She questioned how I could possibly find a job by leaving their program for a less-known and -prestigious university. I didn't say anything and thanked her for the lunch she invited me to and was 30 minutes late for. She crystalized the multiple reasons why every faculty conversation had felt condescending. And I am grateful for her directness, as uncomfortable as it was, for she confirmed in my mind and body why I needed to leave. I didn't want to be like these folks who kept redirecting critiques to be all about me. Who heard critiques as my own problems but never their own. I didn't want to be relatives with folks who dismissed the emotional labor it took to even talk to them. I didn't want to be related to them. I didn't want to become them and do this to my own students. I wanted to keep my humanity and preserve that of future kin.

STEPHANIE: The hardest part about writing this is that the more I've come to challenge myself about what it means to be a good ally, the more I understand the need for me to step back and be quiet. But if I won't pick up my trash, who will?

ANDRÉS: I got the opportunity to listen to Alexis Pauline Gumbs discuss her book *Spill: Scenes of Black Feminist Fugitivity*. Gumbs began her conversation with the audience by stating that her book, among the many different facets it holds and activates, is in fact an oracle. She asked us to think of a question that would lead to our freedom. And then asked us to think of a number between 1 and 150. It was only after we had written it down that Gumbs disclosed that the answer to our query was to be found in her book using the number we had thought of as the page number.

My questions for the oracle: "How do I speak the words I feel are caught wrapped around my throat like a knot? How do I find the words I need to get me through this?"

The abbreviated answer from the oracle that is Gumbs's text: "… the Milagros are in the basement, she is sure of it. the body parts of other women hung like smokehouse family. a warning. what god would want a sacrifice like that? she had to leave" (42).

So, I left.

STEPHANIE: Do I assimilate, separate, or isolate?

AMANDA: As I transitioned to life in Oklahoma, I tried desperately to ignore the nagging feeling that something was not quite right. I reminded myself that being homesick was to be expected, and I had not taken coursework for about four years. "Transitioning back to academia is going to be difficult" was the idea I kept reminding myself. My cohort expressed similar anxieties, but some of my new colleagues kept reminding us that we all worked really well together. I was not fully convinced. Something felt off. Then an incident happened that better defined why I always felt like an outsider with my group and in the department, as well.

STEPHANIE: Will putting myself back together get me tenure? Not unless it's peer-reviewed and garners me "national attention." So I throw myself into my work. Is it assimilation, separation, or isolation? Grief, I think, is what it is.

I listen to the blatantly false stories from colleagues whose allegiance is to academia and the systems that maintain their privilege. I know I can't ever *know* if they are lying to me, but my inner voice has already identified my purpose, and it's infused with what makes the air in my office so damn heavy. I listen closely to what I decide is a reinterpretation of the past, and I use it to reshape the present.

AMANDA: During a social gathering with several members of my cohort, I shared with them an incident that happened while I was walking down Main St. in Norman one evening. A group of about six young white men decided to shout out to me and the two friends who were with me that night. (My friends and I identify as Mexican, by the way). Apparently, our brown skin caught their attention. "Beaners," they called us. That racist word stung and hung in the air for a bit. So many emotions ran through me—humiliation, shame, and outrage. Worst of all was having to internalize all them in that moment. The safest reaction for everyone was to walk away. Never having to confront such direct racism before, I was left to work through the damage that such inflammatory and hate-filled language creates.

Part of the point in sharing my story with my cohort was to let them know that I appreciated how my mentor, Dr. Joshua B. Nelson, helped me cope with the situation. Admittedly, I expected my cohort to respond as Dr. Nelson had or, at least, sympathize with my experience. Instead, one colleague voiced her disagreement that this incident had anything to do with the election. She proceeded to tell me that everyone forgets to mention the qualifier that Trump said in his campaign speech, "Only *some* Mexicans are rapists and criminals." I was too hurt to correct her and inform her that he used the qualifier when he said, "and *some*, I assume, are good people." Another person in the group could not understand why I was so angry. He said that he could identify with their naiveté and stupidity, and I should have immediately dismissed this type of juvenile behavior. He advised that I look at the "intent" of their racial slur. I am still not sure what exactly he meant by that. After listening to their reactions, I took a deep breath and mentally told myself that this was a debate not worth having. I had spent three years with this group trying to build relationships with them. I felt betrayed.

STEPHANIE: I look up and I see an 18-year-old girl I've never met before in my office. A group of men had been following her as she made her way across campus demanding that she go back to where she came from. "America is for Americans," they said, and somewhere in between their threats to rape her and promise to build the wall, she slipped into the nearest building, recognized my name from a Know Your Rights presentation I organized, and came for help.

I think of that little girl throwing her little arms around a world that doesn't realize how much it needs her. I think of her passing down that watermelon dress to her new sister I haven't met yet, and then I accept what I have to do.

AMANDA: I went home and cried. I cried because this incident was a culmination and reflection of other incidents that had occurred during my time at OU. As the only Latina member of my cohort, this incident helped validate my suspicion—I am an outsider. My colleagues would never understand my experiences, and even more depressing to me was that my colleagues did not want to understand my experiences. The usual questions ran through my mind: why did I decide to pursue a PhD? Why am I committed to this program? Isn't it easier to just give up and go back to the community I miss so much?

STEPHANIE: I've got a vision, and after the countless meetings—meetings in the Mayor's office, meetings behind the warehouse on La Quinta Drive, meetings on campus at 10:30 p.m. and then again at 8 a.m.—I'm beginning to formulate a plan. I'm moving downstream, a different person from who I was when I was upstream. I'm going to mine every resource I can from the university because I don't know quite yet what my own greatest resource is.

AMANDA: But along with these questions, I also think about the relationships I have fostered while at OU. Although I have not cultivated the learning community I envisioned, I have formed strong relationships with my two mentors, Dr. Nelson and Dr. Gabriela Ríos. When I think back to the racial slur, I consider the conversation I shared with Dr. Nelson. Or when I think back to my colleagues' reactions when I shared the incident, I also consider the text message I got from Gabi soon after the election asking me how I was coping with everything. My support system at OU is small but strong. During difficult moments, I draw on Shawn Wilson's work on relationality in *Research is Ceremony* where he writes about working with Indigenous scholars who "all understood implicitly the importance of the relationships that we built together, between us, our homelands and our ideas" (83). I share a like-minded sentiment when I reflect on my relationship with my two mentors. In a spirit of "co-operation," both have extended invitations for me to collaborate with them on different academic and research projects (Wilson 83). As I gradually move forward in my research under their guidance, I am slowly forming a much-needed academic community. Their willingness to let me join academic circles like the Calmécac Collective shows me that a supportive community is achievable even outside the El Paso/Juárez borderland.

STEPHANIE: Allyship, for me, is like my beloved game of baseball: it's a story of failures, adjustments, and precision. When I think I've gained a new awareness, created a workable story, and followed my conscience, I think I've made progress. And then I cast that out into the world, only to see it and all its contradictions blow up in my face. Allyship is, as Anzaldúa says about transformations, the story of seeing my stories fail the reality test and doing it all over again ("now let us shift" 560).

QWO-LI: Time slips.

STEPHANIE: Sometimes I think I see the flash of a little watermelon dress in the corner of my eye. In a moment, I'm back there again on my wedding day, smiling at the little droplets of sweat on my now-wife's nose, and thanking that little girl in the watermelon dress for urging me, mid-ceremony, not to throw the wedding rings over the embankment.

ANDRÉS: We survived because of the many kin who imagined us into the future centuries ago.

CATALINA: To the academy: Don't tell me what to write, how to write, which verbs to use, that adjectives and especially adverbs are bad. Don't tell me my syntax is wrong or stuttering, that I don't have enough conflict, that my characters are not round and lushly conceived. I don't care if they are stupid or simpering or underdeveloped or cliché. Let their arteries burst with shamed blood.

Don't crowd my mind with rules and regulations. They bind and gag like vines squeezing blood and breath from me. These stories, lodged in the back of my throat, are trying to breathe. I don't want anyone blocking me, curdling my love for language, advancing their own theories about why this and why not that. I don't want anyone to scold and critique and then encourage. I grew up with nothing but critique, have internalized it as its own type of rotten love.

Leave your critique at the door and say hello to my worlds. Let me find my heart again, my love of storytelling, my Chicana way of doing things.

STEPHANIE: To be the kind of ally I want to be demands a constant rewriting of stories. I need to find a way to rewrite the heaviness that still lingers in my office.

QWO-LI: This moment, to come back together with the Calmécac Collective to tell our stories together, *is* ceremony, *is* resistance. While we aren't able to come together physically as much as we would like, we're woven together through our commitments to each other, through clearing the path for those who are on their way.

ANDRÉS: I didn't know I was part of the Calmécac Collective, even as I was supported by them.

I crashed a conference about two months into the semester because I knew that my mentor was presenting that day. I drove 12 hours to get there just so I could spend some time with them, but really I drove 12 hours to get away from my program. I needed to get out. I needed to talk to someone. I wanted to leave, but felt stuck. And there I was that night, sitting at this small restaurant with my mentor, their intellectual sibling, and my own. I don't quite remember what was the question I was asked that made me open up. I don't quite remember how it all came up. But I do remember someone saying that they had no idea I was carrying so much.

I got validation for feelings of inadequacy and the condescending things I had experienced in just two months. I remember saying I felt scared to leave and was met with examples as to why staying would be worse. I spent less than 24 hours in this small college town before driving another 12 hours back to where I came from. They gave me permission to finally feel at ease and freer to say that what I wanted was to leave. I just had to get through another two months of this.

CATALINA: One day, sometime earlier this year, I decided to stop watching as much television and think of myself as a creative writer. This seems an absurd sentence to write. I don't need to call myself this because most people who know me consider me a writer already and because all writing is creative in my way of thinking. But I wanted to make a public (re)commitment, a decision to go for this life as an artist in full measure. I wanted to build my life around writing and not my writing around my life.

Beyond having my work speak to social justice in some way, beyond allowing stories to come to me unfiltered and ragged, beyond having received inspiration and direction from Anzaldúa's writings and my friends, I did not know how to make a life with art at its center. All my professional life has been tied to academic success, and though I've had my share of it in graduate school and now as a faculty member, I still find myself unfulfilled. I still find the academy to be draining. During this second year, I have returned full circle to the short stories I'd written in my MFA program ten years ago. I reread all of them. I reread critiques from my workshop that I had saved. I found I liked them, both stories and critiques; I thought they had promise, I thought they needed deep revision.

CASIE: My daughter wants to know if I can write all the English letters in cursive. "All of them? *All* of the letters?" I imagine she sees letters like numbers that grow bigger and bigger, stacking on top of each other. More and more. And she asks, "How did you learn *all* of the English letters?" So many letters that make so many words that make so many theories that make so many practices that make so many stories that make so many relationships and undo so many others.

STEPHANIE: I'm still really, really not crazy about living in Florida now. It's the furthest I've been away from the Calmécac Collective, and the closest I've been to snakes. (Anzaldúa says that the snake "is a symbol of awakening consciousness—the potential of knowing within, an awareness and intelligence not grasped by logical thought" ("now let us shift" 540). Is it the snakes I'm afraid of or symbol of acceptance that things will never be the same again?) But once I was walking in a parking lot, and I saw an injured snake trying to get off the boiling pavement and onto the grass.

Too scared to do anything, I walked on. And then I remembered that if we are all made of the same things, those things I love the most are what make up that snake. For the first time in my life, I was within a foot of a snake, and I lifted it up off the pavement with a stick and watched it slither away under a shrub.

QWO-LI: We have a memory older than wounding.

CASIE: "Are we related to trees?" my daughter asks on the drive home from school last week. I look at the trees lining the Houston street through which we are driving. I look at the branches and leaves carved out from their trunks like a tunnel to fit the vehicles that pass under and through them each day. I wonder how long they will live while we keep making those cuts, how long we will live by making those cuts. I wonder if I should explain how our bodies used to go back into the earth and think about the coffin-lined soil that we have now.

Winona LaDuke's work comes to mind (1999). All the trees. All our relations. Indigenous activists at the borders of Peru and Brazil, home and logging industry come to mind. Losing trees. Losing relations. Anzaldúa's words come to mind. "This land was Indian always" (*Borderlands* 25). Relational always. How to give these thoughts I worked through with college teachers and colleagues and students to an almost-five-year-old.

She interrupts my thoughts and asks again, "Are we related to trees?"

"Yes, we are."

"How?"

"We breathe in oxygen and breathe out carbon dioxide. And they breathe in carbon dioxide and breathe out oxygen. We need each other, and if we don't take care of each other, we won't have air."

"So we are related to trees?" she confirms.

"Yes, we need each other."

"And animals, too?"

"Yes, we need each other."

"And we all need air to live, like flowers," she relates.

She moves on to her next topic, and I—I am stuck there, still stuck driving through carved-out trees, stuck trying to understand my relationships to people, things, places who have moved away; to people, things, places I have moved away from; to people, things, places I still want to remain connected to. Still stuck.

Back there.

ANDRÉS: I only spent four months in that program. The anxieties I learned there still pop up sometimes, but less often than they used to. I know this will keep happening; that's just how trauma works. I'm just happy they're no longer consuming my entire life.

My current program is not perfect, nor did it ever pretend to be. We have our stuff too. But at least I don't have to worry that faculty won't have my back. I don't have to question whether or not I actually should be here, because I am reminded every time I walk into a classroom or meeting that my contributions are wanted and appreciated. I don't feel the pressure to perform "graduate student" in ways that make me lose myself, for the purpose of satisfying some form of revenge pedagogy. I don't have to spend my time in courses that only center Foucault and Butler, even if they were never assigned, as if they were the only ones who have ever contributed to our understandings of queer studies. I don't have to belittle my knowledges or my experience in order to not overstep my position as a graduate assistant or a student in any classroom. I don't have to pretend that everything is fine. That I have my shit together. That I know what I'm doing. I'm allowed to be human. I'm allowed to be a full, messy, complicated, don't-always-have-my-shit-together human.

And, in part, this is because of faculty's intentionality in the creation of our program and curriculum. But more importantly, it's because of the many people who have carved out the path for me to even imagine myself doing this work. It's because of the many kin who imagined me into the future centuries ago. It's because of the sacrifices the women in my family made so that I could have opportunities not afforded to them. It's because I, like the other folks in the Calmécac Collective, know that the real work is not one that is measured and counted through awards and publications, but one that is known through the relationships we maintain with those around us. That is what the Calmécac Collective has taught me. That is what I teach my own students. Our work in the world is one built on relationships. So what do my relationships say about my own humanity? About the humanity I see in my own students, even when we don't like each other? How is our work building relationships revolutionary? How do we heal from the trauma non-human academics manifest and recreate as "teaching"? Those are the questions I leave with you, future kin.

GABI: Cherokee writer Thomas King argues, "You have to be careful with the stories you tell. And you have to watch out for the stories you are told" (10). Story, in most indigenous traditions, is a powerful tool for making. One that, as Casie C. Cobos has shown, is born of "flesh-and-bone" bodies and that constitute them as well (2012).

CASIE	**QWO-LI**
"How do you say hello in Cherokee?"	[Singing underneath CASIE in Cherokee.]
"Siyo."	Naiqwo sunale nigalsda
"And how do you say siyo in Spanish?"	Naiqwo sunale nigalsda
"Hola."	Ayvno, ayvno Yihowa
"I can teach my friends 'siyo.'"	Gvyalihelitse Yihowa
"I learn "siyo."	Gvyalihelitse Yihowa

ANDRÉS: We survived because of the many kin who imagined us into the future centuries ago.

QWO-LI: Anzaldúa writes, "Conocimiento is about linking the pieces and mapping the journey of your life, your soul's journey. Rewriting a different way of perceiving, of knowing" (*Luz* 198).

CATALINA: This is where I begin, again.

STEPHANIE: "El arrebato, the first stage: Rupture, fragmentation, woundings, and endings.

A beginning" (Anzaldúa, "now let us shift" 540).

NOTES

The Calmécac Collective would like to thank the Indigenous peoples whose land this was written on: the Anishinabek people of Michigan; the Coahuiltecan people of San Antonio, Texas; the Atakapan-Ishak people of Southeast Texas and Southwest Louisiana; the Multnomah people, who are now part of the Confederated Tribes of Grand Ronde and the Confederated Tribes of the Warm Springs Reservation; the Kalapuya people who are now part of the Confederated Tribes of Grand Ronde and the Confederated Tribes of Siletz Indians; the Karankawa people of the Texas Gulf Coast; the Tawakoni people, who are now part of the Wichita and Affiliated Tribes; the Kiowa Apache, who are now part of the Apache Tribe of Oklahoma; and the Seminole Tribe of Florida.

We would also like to thank the other members of the Calmécac Collective: Marcos Del Hierro, Victor Del Hierro, Aydé Enríquez-Loya, Lisa Fernandez, and Garrett W. Nichols.

WORKS CITED

Anzaldúa, Gloria E. *Borderlands/La Frontera: The New Mestiza.* 4th ed., Aunt Lute Books, 2012.

---. *Light in the Dark/Luz en lo Oscuro: Rewriting Identity, Spirituality, Reality*, Edited by AnaLouise Keating, Duke University Press, 2015.

---. "now let us shift…the path of conocimiento…inner work, public acts." *this bridge we call home: radical visions for transformation*, Edited by Gloria Anzaldúa and AnaLouise Keating, Routledge, 2002, pp. 540-78.

Bartlett, Catalina, Casie Cobos, Marcos Del Hierro, Victor Del Hierro, Qwo-Li Driskill, Aydé Enríquez-Loya, and Stephanie Wheeler. "The Calmécac Collective, or, How to Survive the Academic Industrial Complex through Radical Indigenous Practices." *El Mundo Zurdo 3: Selected Works from the Meetings of The Society for the Study of Gloria Anzaldúa*, Edited by Sonia Saldívar-Hull, Larissa Mercado-López, and Antonia Castañeda, Aunt Lute, 2013, pp. 299-318.

Cobos, Casie C. "An Other Chican@ Rhetoric from Scratch: (Re)Making Stories: (Un)Mapping the Lines and Re-membering Bodies." Dissertation, Texas A&M University, 2012.

Gumbs, Alexis Pauline. *Spill: Scenes of Black Feminist Fugitivity.* Duke University Press, 2016.

Justice, Daniel Heath. *Why Indigenous Literatures Matter.* Wilfrid Laurier University Press, 2018.

King, Thomas. *The Truth About Stories: A Native Narrative.* University of Minnesota Press, 2008.

LaDuke, Winona. *All Our Relations: Native Struggles for Land and Life.* Haymarket Books, 1999.

Mignolo, Walter D. *The Idea of Latin America.* Blackwell Publishing, 2005.

Moraga, Cherríe. *Heroes and Saints and Other Plays: Giving Up the Ghost, Shadow of a Man, Heroes and Saints.* University of New Mexico, 1994.

Wilson, Shawn. *Research is Ceremony: Indigenous Research Methods.* Fernwood Publishing Company, 2009.

CLOSINGS

CLOSING PLENARY

WILD TONGUES/TRANSNATIONAL CROSSINGS

REFLECTIONS ON TRANSLATING ANZALDÚA INTO FRENCH

PAOLA BACCHETTA

Gloria Evangelina Anzaldúa has much to teach us about the freedom of wild tongues, and about translation. In what follows, I engage with her theorizations, meditations and practices relative to both these questions, through my experience of translating some of her work into French.

SITUATED

Before I proceed, I will respect a political desire, a wish, an exigency, advice and counsel, an intense bit of wisdom, handed down to us by Anzaldúa and an earlier generation of Native, Black, Chicanx, and other women and queers of color. In her essay "On the Process of Writing *Borderlands/La Frontera*," Anzaldúa notes (2009: 193):

> One thing I urge you to do when you are reading and writing is to figure out, literally, where your feet stand, what position you are taking: Are you speaking from a white, male, middle class perspective? Are you speaking from a working class, colored, ethnic location? For whom are you speaking? To whom are you speaking? What is the context, where do you locate your experience?

So Anzaldúa, and prior elder sisters and queers, asks us to situate ourselves in relation to the subjects with whom, or about whom, we are speaking.

Respectfully, I will mention that I was born on Turtle Island, in New York, as a non-Lenape person on Native Lenape land. I am from a second generation of parents who are mixed in terms of national heritages, racialization, ethnicity, culture, and languages. My mother's maternal genealogy is with the Wayuu people in the part of Abaya Yala that the Spanish colonizers named Venezuela, and her paternal ancestry is from Turkey. My father is part Italian, from the subaltern *mezzo-giorno* region of Abbruzzo, and part Ethiopian. The mark of colonial patriarchy is evident in my name.

I have been queer all my life. I never went through a heterosexual phase. In the different contexts in which I have lived, queer has many kinds of self-identifications, including dyke (U.S.) or *guine* (dyke in French). I can only multiply-identify. But, at this time, I am especially drawn to one self-designation that was recently articulated by the Black lesbian rapper Janelle Monáe: "free-ass motherfucker" (Spanos). I imagine that if Anzaldúa were alive today she would find this to her liking, too.

My relationship to France and the French language began with exile. I will explain. I was politicized early in my life. By the mid 1970s in Philadelphia I co-founded with other dykes, mainly other dykes of color, an activist group called Dyketactics! (Bacchetta 2019). Our collective simultaneously took a position against colonialism, genocide, slavery and its continuation, the capitalist exploitation of workers, inseparably from our critique of sexism and lesbophobia, and inscribed this stance in most of our political statements. In practice, Dyketactics! supported all the liberation movements of the day—Black liberation, Puerto Rican independence, United Farm Workers, Native sovereignty, etc. And yet, Dyketactics! is perhaps most known today as the first queer collective in the U.S., and possibly the world, to ever take police to court for violence specifically targeting queers. We were brutally beaten by the Philadelphia Civil Defense Squad, the violent "anti-riot" arm of the Philadelphia police force, while attending a peaceful demonstration for LGBTQI rights inside Philadelphia City Hall. In brief, during the demonstration, the riot police attacked, bashed us up, and dragged us down four flights of stone steps. We ended up in the hospital. We took the police to court for anti-lesbian police brutality. Of course, we lost. But, we did manage to use the trial's extensive television, newspaper, and radio publicity to speak out about queer issues to the public. One of the many effects of the publicity was that police everywhere knew about us. At various points, in different sites, Dyketactics! members were arrested, individually, on assorted false charges.

In spring of 1977, while trying to attend the trial of Black liberation activist Assata Shakur in New Jersey, I was arrested on false charges in connection with support for her. I was initially charged with possession of a firearm and carrying firearms across state lines with intent to liberate Shakur from prison. It was a total fabrication. Still, the charges added up to several felonies, to about 40 years in prison. Upon arrest, I was put into the same prison as Shakur; she was in the basement in isolation and I on the top floor in a collective cell. I was able to leave the prison prior to my trial, thanks to Dyketactics! sisters who raised my bail.

I had, on my defense team, one of Shakur's lawyers, William Kuntsler. The charges against me were progressively lessened. At my trial, the State dropped the charges altogether, citing irregularities of the search that made evidence against me inadmissible. In sum, they had nothing to incriminate me: no gun, no plans to break Shakur out, nothing. When I heard that the charges were dropped, I was extremely relieved. But, my lawyers warned me that there were already plans to re-try me. Kuntsler advised me to either cease political activities and go underground, or leave the country. I quickly organized my departure from the U.S.

I first ended up in Rome. For two and a half years, I lived in a feminist squat at the Casa delle Donne (Women's Center), via del Governo Vecchio, in the city's center. Then, due to political repression across Italy including Rome, I moved to France. I spent the rest of my seven years of exile (the time required by New Jersey for freedom from new charges) in Paris. I was undocumented. I was politically active in anti-racism, feminist, and queer movements at once. I ended up living most of my life in Paris. Today, I remain connected to and active in feminist-of-color, anti-racism, decolonial, and queer-of-color movements in France.

As a result, I have no idea anymore what is or is not home. Most of the time there seems to be none. So, today I am sure only of one thing: there is no post-exile.

ANZALDÚA-COMPAÑERA

I came to Anzaldúa's work through a long journey. Across oceans and lands. I was introduced to it well after it was available in the U.S., while in post-exile in Paris. Her writing was a lifeline. Across our differences, there were deep resonances: the multiplicity of our different geopolitics, languages, dimensions and registers of *mestizaje*; a convergence around indigeneity, coloniality, and the mark of southern Europe on our minds, spirits, bodies; our corporeal *prietismo* or brown embodiment; questions of immigration; our queerness. There are also productive differences: Anzaldúa identified as Chicana while I am situated in a kind of multiplicity that can rarely be figured as anything but an always-already otherness status, as excess or as lack, in relation to community, national, and regional normativities.

Very importantly, I found in Anzaldúa a kinship of sensibilities. It has a plethora of dimensions. One of them is the queerness of Gloria's love for all of creation: a horse, a cat, a dog, birds, insects, ancestors and progenitors of all beings-becomings, the unseen, waters, minerals, *terra*, sky, a cloud that slowly sails by, the sunrise, stars, air, wind, rain. In sum, all the beings-becomings and states of being that are travelers with us throughout this life. And, a world of queer sensings, interpretations, socialities, relationalities.

I found in Anzaldúa an uncompromising friend, sister, and comrade creating everywhere total revolution. She had zero tolerance for any form of injustice.

I found in Anzaldúa a brilliant queer theorist whose way of discussing queer—as a sensibility, as an energy, as corporeality, as relationality, as insurgency, and as what Laura Perez would call a special kind of *hallucinatory knowledge*—spoke to my most intimate being-in-the-world (Perez 2018).

I would experience later the shock of Anzaldúa's multiple erasures. While still a graduate student at University of California, Santa Cruz, her work was taught in universities across the U.S. Why was she not awarded a PhD at least for her classic book *Borderlands/La Frontera: The New Mestiza*? Anzaldúa was a path-breaker who first brought queer theory, then a *street theory* in the sense of Kath Weston, into the university (Weston 1991). Anzaldúan queer theory is prior to and more complex than the *colonialism-and-race* amnesiac queer theory that is currently hegemonic (Bacchetta, Falquet and Alarcón 2011). The latter is constructed around an exclusive yet unavowed white queer subject, along the lines of "the feminist subject" whom Norma Alarcón insightfully and critically identified as the presumed (objective, non-situated) "universal subject" (Alarcón 1991). Alarcón also points out that women-of-color writing is systematically reduced to personal narratives to entertain white people; it is rarely considered theory at all. In sum, with Alarcón I do not define white queer theory in essentialist terms according to those who produce it, its speaking subjects, but rather in strictly political terms according to its reproduction, reinforcement, and normativization of *colonialism-and-racism amnesia*. In contrast, Anzaldúa produced queer theorizations that directly critically engage coloniality, racism, class, speciesism, the obliteration of the planet, epistemicide including culturecide and linguisticide, along with misogyny, sexism, and queerphobia. The complexities and beauty of Anzaldúa's queer knowledge production are evident in 1979 in her essay "La Prieta" (2009: 38-50). They appear also in full force in 1987 in *Borderlands/La Frontera*. We find it in writings such as the 1991 essay "To(o) Queer the Writer: loca, escritora y chicana" (2009: 163-175).

It should come as no surprise that while U.S. white feminisms and white queer theory have travelled to France, Anzaldúa's work has remained relatively unknown there until recently. To translate Anzaldúa into French was to confront multiple contextual effacements. As in the U.S., women of color and queers of color in France have been deleted out of the historiography of feminist, LGBTQI, and anti-racism and pro-immigration movements, activisms, artivisms, and intellectual production. Yet, we have been present from the 1970s to today. Unfortunately, we were more marginalized and separate from each other then. Today, that situation is changing. Many autonomous feminist and queer-of-color activist groups, artivisms, and intellectual movements are emerging and producing publications, political events, exhibits, films, performances, and other expressions. This new intellectual production has had little structural impact on the universities. For instance, in the entire French academy, there is not a single lesbian-of-color professor writing on lesbian or queer-of-color issues.

Knowing I would never get employment in a university in France, I moved to the U.S. After holding temporary teaching positions mainly on the East Coast, in 2003 I was hired in the Department of Gender and Women's Studies at UC Berkeley. I have been there ever since. I arrived there just one year prior to Anzaldúa's death. I moved there after a major operation that left me unable to connect with our communities for some time. At the same time, Anzaldúa was also unwell. Thus, though she lived close by, in Santa Cruz, and though we had many common friends, I never had a chance to meet her. When I think that Anzaldúa and I were never in each other's physical presence, it feels strange. Because I am sure that we have spent a very long time in each other's spiritual presence throughout the years. She has, in her present absence and absent presence, given me more than I know how to even receive, let alone articulate.

A major gift from Anzaldúa is her reflections and practices relative to what to do about our wild tongues, about those intimate, corporeal and a-corporeal parts that comprise our whole. About our constituents that dominant subjects find threatening, that they would like to separate, tame, and control.

BIRTHING ANZALDÚA INTO FRENCH

From 2009 to 2011, I had the honor—with my colleague and compañera Jules Falquet—of intensely engaging with and attempting to share with French-speaking audiences some of the offerings by Anzaldúa and her wild tongue(s). Together, we created a first integral translation of a part of Anzaldúa's work for French-speaking audiences: Chapter 7 from *Borderlands/La Frontera: The New Mestiza*, entitled "*La conciencia de la mestiza*/Towards a New Consciousness." (An excerpted version of the same chapter, yet reframed in Deleuzian terms, had appeared earlier.) We published our translation in a special issue of the feminist journal *Les Cahiers du CEDREF* that we co-edited with Norma Alarcón on "Decolonial Feminist and Queer Theories: Chicana and U.S.-Latina Interventions" *(Théories Décoloniales Féministes et Queers: Interventions Ch/Xicanas et Latinas Etatsuniennes* 2011). We included translations of articles by Cherríe Moraga, Norma Alarcón, Chela Sandoval and María Lugones. The issue first appeared in hard copy. It now is freely available on the *Les Cahiers du CEDREF* website to anyone across the French-speaking world with Internet access. In our introduction to the issue, we highlighted Anzaldúa's contributions—to queer, decolonial, feminist, literary and other theories—far beyond the one chapter included.

The process of translating Anzaldúa was a collective poetic, intimate, political and spiritual journey. Anzaldúa led the way, Jules and I accompanied her as best we could. Norma Alarcón and Norma Cantú were also with us. Much of our work, the travelling together with Anzaldúa's words, took place in Jules's apartment, on the last floor of a building in the 10th arrondissement (neighborhood) of Paris. Some of it also happened by Skype while I was based in Berkeley. I felt Anzaldúa's presence with us throughout.

To bring Anzaldúa to a French-speaking public was far from simple. It posed for us a whole array of questions.

One was what to do about Anzaldúa's wild tongue. She expresses herself in multiple languages, all of which are deeply inserted into, and continually co-formed anew with, specific kinds of relations of power, forms of epistemological violence, but also with intimacies, connections, relationalities. We were faced with a sphere of contradictions. We thought we could navigate through this, word by word, if only we could listen well enough to Anzaldúa herself, if only we could work with her spirit, her ideas about language and her sensibilities about translation.

And so, one of the first steps we took was to respect Anzaldúa's refusal to suppress linguistic hybridity. Her refusal is evident performatively in *Borderlands/La Frontera*, with its several languages and linguistic codes. She also theorizes her approach. In her preface to the first edition of *Borderlands/La Frontera*, she states: "The switching of codes in this book from English to Castilian Spanish to the North Mexican dialect to Tex-Mex to a sprinkling of Nahuatl to a mixture of all of these, reflects my language, a new language—the language of the Borderlands" (p. 20). Later, in the chapter entitled "How to Tame a Wild Tongue," Anzaldúa reminds us that lurking within most of these rubrics of languages are ever more languages. She numbers and names them thus: "1. Standard English; 2. Working class and slang English; 3. Standard Spanish; 4. Standard Mexican Spanish; 5. North Mexican Spanish dialect; 6. Chicano Spanish (Texas, New Mexico, Arizona and California have regional variations) 7. Tex-Mex; and 8. *Pachuco* (called *caló*)" (p. 77). In the next sentences, she tells us that her "home" languages are from "the last 5 listed, with 6 and 7 being close to my heart" (Ibid).

To respect Anzaldúa's linguistic multiplicity, her multi-vocality, but also her prioritizations and her linguistic affective relationalities and intimacies, we decided to translate only the English(es) in the plural into French(es) in the plural and to leave, as Anzaldúa herself did, all other languages intact, untranslated, as they are. Because of the great gap between Anzaldúa's context and that of the French-speaking world and because of our concerns about sufficient intelligibility (as opposed to the futile exercise of presuming direct transparency) we added footnotes in which we translated and/or explained many points.

For now, let us consider the relationality of bringing English(es) into French(es). In *Borderlands/La Frontera*, the two *class-and-coloniality* situated forms of English take up the most space. Yet, their authority is undermined in ways that merit clarification. To translate the English(es) into French(es), of course, meant, in the most basic of political dimensions, transposing Anzaldúa's words from one colonial language into another. However, more complexly, it also meant respecting how Anzaldúa appropriated the linguistic coloniality in which we who have been forced to learn to speak English and other colonial languages are saturated. It meant noticing and learning from how Anzaldúa made her way through English(es), made them her own, transformed them until they became something else entirely.

Anzaldúa subverts the English(es), and not only by letting live their pluralization in standard and working-class versions; she also *decolonizes* English(es) as they pass, in one form and another, through her brown, queer body, through her vocal chords, throat and mouth, into the air, becoming part of the life-world, through her hands, and inscribed onto paper. Anzaldúa's words are everywhere, and also are localized, situated, without pretention to neutrality. Our task was to rise into the English, to bring Anzaldúa's situatedness, her subversive adamant otherness, into French. To do so, we needed to respect the geopolitical and linguistic contexts, and the very different kinds of B/borderlands that these languages implicate and represent. We needed to be there with our whole bodies. This was not just a simple linguistic transposition; it was a relationality of love and respect with Anzaldúa, her languages, her spaces, her life.

For my part, I could only draw upon my own subalternly *colonized-racialized* hybridity and my dyke-of-color, "free-ass motherfucker" sensibility. Gloria's words entered my own differently-situated brown body and caused quite a stir in there. They entered my heart, intestines, backbone, lungs, throat, at once. I no longer knew what to think. My body became a vessel. I sat on the floor, looked at Anzaldúa's text in English(es), and spoke it out in French(es). Jules, sitting at the computer, wrote down whatever came out of my mouth. Then, at each turn, we paused. Together, Jules and I gauged the words that had exited me, their accuracy or inaccuracy, by how they felt. Most of the time, they felt just great. But, at times, they made no sense at all. So we discussed them together. We occasionally needed monolingual and bilingual dictionaries, thesauruses, encyclopedias. But, every modality, every tool, had limitations. We needed something more beyond them. We found solidarity in collectivity. There were times when I waited up through much of the day or much of the night in Paris to call Norma Alarcón in San Antonio at what she considered to be a decent hour (she is not a morning person). There are seven hours' difference between Paris and San Antonio. And, Norma is a free spirit, not always in the mood for phone calls. But whenever she was on the other end of the phone line, in our discussions, faced with my linguistic panic, Norma was always calm and loving. I know she intuitively understands that in fact, some words, phrases, sentences, can cause total agony. That some words, phases, sentences, like waves, can overpower you, shove you around, shatter your body across rocks. Throw you into the air. Evaporate you. Because Norma herself, by her own example at UC Berkeley, was the first to directly instruct me in the art of surviving tsunamis.

Today, I know that to translate lovingly is beautiful. I felt the love and the beauty all the while as we translated Anzaldúa. But loving translation can sometimes include torturous moments. One is confronted directly with one's inadequacies of understanding in relation to the beloved other sister. This consciousness can provoke a state of intense anxiety. The risk, the possibility, of inadvertently performing yet another layer of epistemological violence to the text, to the beloved other sister, is always there. Such is movement within and from one colonial language to another, even when enacted by and from one dyke of color to another. How could we know exactly how to fully respect Gloria Anzaldúa's words as we brought them to French(es)-speaking folk? How could I be sure my body surrendered itself only to Gloria Anzaldúa, and not to the coloniality of the languages through which we have been forced to communicate, languages that Anzaldúa subverted, transformed, to make her own?

We were adamant about trying to ensure that Anzaldúa's multi-semic words retain her/their contextual meaning. This made necessary yet another decision: not to try to make the translation conform to what is familiar to a French speaking public. Instead, we wanted to introduce the readers to a new reality: Gloria Anzaldua's. I will try to explain.

As in English, there are *colonial-racial-class* situated variants of the French language. Additionally there is a language in France, created out of standard French, invented by working-class youth of color, mainly Arab and Black, called *verlan*. It is used communicate in front of, and yet below the radar of, police or other authorities, including parents. But, to use *verlan* where Gloria shifts into working class Chicanx English would have meant losing the uniqueness of Anzaldúa's B/borderlands. It would have forced Anzaldúa to become French. It would constitute re-colonization by France. It would have left Anzaldúa vulnerable to abusive singular pluralization, to homogenization. This is what French colonialism desires for all racialized others, across very different kinds of B/borderlands: the convenient reduction of us all to a racialized other-same, and our assimilation into the particular French version of universalism proposed by the colonial and post-colonial French State. This form of deculturalization, cultural elimination, and cultural assimilation constitutes cultural genocide. We need to be aware that sometimes colonialism and *colonial-racism* are located and arrive at you from where you might not expect it.

In the French context, there are many experiences of the stunning and overwhelming power of *colonial-racialized* epistemological violence, of the dominant distortion of words of women of color. For example, some years ago in Paris, a group of white French radical lesbians translated a text by bell hooks. Sounds great thus far, right? Well, they left out all references to racism and in their place substituted references to heterosexism. Similarly, there is now Anzaldúa scholarship that equates her discussion of the B/borderlands with intra-European immigration, thereby inadvertently reproducing, reinforcing and normativising French colonialism. This same gesture of whitening has happened to the concept of *intersectionality* as it has travelled to France, a process that Sirma Bilge insightfully calls "the whitening of intersectionality in Europe" (Bilge 2015). And the enactment of erasing colonized and postcolonial subjects has been brilliantly analyzed by Fatima Aït Ben Lmadani and Nassima Moujoud (2012). This is all part of the total de-historicization, de-contextualization, which makes possible the imposition of false equivalencies. In such an environment, to parallelize Anzaldúa with one or another or even all of the several subalternly racialized communities in France would mean disappearing Anzaldúa. This, of course, we flatly refused to enact. Our concern, instead, was to keep Anzaldúa intact. The French(es) speaking world would just have to deal with her. With her difference.

Yet another question then was this: what to do with the many Spanish(es) and the Nahuatl? We followed Anzaldúa's lead and left them as they were in the text. But, in order to prevent the erasure of those words, phrases and sentences, and to avoid confusion, appropriation, and whitening, we decided to clarify a few things in footnotes. We were then faced with this question: should the terms, phrases and sentences, be translated? Explained? What about our own ignorance and limitations as translators? Jules had grown up in different parts of Abaya Yala and was familiar with several national, regional, and class-based Spanish(es). I was raised until age five and a half by my maternal grandmother in a multi-lingual household. Yet neither of us was fully prepared for the specifically situated Spanishes of Anzaldúa's complex text. We had no pretention of sufficient understanding. So, again, we relied upon those with knowledge. I had long conversations with Norma Alarcón, and, when she was confronted with an impasse, she asked Norma Cantú. Thanks to this process, the translation is a result of loving collective labor performed across lands and seas, temporal-spatialities, and even across dimensions insofar as Anzaldúa, who accompanied us, who guided us, is our ghostly-free-spirit sister, compañera, and ancestor, all at once.

Yet another related major dilemma for us was about contexts in the plural. We needed to make Anzaldúa's work intelligible not only to French-speaking people in France, inclusive of France's overseas departments and territories (Guadeloupe, Reunion Island, etc.), but also across the French-speaking postcolonial world: Senegal, Algeria, Morocco, Tunisia, Cameroon, etc. These spaces, like continental France, are far from the U.S., Mexican, and B/borderlands context. They are also far away from each other. Moreover, the translation would not arrive in the French-speaking world on a blank slate; it would arrive rather *after* hegemonic *colonialism-and-race* amnesiac U.S. feminist and queer theory had already saturated it, and after some translations of Black feminist theory that had first addressed white audiences (such as Hazel Carby's "White Women: Listen!") but which are now amply and productively used by French and French-speaking Black feminists and queers, as well. Anyway, we wanted Anzaldúa to have the right to speak in French in her wildest of tongues, first and foremost to other women, feminists and queers of color, and allies. This is an audience that many people in France suppose does not even exist. We also wanted to recognize Anzaldúa's affinity with all peoples and all beings, and thus to create a translation that could ultimately speak to everyone, across all kinds of situatedness.

Yet another issue around context is this: the entire reading public in metropolitan France—of color and white—has been extensively contaminated by hegemonic discourses about the U.S., including Texas, that travel in dominant mediascapes. On the one hand, there is dominant white popular culture. It includes "information" from the TV show *Dallas* about the mundane lives of boring, rich white people. It is also brought to France via westerns, those colonial *fantasy-productions* with pretensions to historicity in which either white cowboys conquer Native people who are constructed as savages, or in which Native people, who are imagined as always already vanished, serve as a backdrop to white cisgender male heroics, including homo male heroics (i.e., the film *Brokeback Mountain*).

On the other hand, there is in France interest in resistance. The main mode of understanding resistance in the U.S. is via Malcolm X and Angela Davis. Many postcolonial activists and intellectuals in France identify with U.S. Black liberation movements. But, they often imagine Native people as always already vanished. We see here in the reproduction of Native absence the inadvertent reinforcement and normativisation of what many Native scholars call "the logic of genocide" (Barker 2017). In sum, the uneven flows in mediascapes between the U.S., France, and the French-speaking world, their investments in dominant discursive, academic and filmic production and dissemination, has meant that the French-speaking-reading public "knows" the U.S., including its internal resistance, selectively and often through a White-Black binary. This excludes Chicanx, Native, and other subjects and conditions.

Meanwhile, the lives of people of color in France and the U.S., and specifically of women, dykes, trans folk, and other queers of color, are vastly different in many ways due to the differences in colonial practices, positionalities within coloniality, unfolding of enslavement and its continuity in the present, and relations now to capitalist exploitation. France engaged in and is still caught up in multiple kinds of colonialisms, including settler colonialism in Algeria and commercial or administrative colonialism elsewhere, from the Caribbean to the Pacific. France is in denial about slavery and racism. France imagines itself as "universalist," operates through colonial-paternalistic-and-maternalistic civilizational and savior narratives, and forces assimilation upon its internal others. People of color cannot get jobs, wear religious or cultural signs (there is a law banning the Islamic veil), are subjected to police violence, and are incarcerated at disproportionately high rates. There are different controlling images and modalities of control for people of African, Arab, or other descent. However, there have also been workers' struggles and thus for the employed—including people of color—there are more rights, health care, access to education, and other state solidarity than in the U.S.

Given the vast differences across the French-speaking world, and between it and the U.S., we made a decision not to try to invoke parallelism or sameness, or even familiarity. We especially did not want to position Anzaldúa in relation to French political and social movement sectarianisms. Instead, we wanted to translate Anzaldúa in a way that pulls the reader out of her/their/his world and introduces Anzaldúa's world. We put our faith in the readership that they would draw their own lines of relationality, intimacy and friendship with Anzaldúa's text. We put our faith in Anzaldúa's insight and wish that "the text will be different with each reader and reading" (*Reader* 2009: 191). And we have seen that happen in a multitude of ways.

Yet other issues for us were genre and stylistics. Anzaldúa explains: "not only do I code-switch in language, but I jerk the reader around by also code-switching in genre: mixing genres, criss-crossing genres from poetry to essay to narrative to a little bit of analysis and theory. The reader has to put it all together at the end" (2009: 189-190). Anzaldúa may not have foreseen this, but I can assure you: besides respecting all the genres and their specific "criss-crossings," so must the translator "put it all together at the end." Yet, each genre is its own temporal-spatiality in which some things can be said, and others remain silenced (Derrida 1980). Accordingly, not only is the translation of each Anzaldúan genre a world unto itself, but so is the translation of her specific genre criss-crossings. They each have their possibilities for voicings and for silence.

To make present the speech and silence in Anzaldúa, I wanted to reflect upon the dimensions of genre that go where Derrida did not, that live in those places that Gayatri Chakravorty Spivak calls "the space outside language" (181). To translate Anzaldúa entailed making present in French dimensions of Anzaldúa's sensory world. It included the force of excessive blood flow, the fatigue of sweat on skin, the soft smell of home-cooked food, the deep energies of connection with all beings, the calm of the safe space Anzaldúa fled to inside herself, her moods from loving to irritated, and so much more. It meant taking seriously everything that Anzaldúa says and does not say, evokes and does not evoke.

This brings us to an additional thought: affect, both Anzaldúa's and our own as invoked by her words and silences. We needed to be mindful about bringing all of the text, including its capacity to incite a whole array of emotions, into French. This and so much more.

CONCLUDING REMARKS: RECEPTIVITIES

Today, Anzaldúa's work is producing effects in France within the academy, activism, and the art world. The translated chapter from *Borderlands/La Frontera* is part of curricula in women's studies in several universities. Some students are doing dissertations on or related to her work. Some of us engaged in QTPOC scholarship and activism in France, myself included, find Anzaldúa's work, such as the 1979 essay "La Prieta" (2009), inspiring for rethinking queer beyond dimensions of locations in relations of power, beyond identity and beyond our reduction to genders and sexualities. Instead, with Anzaldúa we can re-imagine queer as a sensibility, orientation, relationality to humans and all beings, and as a way of being in the world, in planetarity. In activism, feminist and queer-of-color groups such as *QT Révolutionnaires*, *LTQ Colibris*, and *Transnational Decolonial QTPOC*, are engaging with Anzaldúa's work. Quotes by Anzaldúa have been part of the annual QTPOC Town Hall in Paris, a full day of QTPOC events held at the beginning of annual Queer Week in Paris, since its inception in March 2017. In 2018, Queer Week in Paris included an art exhibition inspired by Anzaldúa entitled "Nosotras." A collective of feminist scholars is now translating the entire *Borderlands/La Frontera: The New Mestiza* into French; they have asked me to write the preface. To celebrate the translation, a group of colleagues, myself included, have organized a three-day international conference on Anzaldua in Paris, May 16-18, 2019. It will include indigenous blessings ceremonies, academic papers, art exhibits, performances, and literary readings, in English(es), Spanish(es), French(es), and Nahuatl. Directly following the conference, there will be a Queer Trans of Color Café event, organized by Decolonizing Sexualities Network, with poetry, slam, and performances. The café will be followed the next day by a blessing organized by Corinna Gould (Ohlone) of Native sacred objects and art objects that were stolen by French colonizers and are housed in a Paris museum. In sum, Anzaldúa's gifts inspire us and bring us together in loving community, especially queer of color community, and allied community, across many continents, across many B/borders.

REFERENCES

Aït Ben Lmadani, Fatima, and Nassima Moujoud, 2012 "Peut-on faire de l'intersectionnalité sans les ex-colonisé-e-s?," *Mouvements*, 72: 11-21.

Alarcón, Norma. 1990. "The Theoretical Subject(s) of *This Bridge Called My Back* and Anglo-American Feminism." In *Making Face, Making Soul/Haciendo Caras*, ed. Gloria Anzaldúa, 356-369. San Francisco: Aunt Lute Books.

Anzaldúa, Gloria. 2009. "La Prieta." In *The Gloria Anzaldúa Reader*, edited by AnaLouise Keating, 38-50. Durham: Duke University Press.

---. 2009. "On the Process of Writing *Borderlands/La Frontera*." In *The Gloria Anzaldúa Reader*, edited by AnaLouise Keating, 187-197. Durham: Duke University Press.

---. 2009. "To(o) Queer the Writer: loca, escritora y chicana." In *The Gloria Anzaldúa Reader*, edited by AnaLouise Keating, 163-175. Durham: Duke University Press.

Bacchetta, Paola. 2019. "Dyketactics!" In *Global Encyclopedia of Lesbian, Gay, Bisexual, Transgender, and Queer History*, Howard Chiang (editor in chief). New York: MacMillan Reference.

Bacchetta, Paola, Jules Falquet, Norma Alarcón. 2011. "Théories Décoloniales Féministes et Queers: Interventions Ch/Xicanas et Latinas Etatsuniennes: Introduction." (Decolonial Feminist and Queer Theories: Ch/Xicana and U.S. Latina Interventions: Introduction). *Cahiers du CEDREF* 18: 7-40. Online at: http://cedref.revues.org/.

Barker, Joanne (ed). 2017. *Critically Sovereign: Indigenous Gender, Sexuality, and Feminist Studies.* Durham: Duke University Press.

Bilge, Sirma. 2015. "Le blanchiment de l'intersectionnalité." *Recherches Féministes*, Volume 28, Issue 2, 9–32.

Derrida, Jacques. 1980. The Law of Genre. *Glyph* 7, 203-204.

Perez, Laura. 2018. *Eros Ideologies: Writings on Art, Spirituality, and the Decolonial.* Durham: Duke.

Spanos, Brittany. "Janelle Monáe Frees Herself." *Rolling Stone*, Rolling Stone, 25 June 2018, www.rollingstone.com/music/music-features/janelle-monae-frees-herself-629204/.

Spivak, Gayatri Chakravorty. 1993. "The Politics of Translation." In *Outside the Teaching Machine.* New York: Routledge, 179-200.

Weston, Kath. 1991. *Families We Choose: Lesbians, Gays, Kinship*. New York: Columbia University Press.

CLOSING BLESSING

SANDRA PACHECO

(Please stand, if comfortable doing so)
Just as we began, let's connect to the ground,
feet firmly planted, feel the top of your head reach to the cielos, arms relaxed at your sides, feeling the energy of the people around you.
As we prepare to depart today, we carry with us sorrow as we learn today of yet another school shooting, this time at Santa Fe High School in Santa Fe, Texas.
We will not merely offer our thoughts and prayers for you
We will offer our continued action in communities,
And, we will teach and write for social change
With joy, gratitude, and blissful fatigue, our time together comes to an end
We thank our ancestors, the four directions, elements, seres divinos for being with us,
Let us take a brief moment to look around,
Con nuestros corazones que saben, y ojitos que platican,
thank each other with a silent gaze,
thank each other for showing up to do the work,
for being present,
for the celebrations and for the struggles
Do you see your otro yo?
Come back to your center, inhale slowly, deeply,

eyes closed,
go inward to your body,
Thank your cuerpo sagrado,
for it too does work unseen that sometimes we take for granted
blood running through venas,
air filling your lungs,
neurons firing in your brain,
your pansitas digesting the gifts of madre tierra,
your skin protecting such a magnificent system…go inward, deeper,
envision the millions of cells,
cells made of the matter and energy of thousands of ancestors that came before us,
each one a tiny miracle holding our histories
We are the love, struggle, hope, and pride of our ancestors
We are the light of the universe, of creator, of the divine
We are Anzaldúans
As we prepare to travel home, may we remember to reach out to our AERA[1]
friends and colleagues holding trauma, carrying susto from their recent flight
from New York
May we show up for each other,
May our journeys home be safe,
May they be peaceful,
Que así sea,
Ometeotl,
Aho.

NOTES

1. On April 17th, 2018, Southwest flight 1389 traveling from La Guardia Airport experienced an engine explosion resulting in the death of one woman who was pulled partially out of her window. Passengers nearby, including colleagues and friends who were returning from the AERA (American Educational Research Association) conference, experienced extreme trauma in trying to assist and/or witnessing the woman's tragic death.

CONTRIBUTOR BIOGRAPHIES

Sonya M. Alemán is an associate professor in the Bicultural Bilingual Department and Mexican American Studies program at the University of Texas at San Antonio. She studies mainstream media representations of communities of color, alternative media content produced by communities of color, and manifestations of race, racism, and whiteness in the media. Her work reimagines a journalism pedagogy that better reflects the lives and experiences of communities of color. In addition, she is invested in improving the educational experiences of students of color. She draws on critical race theory and Chicana feminism to inform both her scholarship and pedagogy. She is published in *Critical Studies in Media Communication*; *Equity and Excellence in Education*; *Review of Education, Pedagogy, and Cultural Studies*; and *International Journal of Qualitative Studies in Education.*

Mariana Alessandri is an assistant professor of philosophy at the University of Texas Rio Grande Valley and is an affiliate faculty of Mexican American Studies and Gender and Women's Studies. She teaches philosophy as a way of life in her classes and writes to make philosophy accessible to people who find it intimidating. She has never outgrown her first love, existentialism, and her favorite philosophers are Søren Kierkegaard, Miguel de Unamuno, and Gloria Anzaldúa.

Ewa Antoszek is an assistant professor at the Department of American Literature and Culture of Maria-Curie Skłodowska University in Lublin, Poland. Her interests include American ethnic literatures with a particular focus on Mexican American and African American writers, women's studies, and representations of space(s) in literature. Her PhD thesis analyzed multiple ways of identity construction in Chicana literature. She is the author of *Out of the Margins: Identity Formation in Contemporary Chicana Writings* (2012) and several articles analyzing issues related to the situation of ethnic minorities in the US. She is also the co-editor of *Inne Bębny: różnica i niezgoda w literaturze i kulturze amerykańskiej* (Different Drums: Difference and Dissent in American Literature and Culture; 2013). Her current research examines Latina authors and artists in the US (re)writing the border.

Lobat Asadi (pronouns: she/her/hers/they) is a PhD student in Curriculum and Instruction in the Department of Teaching, Learning, and Culture at Texas A&M University. Her research projects focus on post-colonial praxis and performance studies for pedagogy that benefits multiethnic and multilingual learners. Lobat has an educational background in journalism, Middle Eastern studies, intercultural relations, and a master's in applied linguistics. Lobat has taught English as a second language in Saudi Arabia and at the University of Texas at Austin. Given her diverse background, Lobat hopes to bring intersectional perspectives from arts-informed pedagogies that address social (in)justices and create culturally sustainable curricula that engages the imagination and promotes creativity.

Paola Bacchetta is Professor of Gender and Women's Studies at UC Berkeley. Her books include: *Co-Motion: On Feminist and Queer of Color Alliances* (Duke, forthcoming); *Global Racialities* (co-edited, Routledge, 2019); *Femminismi Queer Postcoloniali* (co-edited, Verona, Italy: Ombre Corte, 2015); *Gender in the Hindu Nation* (New Delhi: Women Unlimited, 2004); and *Right-Wing Women* (co-edited, Routledge, 2002). She has published over sixty articles and book chapters. She co-translated a chapter of *Borderlands/La Frontera* into French and is writing the preface to the book's forthcoming French edition.

Camille Back is a French PhD student in Hispanic studies and is currently doing research at the Université Sorbonne Nouvelle–Paris 3 on Gloria Anzaldúa's work, Chicana queer feminism, and the emergence of queer theory. As a lesbian feminist and white queer from an Italian, working-class immigrant background, she seeks to propose a critical analysis of white queer theories and some of their paradigms, highlighting the influence of Anzaldúa, whose contribution to the elaboration of these theories has been erased from current genealogies.

Cordelia E. Barrera is an associate professor of Latinx Literature and Co-Director of the Literature of Social Justice and the Environment (LSJE) initiative at Texas Tech University. Her work highlights the need to disrupt mythologies of the American West by incorporating border voices and concentrates on the literature of social justice and the environment. Her current book project explores utopian forms and social dreaming on the borderlands.

Catalina Bartlett is a visiting assistant professor in Writing, Rhetoric, and American Cultures at Michigan State University and holds a PhD in English from Texas A&M University and an MFA from Indiana University. She is at work on a collection of linked short stories entitled *Journey to Chimayo: Stories.*

Samantha Ceballos was born in Brownsville, Tejas, but grew up mostly in Katy, Tejas. She graduated from the University of Texas at San Antonio with a BA in English and is pursuing her MA/MFA in Literature, Creative Writing, and Social Justice from Our Lady of the Lake University. Poetry and prose help her voice what she sees and feels in the chaotic world we all inhabit.

Casie C. Cobos is an independent scholar who received her PhD in English and MFA in Creative Writing. Her work intersects with rhetoric and critical studies with particular interest in Indigenous and Chicana practices and mental illness.

Amanda E. Cuellar is a Latina scholar and a PhD candidate in English at the University of Oklahoma and serves as a programmer for OU's Native Crossroads Film Festival. Amanda's dissertation focuses on ways Gloria Anzaldúa's theoretical frameworks offer a lens to interrogate other Chicanx literature, film, and media.

Qwo-Li Driskill is a non-citizen Cherokee Two-Spirit also of African, Irish, Lenape, Lumbee, and Osage ascent. They received their PhD in Rhetoric & Writing from Michigan State University and are an associate professor and Director of Graduate Studies in the Women, Gender, and Sexuality Studies program at Oregon State University.

Rev. Dr. **Ricardo L. Franco** completed doctoral studies at the Boston University School of Theology. He works with Latinx immigrant communities in the US and Central-South America. His research focus is Latinx religion, particularly the experience of US immigrant communities as a locus of theological/spiritual reflection. Ricardo uses Anzaldúa's vision of Borderlands spirituality as a theoretical framework in order to conceptualize and to interpret the ontological, epistemological, and ethical dimensions of the spiritual practices of these communities.

Jessica Gonzales is an interdisciplinary artist born and raised in San Antonio, Texas. Through the use of digital media, photography, and poetry, she explores history, identities, and self-preservation. She has exhibited her work at the Movement Gallery and Centro Cultural Aztlan. She is the daughter of a Vietnam veteran and an agricultural migrant worker. She studied English and Women's Studies at Texas A&M–San Antonio.

L. Heidenreich grew up in down-valley Napa and, today, is an associate professor with the History Department at Washington State University where they enjoy working with the graduate group Camaradas. They are the author of *"This Land Was Mexican Once": Histories of Resistance from Northern California*, and, more recently, worked with Antonia Castañeda, Luz María Gordillo, and Deena González to edit *Three Decades of Engendering History: Selected Works of Antonia Castañeda*. They are looking forward to the release of *Nepantla2*, by Nebraska, in fall of 2019.

Larissa M. Mercado-López, Associate Professor of Women's Studies at California State University, Fresno, earned her PhD in English Literature at the University of Texas at San Antonio. She is the co-editor of several volumes of *El Mundo Zurdo* and collections of critical essays on Latinx literature and Chicanx children's literature. Mercado-López is also a children's book author and an editorial board member for the National Center for Institutional Diversity Public Scholarship Initiative.

Andrés C. López is a Latinx trans and queer writer, poet, musician, and scholar. His activism, pedagogy, work, and artistic projects center the lives and experiences of queer and trans folks of color. Andrés is a PhD student in Women, Gender, and Sexuality Studies at Oregon State University.

Rebel Mariposa comes from an ancestral line of healers and artists. She has her bachelor's in psychology from the University of Texas in Austin. She has curated art shows in California and Texas for over ten years. She is a co-creator and founder of Texas's first vegan restaurant with a full bar and community venue: La Botanica SA. She also owns and operates a skin, body, and soul care company, The Alluring Alchemist. You can learn more about her at Rebelmariposa.com.

Yvonne Montoya is a choreographer, independent scholar, and founding director of *Safos* Dance Theatre. From 2017-2018, Montoya was a post-graduate fellow in dance at Arizona State University's Herberger Institute for Design & the Arts, where she organized the inaugural Dance in the Desert: A Gathering of Latinx Dancemakers. Montoya was adjunct faculty at the University of Arizona's Department of Mexican American Studies from 2006-2012. www.yvonnemontoya.co

Dr. **Sandra Pacheco**'s teaching, research, and activism focuses on Chicana, Latina, and Indigena feminisms, spirituality, and critical psychology, with an emphasis on social justice. Her most recent work focuses on curanderismo. She apprentices regularly in Oaxaca, Mexico with Doña Enriqueta Contreras and Pastora Gutierrez Reyes, curanderas within a Zapotec tradition. She is co-founder of Curanderas sin Fronteras, a women's healing collective dedicated to serving the health and well-being of underserved communities through traditional medicine.

Eliza M. Pérez grew up in Pharr, Texas, a small frontera city in El Valle del Río Grande. She is the daughter of Mexican immigrants from Nuevo Leon and San

Luis Potosi. Eliza is a queer double Capricorn, rising Scorpio, who enjoys graphic design, baking, and zines. She has worked as a cultural arts programmer at the Esperanza Peace and Justice Center in San Antonio, Texas since 2015.

Sara A. Ramírez, Assistant Professor of English at Texas State University, earned her PhD from the University of California, Berkeley. Her interdisciplinary research focuses on representations of historical and intergenerational trauma in Chicanx cultural productions. She teaches literature courses that focus on Chicana and women of color feminist narratives. She is also the first member of a collective working to revitalize the historic Third Woman Press.

Gabriela Raquel Ríos is an assistant professor in the English Department at the University of Oklahoma. Her research traces how indigenous communities create knowledge, resist colonialism, and continue/reshape culture and "tradition" within shifting historical, political, and social contexts, with a focus on Latin American and Chicana/o/x sites of production.

Lilliana P. Saldaña is an associate professor of Mexican American Studies at UTSA with research interests in Mexican American teacher identity and consciousness, Chicana/o schooling, and epistemic struggles to decolonize the curriculum. She has published in nationally recognized journals, including *Latinos & Education*; *Decolonization: Indigeneity, Education & Society*; and *Association of Mexican American Educators Journal*. She currently serves as Associate Editor of *Chicana/Latina Studies*, the flagship publication of Mujeres Activas en Letras y Cambio Social. As a local scholar, Saldaña works to bridge community and academia through teaching, research, and service. She currently serves as co-chair of the board of the Esperanza Peace & Justice Center and is involved in local and state-wide organizing efforts to implement MAS in Texas K-12 public schools.

Sonia Saldívar-Hull is a professor of English and the founding director of the Women's Studies Institute and the Women's Studies Program at the University of Texas, San Antonio. Her publications include *Feminism on the Border: Chicana Feminist Politics and Literature*, and multiple book chapters and articles on Gloria Anzaldúa, Sandra Cisneros, and Helena Maria Viramontes, among others. Since 1997, she has been the co-editor of the book series Latin America Otherwise, published by Duke University Press.

Victorria Simpson-Gervin is a recent graduate of the MA Graduate Program at the University of Texas at San Antonio, where she received her Master of Arts in English. She also received her Bachelor of Arts in Women's Studies at the University of Texas at San Antonio. She is currently applying to PhD programs in an effort to continue her education. Her research interests focus on narratives of health, illness, and healing.

Mario I. Suárez (pronouns: he/him/his) received his PhD in Curriculum and Instruction from the Department of Teaching, Learning, and Culture at Texas A&M University. His research interests involve queer studies in education, STEM equity, and curriculum studies. Mario was born and raised in Eagle Pass, Texas, a small town on the Texas-Mexico border. He has been through a very long and challenging journey ever since coming out as a transgender man during his second year teaching high school mathematics at an economically disadvantaged school in Austin, Texas. He hopes that his journey as a transgender person of color can help bring awareness to the hardships that intersect when race, gender identity, and socioeconomic status are not within the majority. He is currently an assistant professor of cultural studies in the School of Teacher Education and Leadership at Utah State University.

Fabiola Ochoa Torralba was born in Guerrero, Mexico and was raised on the west side of San Antonio, Texas. Trained as a cultural worker and grassroots organizer, they engage art making as a transformative practice for building community, civic engagement, and social-cultural awareness. They enjoy facilitating dance making opportunities for movers of all backgrounds and interdisciplinary collaborations that explore the intersection between performance and action.

Stephanie K. Wheeler is an assistant professor in Writing and Rhetoric at the University of Central Florida. Her research focuses on cultural rhetorics as they relate to the intersections of disability and race, specifically the relationship between disability and meaning-making in historical and rhetorical constructions of eugenics.

Claudia Zapata is a doctoral candidate in Southern Methodist University's RASC/a: Rhetorics of Art, Space and Culture: PhD Program in Art History. She received her BA and MA from University of Texas in Art History. From 2010 to 2014, she served as the Curator of Exhibitions and Programs at the Mexic-Arte Museum in Austin, Texas. She is currently pursuing her dissertation project, "Chicano Art is Not Dead: Politics on Display within Major U.S. Exhibitions."

Aunt Lute Books is a multicultural women's press that has been committed to publishing high-quality, culturally diverse literature since 1982. In 1990, the Aunt Lute Foundation was formed as a non-profit corporation to publish and distribute books that reflect the complex truths of women's lives and to present voices that are underrepresented in mainstream publishing. We seek work that explores the specificities of the very different histories from which we come, and the possibilities for personal and social change.

You may buy books from our website or by phoning in a credit card order.

www.auntlute.com

Aunt Lute Books
P.O. Box 410687
San Francisco, CA 94141
415.826.1300
books@auntlute.com

This book would not have been possible without the kind contributions of the Aunt Lute Founding Friends:

Anonymous Donor
Anonymous Donor
Rusty Barcelo
Marian Bremer
Marta Drury
Diane Goldstein
Diana Harris
Phoebe Robins Hunter
Diane Mosbacher, M.D., Ph.D.
Sara Paretsky
William Preston, Jr.
Elise Rymer Turner